FIELDS OF FREI

Breaking through fear in

personal and professional life

John Holt

First Kindle Edition 2014

Cover design: Sylvia Merrett

Cover Photo: freedigitalphotos.net

© **2014 Kindle Edition**

© **2015 Paperback Edition**

ISBN No:0993265804

Published by John Holt ASP

info@johnholt-authentic-self-purpose.org.uk

CONTENTS

FOREWORD BY STEVE PAGE:

These are not the musings and reflections of a man hanging up his coat and (Chesterfield FC) scarf, putting on his slippers and supping a pint, satisfied that his contribution to the world is complete. Rather John shares with us highlights from his life as he eyeballs death, toe to toe, unwavering in his willingness to explore the searching questions death fires at him: about what has made him who he is; what he values above all else and how he makes sense of this mortal life, body, soul and spirit. John offers us a generous gift, his personal version of what William Bloom (2011) describes when he writes, 'It is wonderful and redemptive how the human spirit can wake up in times of discomfort, pain and challenge. Our compassion and witnessing consciousness can emerge and grow in the most uncomfortable situations.' (p. 127)

In part John's response to being confronted by his mortality, in his own words: ....*comes from within, from our own choice to actively live, to really choose to live and to go on choosing life, whatever our current illnesses, fears, trials, grief and tribulations; to continue to believe in ourselves, and to go on believing, whatever the cost, as we simultaneously love through our work, and facilitate and celebrate the emergence of the magnificent human and God given potential within others.* (Chapter 4)

This is a book about the personal biography of a psychotherapist, coach, supervisor, trainer and consultant and how personal history informs professional understandings and approach. This is a book about a spiritual journey; making sense of being a consciously spiritually aware person without any single traditional framework to define (or limit) that spiritual awareness. This is a book about facing our worst fears with openness, honesty, integrity and courage and the transformations that makes possible. This is a book about love, relationship, and authenticity.

As the focus shifts from one strand to another you may find some hold your attention more fully than others. Having known John for over twenty years, as a colleague and a friend, I want to read more of his stories, especially those that make me laugh: about biking, his mother's spiritualism, men's workshops and his other adventures. You may be more captured by understanding how he has developed his ways of working and the thinking behind his personal philosophy of therapy and facilitation. You may be inspired by how he has formulated his particular take on what it is to be a humanistic psychologist by pulling together his experience of working with disadvantaged young people caught up in youth justice, with what he has learnt through Hakomi, self and peer assessment and organisational consultancy. Or perhaps you are reading this to find out more about how John has faced his diagnosis of terminal disease, how he has delved through layer upon layer of fear, pain and uncertainty to find a place of fierce serenity and how his spiritual life has grown in so doing. Whatever brings you to read this book, I encourage you to be open to being taken by surprise by every strand, as well as focusing on what matters most to you.

I know that some people have advised John to choose a single focus for this book, but he stood his ground and has taken on the challenge of weaving together a number of the most important strands of his life. In doing so he gives us an opportunity to see how the core strands of living a life with awareness and integrity can bind to each other to build a single, strong rope.

I have felt privileged to be one of the large midwifery team assisting John to bring this book into the world. I hope you enjoy reading it and find words that speak to your heart and mind as John writes to you from his.

Steve Page

(Counsellor, supervisor and author of "The Shadow and the Counsellor"[1999]; Co-author of "Supervising the Counsellor: A cyclical model"[2001]).

August 2013

Bloom, W. (2011) *"The Power of Modern Spirituality"*, London: Piatkus.

EARLY THOUGHTS, MAY 2011:

My Last Will and Testament: A letter to fellow professionals both old & new

These writings are offered primarily to fellow professionals who work as counsellors, psychotherapists, facilitators, healers and coaches, and to supervisors of these professionals. However, I also hope they may be of help and interest to therapy clients and also to anyone facing their own fears over receiving a terminal diagnosis, or being alongside loved ones dealing with such a diagnosis.

Effectively the writings constitute my "Last Will and Testament" on the subject of choosing to work and live beyond the confines of fear in my personal and professional life because, as things stand, I may not be given or have time to write anything more before I die.

I have an illness which my Consultants tell me is now incurable: it is "carcinoid syndrome", a form of cancer with a primary tumour in the small intestine, and secondary tumours which have spread to my liver. As a result of the toxins thrown off by the tumours in the liver, I also have pure right ventricle heart failure, with malfunctioning heart valves and an over extended right ventricle. As far as I can tell from what my Consultant Oncologist has said, and what I have gleaned from the Internet, statistically I have a likelihood of surviving for a further 3 years at most from the time of the initial diagnosis in 2010. I have begun writing this book in earnest, in May 2011, so I have no idea if I will still be around after 2013.

However, I am choosing not to accept the above as inevitable, in fact I am very active around my own healing and I continue to be very active in my own professional field.

Nevertheless I am also a realist and accept that just as I may recover from this illness, I may also die from this illness. I am still choosing life but perhaps the choice will one day be taken away from me.

I am aware that some part of me believes I have been given time to write this book and that once it is written I will die. That might suggest I have a good incentive to never finish the book! But I think it is also a good discipline to hold this thought, whether it turns out to be true or not: because I experience it as a breathtakingly powerful choice to hold such thoughts and feelings whilst contemplating my own death. In so doing, I am taken by a strong energetic surge directly into the world explored by Carlos Castaneda in his "Don Juan" writings.

For those unfamiliar with him, Castaneda was a Peruvian-American author and anthropologist. Starting with, "The Teachings of Don Juan: A Yaqui Way of Knowledge", published by the University of California Press in 1968, Castaneda wrote of events that he claimed took place during an apprenticeship he served with a Yaqui Indian Sorcerer, Don Juan Matus of Sonora, Mexico, in the period between 1960 and 1965. The authenticity of the book and subsequent series of books has been a matter of debate and controversy since they were published. However, controversy or not, what Castaneda and Don Juan enabled me to do, was to breathe deeply into my fears and face them directly, especially in relation to my possibly impending death.

The wisdom communicated in much of the writings spoke to me when I first read the books in the late 1960s and early 1970s and today has an even more powerful resonance for me. In particular Don Juan suggests there is deep wisdom in beginning an active dialogue with my own death, and regarding death as my wisest friend who will loyally serve me with the truth up to and including the moment he/she lets me know it is time to leave this life.

In my journey through this illness so far, I am aware that I feel a need to write this book for myself as an authentically truthful description of this "dialogue with death" and therefore absolutely central to my truth as it unfolds around my illness and my life, as I continue to work as a counsellor, psychotherapist, coach, supervisor and facilitator.

I have been working in the helping professions for most of my adult life. Through cumulative experience which dates back to the mid-1970s and the more visceral aspects of my lived experience as a person travelling on a potential 'terminal illness journey', I feel I now have something to say to my fellow professionals from a place of 'eldership' both as a practitioner and as a person with considerable life experience. What I say may hopefully be of interest and real help to them, and more importantly, given the short time that may be available to me, may be a useful contribution from an 'elder', to the body of knowledge within this professional field. After all, perhaps after all this time, I recognise I know a lot, and as an elder it feels necessary to share it whilst I still can! Paradoxically, it also follows that the "more I learn the more I realise how much I probably still don't know" about the realities and mysteries of the world, so 'eldership' may be a rather more limited concept in my case than I imagine. But it still seems important to me that I speak my truth whilst I have time to do so, both as a professional within this field and also as a man facing a major life challenge.

This book, given the title, is also of course about my relationship with, and knowledge of fear. John C. Parkin in his wonderful work publicised via his Website (*www.thefuckitlife.com*) and his new book, (Parkin, 2012), suggests fear of death is at the root of ALL human anxieties.

Furthermore, I read in Pat Rodegast and Judith Stanton's book, (1985) that cancer is all about fear – and that fear is our biggest denial, as human beings, of the existence of God.

So perhaps, as I walk this road and search for meaning around my illness, I am beginning to understand why I have this opportunity to reflect and speak my truth: Over the last year or so I feel the only way I have been able to deal with this illness and my possible death, has been to very deliberately and consciously face my fears one by one, really come to know them and how they impact upon me both personally and professionally.

Through this, I feel I have learnt a great deal about fear, but I am still surprised by new aspects of fear that surface within me. One relatively recent manifestation has been some level of anxiety about how my "truth" around the professional aspects of what I write might be received, once this book is published.

Twenty seven years ago I was completing an MA dissertation in Criminology. As I neared the end of that process, I began to realise that I was very reluctant to achieve completion, because I recognised that I was uncovering new material all the time in my research and if I did complete, somewhere someone would point out that a piece of new research meant my writings were out of date or in fact incomplete. This was pure fear linked to egoistic concerns about my professional reputation, and also nonsense: I simply needed to have the courage to stand by my words as a statement of my accumulated truth in that moment. Which I suppose is what I am doing right now in my 'dialogue with death'.

So instead of worrying that what I have written may be seen by others as, 'simplistic... naive... just a narcissistic ego exercise', or whatever, I need to remember this is simply my truth and my honest attempt to describe it accurately at all levels. I invite you to make of it what you will, and to also ask yourself why you have come to any particular conclusions you have reached. Depending on your reactions and reflections, it may reveal more than you had realised!

A work colleague Em, suggested to me at one point, that I am offering, "a piece of essential modelling" of how my personal and professional journey has shifted my own perspective.

In that context, I have come to realise how far down I have had to dig to fulfil the role of counsellor, therapist, coach, supervisor and facilitator, from a place of deep meaning, choice and intention. I consider these things to be essential elements of the role. I have had to dig very deep indeed as I reflect on my possible death; however, it is also my belief that a very deep level of self-examination and personal honesty is required of every practitioner who chooses to work seriously and ultimately professionally in this field.

We are required to dig very deep if we aspire to fully fill the role we have chosen as a professional within the 'helping professions'. This goes significantly beyond the notion of becoming a highly skilled technician with a wide 'toolbox of techniques'. It is about developing a lifelong craft and an embodied relationship with the authentic personal and professional Self, our clients, our supervisees and the wider world.

Perhaps for that reason, I am weaving together three themes: *my personal narrative from childhood to adulthood; a record of my journey through debilitating and life threatening illness; and finally reflections on my accumulated wisdom and experience through a lifetime of developing my craft within my chosen disciplines, working as a*

practitioner within the helping professions, applied social policy and applied psychology.

Developing a lifelong craft within the context of an unfolding and embodied relationship with the authentic Self, requires a willingness to repeatedly choose expansiveness and a clear focus for my work, especially in those moments when I experience fear. As my colleague Em commented to me and other peers on a previous occasion, "intention is everything" in this work.

I will expand upon this theme because I feel we often significantly underestimate what is asked of us when we choose to work in this field. In fact my belief is that this professional field demands much from practitioners, in order to fulfil the greatest potential in the role; whether it be as counsellor, therapist, clinical supervisor, coach, coach supervisor, group facilitator, healer or trainer.

My 'Last Will and Testament', and the chapters that follow, are my contribution to how I dealt with, and am continuing to deal with this challenge in my own personal and professional life.

On some level, this book may also represent my final 'dance with death' and if so, I choose it to be both an act of surrender and also an act of power. I offer it with deep gratitude for everything I have learnt, and everything and everyone I have been given the capacity to love in this life.

Thank you.

John Holt

Ballycastle
County Mayo
Eire
May 2nd, 2011

CHAPTER 1:

Envy and "En vie" - Confrontations with a house brick

I was 4½ years old. The 1950's: on a council estate, Inkersall Green, Chesterfield, North Derbyshire.

I was standing on the pavement, on the corner of Crich Road and Hillman Drive. Behind me, a grassy area in front of a brick wall which formed the boundary of our garden. In front of me, across the pavement on the other side of the road, was a big lad, aged about 11 or 12, who I had seen before many times.

Today, to my surprise, he began to talk to me. He was friendly, with a warm smiling face. I felt very pleased, that he wanted to talk to me and very comfortable because somehow I expected it. It was natural because I was discovering that the world was interested in me and I loved the world. It was a place of great curiosity and wonder, which I was really beginning to explore, beyond the familiar boundary of our garden gate.

As we spoke, out of the corner of my eye, I saw his right arm swing back behind his head. He continued to smile and laugh with me. I felt happy, full of joy and playfulness. His arm moved forwards, I was vaguely aware of some shadowy shape moving towards me through the air, but I really didn't know what it was. I just accepted it as yet another wonderful and curious thing happening in my world.

Suddenly my head exploded with a deafening bang of total blackness. He had hit me square between the eyes with a full house brick: My face flooded with blood, obscuring my sight.

I turned and ran blindly home, screaming in pain

***

Why would a 12 year old boy do such a thing to a 4½ year old? It is only in recent months that I have begun to understand the answer to that question.

I had completely forgotten and buried this incident deep in my unconscious for around 34 years. At the age of 38, I was struggling with a debilitating illness, referred to as Myalgic Encephalomyelitis or M.E.

I had been ill for months and nothing I tried seemed to help. I had been told of a healer, Dorothy Lewis, who lived in Reeth, North Yorkshire. I went to see her for healing sessions as an alternative to months of frustration in receiving no helpful action from the allopathic medical profession. My first session involved a form of medical dowsing where Dorothy scanned my energy field. She made notes of what she was discovering. Written down there, amongst other things, in bold letters was, "severe trauma age 4½". I had no idea to what this was referring.

The following weekend, I went back to visit my mother in Chesterfield, and asked if she could give me any information about a "severe trauma" when I was 4½. She told me of the shock she felt one day when I suddenly I ran into the house, screaming in pain with my head covered in blood. She said I had told her a boy had hit me and I had given her a description of him. Apparently my brother, who knew this boy from school, went round to his house shortly afterwards to, 'have a quiet word with him'. Such are North Derbyshire euphemisms and such is the rock solid loyalty of a much loved brother.

It was only after my Mum had shared these fragmented memories that everything that happened around the house brick incident came flooding back into my consciousness. I remembered everything. I saw it all in vivid colour. I remembered the sunshine. I remembered the feelings of joy and enthusiastic energy I had. I remembered my sense of openness towards the world. I remembered the power of the explosion and how that whole world suddenly and violently turned black.

This remembering was the beginning of my healing from ME and it was somehow connected to finding the courage to choose to be open to looking the world squarely in the eyes again, without blinking or turning away.

I recall a video exercise we did when I was studying at Leeds University for my social work qualification in the late 1970s. An elaborate role play stage had been set by a local BBC TV Look North producer, where we were filmed interviewing a pretend client with a multiplicity of problems. When the video tape was played back, I could not believe how much time I spent rapidly blinking as the client piled on the details of his impossibly chaotic and catastrophic life story. The more complex his reasons for not being able to receive help from me, or more pertinently be unable to help himself to some level of effective personal power, the more I blinked rapidly. That was how I used to cope with the complexity of life. Choosing to look life (and death) squarely in the face without blinking or turning away has been an incredibly tough challenge for me.

In early February 2011, I was reading a newspaper and an advertisement image jumped out at me and powerfully caught my eye. I have had such feelings many times before: an instantaneous recognition that something deeply synchronicitous is happening in that moment. It was an advert for a Peugeot 207 car. The caption read, "Beware of the consequences of Envy", and a house brick was in flight towards the car, thrown by someone. The brick was made up of a form of letters into the word, Envy.

I was meeting with my spiritual director Brenda that week and I took the advert with me. We discussed it and its significance to what happened to me when I was 4½ years old. Brenda is strongly drawn by the power of language and symbolism. She explained to me that one way of seeing the word envy was as a play on words from the French: "En vie... in life... on seeing with life... seeing from". My capacity to be fully in life and viewing my experiences from that perspective, was blocked in me from the moment the brick hit, but it seemed I retained a half memory somewhere; a passionate desire to find my way back to seeing the world from a place of deep wonder and nourishing human connection.

Brenda saw this retained half memory as both a reflection of what she termed a 'warrior stance' within me and also as a subsequently chosen life statement: about both my initial early years' discovery of the apparent nature of things and also about my emotional opposition to the received wisdom of the nature of things, where a view of the world is held from a reactive place of being wounded by another. My greatest resistance to such received wisdom would be found in my refusal to accept that a typically and reactive response to feeling the presence of human fear, should inevitably be manifested in acts of brutality. Somewhere inside of me I knew there had to be an alternative way of living to that.

The knowledge may have been buried within me for 34 years but it was not lost. The brick gave me a task to move beyond the way human beings can be, because I knew it was not the way they should be. Brenda's final comment was, "the challenge of your life has been to resist sliding into paranoia".

In the light of my reading and explorations in writing this book, I am recognising that, like others, I may oscillate between paranoia and what Brenda terms "metanoia" as I learn the lessons of life. For now, it is enough to say that my desired place seems always to have been to live in the world from the stance of metanoia rather than paranoia, but like I assume that most people would, I found this to be an exceptionally difficult process.

What did Brenda mean by her use of the term metanoia? She recognised its Greek origins and was aware of both its theological and also secular connotations. She saw its roots in Ancient Greek as describing a state of mind beyond perception, or in her words, "as a complete change of mind from what went before".

In a theological context, she commented that the King James translation of the Bible had misunderstood the term, and instead of seeing it as a "complete change of mind" she felt it had been mistranslated as "repentance", which for her also meant the mistranslation carried profound theological implications. In my view, it is not so much about repentance but more a case of a paradigm shift to a new and positive way of seeing the Self and my place in the world.

In a secular context I feel she would see it in the way I would, as a form of psychological reconstruction after a crisis. In my own story and application of the term I would relate to it in both contexts. The theological aspects have begun to become much clearer for me as my story has begun to unfold, however the psychological interpretation also applies to my story and my journey through life.

It seems extraordinary to think that a 12 year old could be envious of a 4 ½ year old. Perhaps he was somehow seeing my joyful openness to the world and the complete absence of fear in me and it was that he envied, and it was too painful for him. Quite possibly, this contrasted with his own lived experience of 12 years of gradual, or brutal, exposure to the fear of life, and the only tolerable response to this contrast of experience was violence. Creating pain in me would then reduce any perceived gap between us and may well have temporarily reduced his pain.

Whatever was happening for him, from my point of view, I met fear of life and fear of the world that day, probably for the first time. I shut down much of my trust in the world and trust in my own judgment of the world. I could not trust myself nor trust others; it was too dangerous to get close to anyone; I set up a deep pattern of mistrust in my life from that point onwards.

This was the start of decades of repeated non-conversations with house bricks in my daily lived experience. I hid from the world and from myself. I looked out at the world with suspicion and hyper vigilance. I was not welcome here. It was not safe here. I would tend to experience trauma around new and potentially threatening experiences.

My continued existence was under severe threat. My whole life was in danger. That was the 'lesson' I learnt.

***

Pat Rodegast and Judith Stanton (1985) suggest that when we choose to incarnate into this human life, we, "enter into a perceptual falsehood". It is an illusion and if we treat it as "truth" we can, "become embittered, fearful and ill" (ibid; P6). They suggest that each soul, "enters into a physically symbolised reality of that soul's conscious resistance to the Inner Light" (ibid; p6) and from that place, life is experienced predominantly from the perspective of fear. Instead they recommend that we should come into life, "assuming the perspective of the creator of that life" and see it all as a, "wondrous and valuable learning experience" (ibid; P6).

This suggests to me that we need to accept a high level of responsibility for our chosen perceptions and actions. My perception is that whether we acknowledge it or not, we are all on a path of self-responsibility. To a much greater extent than we give it credit, we create our own experiences of life. Whatever we weave as our own personal story, our view of the world and our place in it, becomes the narrative from which we live out our experience of life. We can either choose to do that from a place of self-responsibility and self-empowerment, or from a place of inaction, passivity, blame, paralysis, or apocalyptic thinking rooted in fear.

In my work as a counsellor and psychotherapist, I recognise the moment when a client shifts their perception and in so doing also shifts their energy from a preoccupation with finding a form of external salvation, to an acceptance of the possibility that they can create internal solutions through the exercise of their competence and power. In therapeutic jargon, this is known as, 'a shift from an external to an internal locus of control'.

When I experience this shift in a client's perceptual, energetic and possibly also relational field, I know big changes are about to happen in the way they perceive the world and choose to be and act in the world. I believe this represents a willingness to trust in the Self, especially the internalised adult aspect of the Self, and to trust in the world's response to the Self. It offers an opportunity to exercise healthy power in their way of being and living in the world.

At this point I notice a desire in me to shift the focus of my writing for a short while to a wider perspective on our human condition. In terms of Jung's notion of what he termed the collective unconscious, I believe what we do at the individual level also adds to the collective mental and spiritual health of the human family and creates a parallel reduction in the existence of toxic relational patterns in the collective human experience.

Buddhist writer Joanna Macy (Macy, 1991) regards the world less as a classroom for human growth and development and more as an opportunity to experience (as promoted in the title of her book) "world as lover, world as self". From this perspective the significance of an individual's decision to live life with a high degree of self-responsibility, cannot be overestimated.

When we grow the whole world grows. When we expand our consciousness the world expands its consciousness. Fundamentally, in the way I would term it, we can choose 'inclusivity and expansion' or 'exclusivity and contraction' within the Self. Inclusivity and expansion, especially coupled to a willingness to see the world as lover, world as self, inevitably reduces the likelihood of engaging in what I would recognise as destructive shadow projection, in the unconscious psychological process of projective identification of the presence of so called evil in others, and its apparent absence in the Self.

To say a little about each term I have mentioned above:

The Jungian concept of shadow projection is a common occurrence in patterns of individual and collective behaviour and communication. For me the human shadow represents disowned aspects of the Self that are too uncomfortable or painful to acknowledge, whether for an individual or for a social group. As a consequence, the shadow material is unconsciously projected on to others, becomes visible and the individuals or groups identified as carrying it are criticised and often ostracised.

This process deepens when specific aspects of the human shadow may be highlighted as particularly visible in others and singled out for strong criticism or condemnation. This process of projective identification is stronger the more uncomfortable the material is for the person who is unable to see it in themselves, whilst simultaneously and powerfully identifying it in others.

In a collective sense I remember these shadow processes very clearly when recalling the overblown rhetoric of the Reagan Administration in the USA, who often referred to Russia and its geographical satellites as the 'evil empire'.

In contrast to the potentially life enhancing aspects of inclusivity and expansion which seem to project very little shadow material onto others, exclusivity and contraction seem to inevitably lead in the opposite direction and almost always, in my experience, towards a way of living and being in the world which in terms of its relational qualities seems perceptually distorted, psychologically and emotionally toxic.

If this split thinking is focused on the intrapersonal relationship with the Self, we will also or instead develop a powerful internal critic which despite any best efforts we make, will shame us, diminish our achievements and ultimately lock us into a fear based certainty that whatever we do, we will never escape our basic unacceptability to ourselves and to the world.

It seems to me that most pain in the world, most fear and most destructive acts stem from an unwillingness to even acknowledge the existence of these aspects of the human shadow in every human being. If we come to believe some people, or even some countries, are born evil (but fortunately we are not), or others are good but we never can be so, we deny the universal human capacity for evil and we embark to a greater or lesser extent on a crusade or jihad (the language of preference changes with geographical or theological differences) to eradicate the evil Other. Arguably, even more destructively, if we are unfortunate enough to see the true Self as the Other we are on the road to suicide.

I believe these processes are the root of much violence, declarations of war, terrorism and human isolation and quite possibly the apparently inexorable drive towards selfishly motivated destruction of the planet itself. And if the deeper reality really is, 'world as lover, world as self' then in Buddhist terms these are also processes of self-hate. How insane is that?

There is also of course a wider political and contextual reality which has been constructed, created and maintained by collective human choice of those with access to material wealth and political influence, to exercise power in particular ways. Political theorist Gramsci referred to the ruling perceptions of the elite as an ideological hegemony. The ones with power define what is normal and what is not, what is acceptable and what is not. In this hegemonic world, rooted in particular beliefs and ideologies, people are defined, categorised and further redefined by those exercising political, ideological and economic power. It seems in our modern western societies that we use this power to the advantage of the few and the disadvantage and damage of the many.

From my previous studies in Criminology, it became very clear to me that in our society this hegemonic thought process and these ideological constructs, work powerfully to control and direct collective social perceptions and social groups. Time and again it was possible to observe that the first people in society to become marginalised and disenfranchised were the poor, the culturally different and those deemed, one way or another, to be abnormal, criminal or mentally ill. To take a stand against this hegemonic view quickly tends to invite categorisation and marginalisation as bad or mad, and therefore in possession of crazy or dangerous viewpoints, which cannot be taken seriously.

It has been my experience that a lot of self or officially diagnosed depression and low self-esteem felt by many users of mental health services, has often been as a result of this social and political marginalisation, where the understandable anger of the User is frequently turned inwards as a less risky course of action, and then becomes re-channelled as depression. Undoubtedly some people struggle with particular and severe imbalances in their personality, however it is very easy for Users of mental health services to fall into almost automatic self-pathologising and thus complete a very toxic ideological closure around a view of the Self, mirrored by the categorisation and codification of the powerful elite in society and their media propagandists who peddle the kind of authoritarian populism promoted by American and UK shock-jocks and much of our tabloid press.

So, taking a risk to expand and grow under these circumstances is often an act of considerable courage, which needs to be supported and acknowledged as such.

We do not live in a value free world and I feel it is sometimes incumbent on professional healers to acknowledge this actively in their work with clients.

Further reading:

(Hillman. & Ventura, 1993): an articulate exploration of the place of personal politics in therapy.

(Taylor, 1981): a thorough exposition of the existence and toxic influence of authoritarian populism in society.

(Glasgow University Media Group 1976; 1980; 1982): a study of the malign influence of ideological hegemony in the British media.

FOOTNOTE:

"Myalgic Encephalomyelitis represents an acquired complex and debilitating disorder that is characterised by profound fatigue and cognitive problems which do not improve with bed rest and becomes worse with physical and mental exertion". www.fatigueanswers.com .

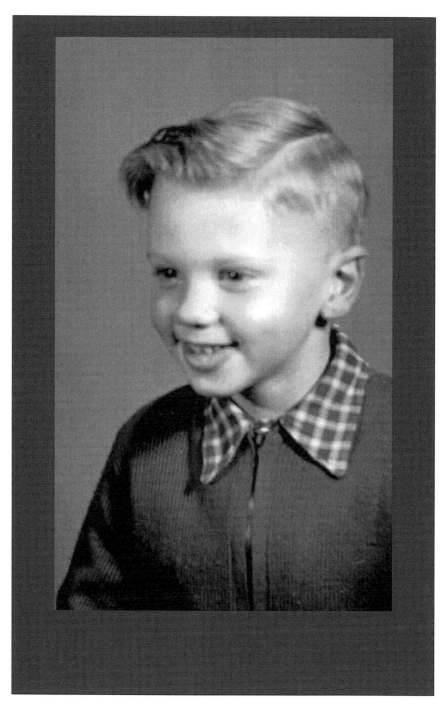

John aged 4½ before brick incident

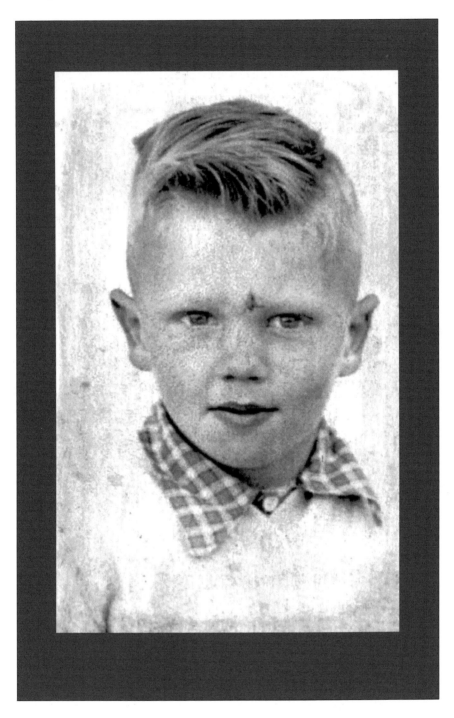

John aged 4½ after brick incident

CHAPTER 2:

Hyper vigilance, self-reliance and endurance

I trained as a therapist and facilitator, in Humanistic Psychology (with the UK based Institute for the Development of Human Potential [IDHP]) and the Hakomi Method: a body centred psychotherapy developed by the USA based Hakomi Institute, located at that time in Boulder, Colorado.

During the Hakomi Training we spent a five day block exploring what are referred to in Hakomi as "Character Strategies" *(see Appendix One, p. 357)*. These are highly creative but crisis focused responses to powerful original trauma, particularly trauma experienced during childhood. Essentially they are mechanisms to rapidly remove the emotional self (if not the whole Self) from the immediate pain of grief.

The concepts were originally developed by Ron Kurtz, Pat Ogden, Jon Eisman and others at the Hakomi Institute and build on a reframing of the American Psychiatric Association "D.S.M" ("Diagnostic and Statistical Manual of Mental Disorders"). It was an attempt to move away from over-medicalisation or over-pathologising of mental health. The language chosen reflects grief reactions caused by losses or absence of critical nurturing during infancy and early childhood.

Given that authors Robin Skynner and John Cleese, (1993) suggest that around 80% of the population experience some form of critical loss or lack of emotional nourishment in childhood, it is I think unwise to readily over-pathologise the resulting mental health difficulties that adults experience.

The considerable dangers of this can be seen in a brief look at relatively recent developments in the formation of the forthcoming fifth edition of the "DSM" and how the issue of 'bereavement' and typical grief responses to loss are being addressed.

The previous edition "DSM-IV" was published in 1994 and "DSM–V" was due for publication in 2013. Whereas DSM-IV clearly distinguishes the normal and expected grief reaction after bereavement from the more persistent symptoms of clinical depression, it is currently rumoured that DSM-V will specifically characterise bereavement as a depressive disorder, even including people experiencing two weeks of mild depressive symptoms, following the loss of a loved one.

Thus at a stroke, this appears to turn normal human grief into a psychiatric diagnosis and erroneously label 'mentally healthy' people with a psychiatric illness. Although normal bereavement processes are often extremely painful, they are (in the course of a lifetime) relatively short-lived (usually at most, up to around two or three years after the bereavement) and 'benign' in the sense that ultimately, bereavement does not severely impair function or increase the risk of suicide in the way that is quite possible with other forms of clinical depression with a less immediate trigger.

Furthermore, of course, there is the attendant danger that it will present the pharmaceutical industry with significantly increased opportunities to market and sell drugs to medical professionals and thus encourage unnecessary treatment with antidepressants and antipsychotics, both of which are increasingly used to 'treat' depression and anxiety. Given the tendency of many antidepressants to mute or mask emotional symptoms, their routine use in bereavement can only be a retrogressive step. The natural processes of grief require the natural flow of emotions in order to follow an organic process towards emotional ' healing' from the deeply painful experience of bereavement.

In contrast to such dangers of over medicalisation, the Hakomi approach utilises these diagnostic frameworks in a rather more humanistic and holistic way. It encourages a movement away from over-medicalisation and over-pathologising of symptoms, towards the possibility of partnership work with clients to affect perceptual, intrapsychic and interpersonal relationship and behaviour change.

This change is based on the client's self-determination and choice to:

- firstly accept and utilise increasing levels of personal responsibility for their actions and what they choose to believe about the world and their place within it;

- secondly to develop a more robust level of confidence and trust in the ability of the adult Self to increasingly cope with the emotional challenges of life.

The therapist is in the privileged role of supporting and encouraging the unfolding of these processes.

According to the Hakomi Institute, "Character Strategies" *(see Appendix One p. 357)* can offer the opportunity to develop particular strengths, but they are also potentially very self-limiting in that their motivatory base is fear (of experiencing grief), and often as a consequence, will lead to behavioural patterns of rigid self-protection and over emphasis on survival, which will also entrench deeply frozen grief within the client's emotional world.

Very often, an over emphasis in a particular area will also limit opportunities to develop complementary life-skills in other areas, creating what is known in Hakomi as an "insight barrier" which blocks sight of other possible or complementary options. For example, the development of particular strengths in what Hakomi called the "Burdened and Enduring" Character Strategy (an ability to withstand considerable psychological and other forms of pressure, endure considerable levels of stress and be determined to see things through) is likely to block the person's awareness of the life enhancing possibilities of natural expression of spontaneity and sense of fun.

The ultimate aim is to balance both "strengths" and what Hakomi terms "underdeveloped complements". Assuming that the majority of us experience some lack of nourishment in early childhood, we can move beyond this in a healthy self-determining way by seeking to know our particular strengths formed around a particular defence position and then choosing to develop what might have been masked or missed to balance over emphasis on a strength in the form of nurturing an underdeveloped complement.

The issue is not one of inherent illness or personality defect, but instead one of eventual self-education and self-empowerment. This is a long way from the somewhat apocalyptic DSM notions of "diagnostic mental disorders". Rather, it is recognition that the road to personal growth and emotional freedom can potentially be open to all of us, through a developmental commitment to increasingly know ourselves, accept adult levels of personal responsibility, gain confidence in the Self, and so exercise increasing personal power and choice in the world.

For the sake of flexibility, realism and balance, it is of course necessary to acknowledge that a small percentage of the population do struggle with distinct, severe and enduring mental health problems, which do require considerable psychiatric support; possibly including the careful use of medication, and those people would not be helped nor supported in any useful way, by psychotherapy sessions alone.

Curiously, as a previous practitioner in the Criminal Justice System, even though I am not at all suggesting behavioural parallels between the two populations, there is a similar ratio of a relatively small number of offenders who need to be incarcerated for the protection of the public and themselves. At the time I was practising it was calculated that figure amounted to less than 5% of the total prison population, and that the majority of incarcerated prisoners were largely persistent petty offenders. In other words, around 95% could be effectively worked with in the context of community based responses to offending behaviour, often with a much lower reconviction rate than those who served prison sentences.

I have certainly worked with a few therapy clients in my career that had severe mental health difficulties which could not be contained nor realistically alleviated on the basis of weekly counselling or psychotherapy sessions. In one case, after a number of increasingly manic episodes, it came as a considerable relief for the young man I worked with to recognise he needed more support than I could offer. Furthermore, the psychotherapy sessions we undertook enabled him to re-negotiate a much more helpful and effective working relationship with both his community psychiatric nurse and his psychiatrist.

However, the vast majority of clients I have worked with since the 1980s have not required medication. Instead they required therapeutic support, consistent positive regard, attentional non-violence, and encouragement towards expanding mindfulness and self-education in respect of their own internal processes and habitual responses to their environment, especially to stress in their environment.

By way of illustrating a range of possible self-motivated responses to life difficulties, I am outlining in *Appendix One* (p.357) a broad perceptual framework for potential clients to understand: the typical defensive responses of the adapted self; potential learnt strengths that can be drawn upon to effect personal growth, and what might also be developed to create a more flexible and responsive way of living more easily in one's world.

In my case, utilising the terminology of Hakomi Character Strategies, the adoption of a "Burdened and Enduring" strategy may have been principally as a result of the brick incident experienced at the age of 4 ½. In addition, but at an earlier stage during my first year of life, I believe that I also adopted a "Sensitive-Analytic" stance. This I understand to be the consequence of my mother's possibly inevitable emotional absence from me, during the first nine months of my life due to her hidden grief for her own mother, whom she knew to have a developing terminal illness. My maternal grandmother died when I was 9 months old.

The Sensitive Analytic strategy is based on a perceived crisis around visibility and safety in the world. For me this is likely to have been considerably amplified and perceptually confirmed by the brick incident. I would explain it in these terms: I understand that any significant level of emotional absence experienced in the first few months of life would probably leave me feeling under protected in the world. If I add to this the powerful shock of the brick incident at the age of 4 ½ it would not be surprising to recognise that I had developed a belief that I was not safe in the world. As much as I can remember, I can sense feeling generally unwelcome and not wanted, from an early age. I believe I even felt this to such an extent that at some level I clearly believed that my continued existence was in serious jeopardy.

As a consequence of this combination of Sensitive-Analytic and Burdened-Enduring elements I developed behavioural patterns of hyper-vigilance and invisibility, to protect myself. This resulted in a marked ability to register, retain and read information about everything in my immediate local environment, at cognitive, observational, energetic and intuitive levels. Clearly what was absent from this list of abilities was the emotional level. It was not safe to directly relate to the world from a relaxed place of emotional sensitivity. I certainly had acute emotional sensitivity, but it existed in what I regard as a deeply wounded form.

I can now see this in retrospect, as at least an excellent partial grounding for my work as a therapist from an Integrative-Relational perspective: as such I am able to offer a relatively safe and relationally intuitive and unobtrusive environment to clients, but at some considerable cost to myself. It remained this way until I had worked on my own fear issues and also more fully understood the importance of energetic self-acceptance and self-protection.

I remember my early adult life as a time when I could 'read' what was in other people's hearts but I rarely trusted their continuing good intentions. I also believe (from what I later learnt with the Hakomi Institute and what I began to more accurately observe around my own feelings and behaviour), that I additionally developed character strategies of Self-Reliance and an Industrious and Over-Focussed stance in life.

In my experience, these are often complementary developments added to a Sensitive-Analytic base, as the person attempts to remain unobtrusive and safe in the world whilst continuing to develop and grow on some level in response to an ever changing environment. These additional strengths enable the person to develop the ability to withstand very high degrees of stress and pressure (because keeping one's head down and enduring threats is the safest thing to do); to rely on themselves (because it is not safe to trust anyone) and to work very hard (because that is probably the only way one will be offered love and affection, if one is lucky, somewhere in the world).

From a positive angle these strategies offer a valuable self-sustaining presence in the world, with the attendant ability to keep going where others might buckle under the strain. Essentially however, they are self-defeating unless they are understood, and underdeveloped aspects of these positions are grown to complement the strengths that already exist.

My own 'self-defeat' manifested itself in the 1980s when I developed Myalgic Encephalomyelitis (M.E.). I was working under a sustained and intense level of pressure when I contracted M.E. It was a time in my life when I was holding responsibility for managing a high powered consultancy and training unit within the traditionally underfunded Voluntary Sector, with a severely depleted and disaffected workforce, including one member of staff who had become very suddenly bereaved and another staff member undergoing disciplinary action. Something had to give and eventually it was my health which dramatically and suddenly collapsed.

The underdeveloped aspects of my particular set of character strategies are:

- A flowing comfort with living in an emotionally relational world.
- An ability to recognise self needs and to clearly ask for help around meeting those needs.
- An ability to be both visibly spontaneous as required and also assertive in relation to personal boundaries and exercise of personal power in the world.

- And last but not least a belief that I am naturally loveable for whom I am and that I do not have to work hard simply to be loved by others (or by myself).

Therefore, my challenge has been to develop trust in myself and the wisdom of my own heart. I was very sensitive and easily wounded by myself or others' responses towards me and I lost trust in what my heart was telling me, especially when I felt afraid and was suspicious of myself or the motivations of others. I also found it hard to believe I could be loveable simply for being me, or as I would term it these days, being my authentic Self.

Most of the DSM diagnostic framework suggests that an over emphasis on a particular way of acting in the world is a malfunction of healthy thinking and perception. In contrast, Hakomi suggests that these are understandable defensive responses developed in the first instance to minimise the visceral and possibly life threatening effects of primary grief, and secondly to enable the person to experience the world from a place of greater emotional safety and self-protection.

These creative responses to a perceived threat to personal safety, suggest human experience and subsequent perception is not only a result of a particular way of thinking but also of a broader way of 'being' in the world, based on emotional and somatic as well as cognitive functioning. It is not only the 'head and brain' that is involved in this process.

In recent years there has been a growth in literature within the field of ecopsychology, which reminds us that human experience has, and always has had, a direct perception of the world and nature through the "intelligence of the heart" as well as what the "head" might have concluded. Stephen Buhner's work is especially interesting in this area (Buhner, S. H. [2004]).

From this perspective, Buhner asserts that the heart is not a mechanistic pump, but is in fact a second brain: in the words of Matthew Wood, quoted in the book, *"The informed, intelligent core of our emotional, spiritual and perceptual universe"*, (Buhner, 2004).

Often without knowing it, human beings relate to each other from the heart. If we choose to think, act and feel from the heart in relation to others, we can dramatically alter our own and others' experiences of the world, its potential and our own potential for generative co-creation. This will take us beyond the restrictions and confines of a particular Character Strategy or combination of strategies, if we are able to move even just a little beyond habitual patterns of thinking, physical sensation and emotion, as typical responses to anxiety and fear.

My memory of how I dealt with my maternal grandfather's death at the age of 11yrs is still very vivid. As I reflect on how I experienced the night before his death and the morning after when I found him dead in bed, I am struck by two things: despite what I have said in this chapter about my earlier life experiences, how comfortable I felt with him at the level of relating from the heart, as we spent a very emotionally warm and close evening together; and how quickly my heart response moved into a sense of responsibility and protection towards my mother, in the moments before breaking the news to her of her father's death. I was fully conscious at the time of exactly how I was going to word things in breaking the news. I was seeking to do my best to offer as much empathy and protection as I could in impossible circumstances, when I was already feeling grief myself.

I knew I had to communicate an overall truth, but I chose to do it in the gentlest way I could imagine at the time. I suppose that is why I felt I left childhood behind in those very powerful last moments before I entered my parent's bedroom to let mum know that something awful had happened.

***

I think I left childhood behind me when I was 11 years old.

After my maternal grandmother died, when I was 9 months old, my grandfather came to live with us. Our family unit consisted of Mum, Dad, my Brother Glyn who was 7 years older than me, and Granddad, Luther Wheatley. By the age of 11, I had already seen my Brother leave home and my family world was about to get dramatically smaller.

It was a Friday evening, with my carefully saved spending money, I had just bought a harmonica and I was attempting (very badly but nevertheless with considerable enthusiasm) to play it. I was at home with Granddad, Mum was out at her choir practice and Dad was also out somewhere. I remember enjoying a wonderfully warm and intimately affectionate evening; the fire was burning in the hearth, I was blowing hard on the old 'harp' and Granddad was lost in paroxysms of helpless laughter at my attempts to create music. I went to bed that night feeling very loved and appreciated, even if I was making a terrible noise.

I woke up next day around 9am and went to the bathroom. I heard Mum's voice asking me to call Granddad who, unusually, had not got up early that morning to make the fire downstairs as he usually did.

Mum and Dad were in the bedroom next door to the box room which was my Granddad's room.

I opened Granddad's bedroom door, saw his neatly folded pile of clothes on the chair next to his bed with his Chesterfield F.C. season ticket resting on top of the clothes. I saw my Granddad lying in bed; I saw the grey pallor of his skin and immediately I knew he was dead.

I felt the power of the moment and an enormous silence in the world which only I could break.

I immediately felt the responsibility resting on my shoulders as I considered how to give the news to my Mum.

I entered Mum and Dad's bedroom and said, "Mum, I don't think Granddad is very well"...

***

The Messenger

Thinking back

I see the image

I feel his gentle laughter

it falls softly in the quiet evening

A NEW DISCOVERY!

my first harmonica

played badly, perhaps

but with real feeling!

He watches my gallant efforts

unable to hide his smile

tears of laughter

a gift of warmth and sharing

I see the real me

it feels so good

and it seems so long ago.

Something ended then

a short night

but a new world come morning.

I head towards his room

lingering memories are fading in the hardening light

something is wrong here

I see his face

cold, peaceful, in another world

my heart knows

as I search in vain for a different reality

Next door

my parents are awakening.

in here I feel the awful chilling truth

In this deep silence

the whole world waits

in this deep silence

the child in me is dying

The messenger

hides his memories away

and sadly walks

towards their bedroom door.

(December, 1985).

Above: John aged 6 months with Grandma Wheatley
Below: First home, council 'prefab', Mastin Moor, North Derbyshire

Above: John with elder brother Glyn, and Mum
Below: Council House, Inkersall Green, North Derbyshire

Grandad Luther Wheatley

CHAPTER 3:

Betrayal and retreat into the Self

Buhner's concept of "the intelligence of the heart" gives a hint of the potential power of therapeutic healing, growth and of generative co-creation possible in the encounter between therapist and client. This is especially so if both parties become aware of such possibilities when applying mindfulness to their therapeutic and emotional dialogue. The awareness of the existence of "heart intelligence" as well as awareness of necessary "cognitive functioning", would offer the opportunity for direct co-creation in the immediate and developing therapeutic environment of the therapy room (perhaps in the form of negotiated and mindfully observed results of therapeutic-relational 'experiments') and also perhaps simultaneously, by inference and application through energetic impact in the wider world itself.

The potential for co-creation through therapeutic and relational dialogue would be invaluable to men in particular, because they are largely socialised to separate heart from head and to give greater importance to logical thinking ("Logos" in Jung's language) than to symbolic and emotionally creative sensing and feeling ("Mythos" in Jung's terminology as a contrasting aspect of the collective unconscious). The work of Robert Bly, Michael Meade, James Hillman and others has provided a way for men to revisit the place of being where both "mythos" and "logos" can be balanced and made much more equally accessible as a creative and therapeutic life resource.

Robert Bly, in his book, "Iron John", an attempt at a balanced "logos and mythos" critique of the Grimm Brother's Folk Tale "Iron Hans", (Bly, 1990), talks of the 'golden ball' of childhood which contains elements of both logos and mythos. *"the golden ball reminds us of the unity of personality we had as children – a kind of radiance or wholeness, before we split into male and female, rich and poor, bad and good"*. The child gives off a *"radiant energy from the inside"*. Bly considers that we lose the "golden ball" around the age of 8, and that, *"once the golden ball is gone, we spend the rest of our lives trying to get it back"*

I do wonder whether substantially I lost mine at the age of 4½ rather than 8. I can recall glimpses of that "radiant energy" after age 4½ but only in brief patches. They occurred mostly in the presence of animals, not in the presence of human beings. I remember having a deep love of animals which stays with me to this day, and I'm sure comes from my mother's influence. I remember clearly that I had no fear of any animal and no animal seemed to have any fear of me. I would automatically reach out my hand to any dog, including those regarded by their owners as 'fierce' and the dog would invariably come to me and rest by me. I also recall sitting in the park on a park bench whilst on holiday in Scarborough with my parents, and experiencing wild birds landing on my knee and sitting looking at me for quite a while before they flew off.

Perhaps the process of loss was completed after the age of 8, during that transitory time when I moved from Infant School to Junior School, a time when I recall that I began to feel the pain in my parents' relationship with each other. As I moved further beyond the age of 8 towards adolescence, I also remember being increasingly wary of the world, and fear was building in me about being in the world itself. A critical moment, perhaps symbolic of this internal shift and growing anxiety, was a time around the age of 11, when I reached out to a dog and instead of coming to me as I naturally expected, it 'went for me'. I was shocked and remember feeling very confused and no longer trusting of my own intuitive judgment about what or who was safe and what or who was not.

Certainly by the age of 11, it seems that I expected the world to bite me and it often did. My brother was leaving home, it was shortly before my Granddad died and I suddenly found myself isolated, one of a family of four, not one of a secure and protected family of five. Then very shortly afterwards, by the time I was 12, I was in a family of three, living in the middle of an exposed environment where I could sense my father's discontent with life and my mother's quiet desperation.

By the time I was 11 I was also already used to being routinely humiliated in front of my class at Junior School, every Friday morning (during feedback from mental arithmetic tests) by my class teacher 'Frank B' who had been a childhood suitor of my Mum. Unfortunately for him, she had repeatedly rejected his advances, in favour of other suitors and then eventually she chose to be with my Dad. Frank seemed to have a great delight in letting people know I had scored badly in my weekly mental arithmetic torture sessions. I now suspect this glee was an amplification of mountains of 'schadenfreude', connected to his negative feelings about my Dad. For those not familiar with the word, by 'schadenfreude' I mean pleasure derived from witnessing the pain of others.

Like many young people of his generation, growing up in a working class community, Dad left school at the age of fourteen, as my grandparents could not afford to allow him to stay in education, even though he was academically very gifted. Before the Second World War, Dad worked as a railway clerk in Darnall, a small railway station in Sheffield. The War introduced him to a life serving overseas in the RAF, and after being demobbed he undertook a post war

51

'crash course' in teacher training at Sheffield University. He eventually became a Primary School teacher, with a particular flair for mathematics.

Frank was well aware of my Dad's (by then) county-wide Education Department reputation, as a quiet genius at mathematics and gifted original thinker. Being my final year class teacher, Frank also knew very well that I lacked ability, and or confidence, at mathematics, especially when asked to answer 'put you on the spot in front of your classmates' type mental arithmetic questions. At an earlier age I had intuitive wisdom but little common sense. I knew already four years previously, by the age of 7 or 8, that I would have future problems with Maths. Even at that age I had an ability to 'witness my own process', and I can distinctly remember the day at Infant School when we were given a choice to 'learn our times tables' or go out to spend time in the school grounds in the sunshine. Unwisely, I of course chose the latter and was fitfully aware by the time I left Infant School, that I had not learnt my times tables.

This was one critical element amongst many, as I became older, of my growing fear of my father, as I was well aware I didn't know my times tables and I lived in anxiety of being found out both by Dad and also by my teachers and classmates at School. By the age of 11, my moth like fear was drawing me inexorably towards the sadistic flame of Frank's weekly public humiliation. He never allowed me to hide, but crucially he never helped me either; apparently preferring instead to savour the moment and, I assume through causing me considerable pain and shame, eke out some small weekly revenge on Dad for succeeding in marrying my Mum.

This public humiliation considerably deepened and continued at Grammar School. By the age of 14, I had the misfortune to be 'taught' by a particularly sadistic Maths teacher who seemed to create an illusion of power and security for herself by humiliating those she perceived as weaker than her. My class mate "Kenny S", and I, were equally bad at Mathematics and every week without fail, she asked each of us in turn to stand up and answer a mental arithmetic question. When we couldn't she would invariably retort, "You are stupid boy. Say, 'I'm stupid Miss". Kenny and I would mumble such a reply and then she would demand we said it very distinctly and loudly. It seemed we had no option, so when we did, she then invited the class to, "Laugh at them and their stupidity". The (no doubt fearful) pupils always joined in to order, presumably relieved that it was us up there being publically pilloried and humiliated, not them.

As our school was a mixed gender school and by then I at least was feeling the first hormonal stirrings of sexual attraction to girls, this weekly humiliation was absolute torture. I experienced and also anticipated this with terrible fear; at the same time I regarded the Maths teacher and many of her colleagues, who had a similar fear based approach to education, with absolute contempt. Kenny took the first opportunity to leave at age 16. I stayed on because I was too frozen to even be aware I had any other options.

To this day, I am passionate that if anyone seeks to hold office as a teacher, they should be absolutely committed to facilitating education by love, not by fear. If they cannot do that, they are not fit to be regarded as teachers. I recall how excited I was after I learnt I had passed my Eleven Plus, and was going to Grammar School. I was enthusiastic and committed to learning and self-education. It is a damning indictment of the way I and many unfortunate others were educated, to reflect that it took less than twelve months for my Grammar School to practically destroy that child-blessed enthusiasm within me.

As I understand it, a teacher's sacred task is a facilitative one linked to blessing the potential in children. From a facilitative perspective, the root of the word educate is 'educare' which means 'to bring out what the person already knows'. I have never seen this done successfully through use of fear. I experienced much of my time with teachers as a deep betrayal of this sacred trust. It was a further contributing factor in pitching me headlong into a 'retreat into the Self'. By the age of 17, I was a lost soul.

I was delighted to find a website (*www.sathyasaiehv.org.uk*) which promoted "education through love" as part of a contribution to the "National Curriculum Citizenship Programme". Sathya Sai is quoted on the website as follows:

"Education has two aspects; the first is related to external and worldly education, which is nothing but acquiring bookish knowledge. In the modern world, we find many well versed and highly qualified in this aspect. The second aspect known as 'Educare' is related to human values. The word 'Educare' means to bring out that which is within. Human values are latent in every human being; one cannot acquire them from outside. They have to be elicited from within. Educare means to bring out human values. To 'bring out' means to translate them into action"

In continuing the theme of personal 'betrayals', not only do I recognise that I may be articulating at a personal level, the destruction of a 12 year old's enthusiasm, which reflects a society level based betrayal of human values through toxic forms of education and teaching; I also recognise in terms of my own life narrative, a need to articulate another passion and betrayal, this time connected with my ancestors, the communities that supported them, and my county of birth, Derbyshire.

One of my Dad's earlier experiences had been teaching at Creswell Junior School, North East Derbyshire, when the coal mining disaster happened at Creswell Colliery, in the village, on the 26th September, 1950, just over a year before I was born.

In the disaster, 80 men were overcome by smoke and fumes and perished underground. 23 of those men's bodies remained underground for a year until it was safe to move them. Dad later recalled having to break the news of the disaster to some of his class pupils, and also to repeatedly deal with the aftermath of much grief and sorrow for months afterwards. It was said that word of the disaster spread quickly around the village and many off duty miners rushed to offer any assistance they could. One miner, who had broken his back several months before, went down the stricken pit wearing a back brace, to rescue his fellow workers.

Whichever way I read this, from both the perspective of my Dad's actions and also from the actions of the anonymous miner, I regard such commitment as deep human love **in action**, and I regard such gestures as the essence of meaningful life on this earth.

M. Scott Peck in his seminal book "The Road Less Travelled" (Peck, 1978), defines 'love' as, *"the will to extend one's self for the purpose of nurturing one's own or another's spiritual growth"*. In other words, *"love is an act of will"* (it is not simply a 'feeling'), *"namely, both an intention and action. Will also implies choice. We do not have to love. We choose to love. No matter how much we may think we are loving, if we are in fact not loving, it is because we have chosen not to love and therefore do not love despite our good intentions"*.

By the time I was 11, Dad had secured a Headship at Duckmanton Primary School (located in a pit village about five miles as the crow flies from our council estate and close to Markham Colliery where there was a further pit disaster in 1973)

On July 31st, 1973, at the age of 22, I was on a student working holiday in the USA, employed as a janitor and odd job man at a local telephone company in Madison, Wisconsin. I had been away from home for weeks and felt I had lost touch with any news about the world outside of the USA. I came home after my shift at the company and turned on the TV, which being located in the Midwest hardly ever reported on anything at all outside of the USA.

Imagine my shocked surprise therefore when I returned home that day and turned on the TV at the precise moment that the TV Company was broadcasting a news story about a mining accident in England, at Markham Colliery, North Derbyshire. 18 coal miners had lost their lives at Markham, and a further 11 were seriously injured: it was another major pit disaster.

A descending cage carrying the men failed to slow down as it approached the bottom of the mine shaft and 18 miners were killed instantly in the impact. The accident was caused by a fracture of the brake-rod, when a slowly growing metal fatigue crack reached a critical stage and the brake-rod parted.

The mine was closed in 1994, ten years after the Miner's Strike, during which Margaret Thatcher had talked of and promulgated the notion of striking miners as "The enemy within". Some enemy! These people were not enemies. Many of them gave their lives for their country and their communities. At the time and ever since, I have felt it nothing less than an obscene betrayal of a heart based community, to hear people recollect events of the 1984 Miner's Strike as if the government of the day was the patriotic champion of democracy.

This historical narrative and frequent distorted re-writing of history, about miners from my beloved Derbyshire and those from neighbouring South Yorkshire, still has the power to stir rage and anger in me. I heard many stories from my grandparents about the extreme hardships in local mining communities, created by historical industrial relations policies. Both my Paternal and Maternal Grandfathers lost their jobs after colliery management 'lock outs', following the General Strike in 1926. They were both good men, as were very many of those attacked by mounted police, 12 miles away at the "Battle of Orgreave" many years later, on the 18th June, 1984.

The 'Battle of Orgreave' was a confrontation between police and picketing miners at the British Steel Coking Plant in Orgreave, South Yorkshire during the 1984 Miners' Strike. In 1991, South Yorkshire Police were forced to pay out half a million pounds to 39 miners, who were falsely arrested during events at Orgreave. During the 'battle', police mounted on horses charged miners time after time. Some miners fought the police officers, many were arrested, and some were severely beaten with truncheons by policemen on horseback.

Ninety-five picketers were charged with riot, unlawful assembly and similar offences after the battle. A number of these were put on trial in 1987, and if convicted would have faced very lengthy jail sentences. But the trials collapsed, all charges were dropped and a number of lawsuits were brought against the police for unlawful arrest and allegedly corrupt procedures, when in particular questions were raised about the evident forgery of police statements and police signatures on statements. South Yorkshire Police later agreed to pay £425,000 compensation and £100,000 in legal costs to 39 miners through an out-of-court settlement.

It appears that such police behaviour was not an isolated incident. In 2012, further startling revelations of the corrupt practices of South Yorkshire Police came to light in the alleged doctoring of evidence after bot'h the Hillsborough Disaster and the Battle of Orgreave'. This is nothing short of a fundamental betrayal of democracy. I would never forget my roots, my ancestors would not allow it - but in 2012, no pits remain in Derbyshire and virtually none in neighbouring Yorkshire. The close knit communities around the mines, so common in my childhood, are no more.

In 2009, the BBC commemorated the 25th anniversary of the 1984 Miner's Strike with a series of programmes. For a while I experienced this as a fitting reconnection with the heart of human experience at a very difficult time in our national history. Until that point, I had felt much received media wisdom had effectively consigned the Miner's Strike to deliberately forgotten history. It had become a footnote, as Marxists might see it, an aspect of the "fetishism of commodities" that passes for much current affairs coverage of news stories in these modern times.

Any serious study of the workings of the British media would reveal that 'News' is more often than not, selectively chosen, within the parameters of the particular ideological constructs of the current ruling 'hegemony'. It is then analysed, categorised, commoditised and finally filed as one of many historical objects that constitute our collective historical narrative. The deeper reality is that human meaning and significance is often lost or devalued to the point of the received wisdom of historical objectification. At times, all aspects of soul and human meaning appear to have been removed.

I can become very strongly stirred by music, especially where it connects with the more radical aspects of the Folk tradition. Often I feel the work of creative artists active in the folk and roots movement, like Derbyshire based John Tams and Barry Coope, or the work of the South Yorkshire based singing collective 'Coope, Boyes and Simpson', is regarded by some media and political commentators as naïve atavistic recall of things best forgotten. If this is so, then I feel such judgments reflect the views of those who will not or dare not see the truth.

In my reality, John and others sing and remember as an act of love and with a determination to never let the songs of the heart die. If the song of the heart dies in our collective human memory, then all human meaning eventually dies too. These creative artists are warriors of the heart and they are vital to all that is best in our continuing humanity.

In his 2005 recording, 'The Reckoning', John Tams adapted the traditional song, "Man of Constant Sorrow", to include lyrics which honoured the miners and their families who live through the 1984 Miner's Strike. It included these lines describing abandoned mines, *"And they shut them down and left them, buried coal for evermore. Now the market place stands empty, but there's still a sign that says "remember '84". We remember 84"*. In the sleeve notes of the record, John writes, *"Who'll sing the anthems, and who'll tell the story, will the line hold. Will it scatter and run. Shall we at last be united in glory only remembered for what we have done?"* (Extract from John Tams, [2005], The Reckoning, Topic Records.)

Much as I am now able to see my father's better qualities in retrospective historical reflection, and recognise his active role in mining and post-mining communities of North Derbyshire, it is also true to say that I became very estranged from my father from age 11 or 12 onwards, after I had passed my 'Eleven Plus' exam and gone to the local Grammar School in Staveley, a North Derbyshire mining & steelworks town.

59

The local Grammar School was, in my eyes, always a pretentious establishment, surrounded by pit slag heaps but nevertheless aspiring to create a culture mirroring the misplaced and inflated pride of a public school. It did this by, amongst other things, adopting "Gaudeamus Igitur" and "Forty Years On" as the two official school songs, both well-known songs sung in highly regarded public schools of the time.

Although I loved learning and had a very active brain, I despised the place, its values and the pretentious fear based education system that appeared to thrive on the pain and discomfort it engendered in many of its out-of-place pupils, and I certainly felt out of place there. Furthermore, fear there was definitely like a cancer, in the way I experienced it, spreading through the school and haunting the corridors and quadrangles. By the age of 12, I was becoming increasingly disaffected with the place.

I remember feeling and being intimidated by the Deputy Headmaster (known colloquially as "Sonky") who had been at the school, initially as a student teacher when my Dad had been a pupil, and had in fact been there ever since.

He roamed the corridors in a flowing academic gown and seemed to contaminate the environment. He told me one day to "carry some books" for him to the Headmaster's Study. As a naïve 12 year old boy, I was very nervous around him, misunderstood a couple of demands and also dropped a pile of books twice. I was thoroughly intimidated and felt the terrifying force of his voice shouting very loudly in my ear, "You are really stupid boy".

I was acutely aware of my internal reaction to his accusation-judgment: I heard an angry voice speak within me in a very distinctive tone. It must have been a powerful response to his insult, as I can still hear the voice speaking inside me to this day. It said, "I'm not stupid, I can't be, I think too much".

From that moment onwards I had a growing and unmistakeable contempt for the values of the school and its emotional stupidity. I started on the road to rebellion from that rather lonely place of personal truth.

I was so thoroughly disaffected by the age of 17, that I truanted for a whole year (after I had "signed in" every day) and spent my time sitting under the veranda of the local Miners' Welfare cricket pavilion, furiously growing my hair and thinking dark thoughts about the oppressive institution which claimed to be attempting to educate me.

It was an automatic process in our school, that every sixth former was made a School Prefect and expected to uphold the school values. I think this had been going on in one form or another, with senior pupils, ever since the school was established in 1572. Neither I nor another disaffected youth Andrew T. were invited to be School Prefects. I could say possibly, but I suspect almost certainly, the first exceptions in almost 400 years! I was told later, that when asked by a pupil, "Why are Holt and T. not here?" the Headmaster had replied, "Well, they are not on our side are they?"

Nevertheless, I had done admirably well growing my hair, as Bob Dylan once sang; *"I'm going to grow my hair down to my knees so strange, that I look like a walkin' mountain range".*

By the end of the first year of Sixth Form, my hair was two thirds of the way down my back. Magnificent golden tresses although I say it myself! No one had ever grown their hair that long before at our school. In fact I heard a few months later that the Headmaster had demanded another younger pupil get his hair cut. The lad refused saying, "I'll get mine cut when Holt gets his cut". A fair point made I believe.

The Headmaster saw me in the corridor one day and called me into his office. "Get your hair cut Holt, or don't bother coming back". I went home that lunchtime and cut half an inch off the bottom of my hair. Later the next morning I was in school and the Headmaster sought me out. "You haven't had your hair cut"... "Yes I have"... "No you have not"... "Yes I have"... "Right, I'm throwing you out of school, go home".

I went home for lunch on my pushbike. After lunch Mum said to me, "What time are you going back to school John?" I replied, "I'm not, I've been chucked out"

This was the signal for wild parental activity. Mum (who hated using telephones) immediately phoned my Dad. He clearly knew our Headmaster well from the county wide network of Head Teachers' gatherings. He must have done some hard bargaining on my behalf. That evening Dad told me to get back to school next morning.

I recall it was later still that evening, when Mum and Dad cornered me in the kitchen, physically held me down in the kitchen chair and hacked off a few inches of my hair (no longer a walking mountain range, but at least I still looked like a walking hilltop). I could have stopped them I suppose. I had the physical strength to fight off ten Mum and Dads by then. Although I was furious, I let them cut my hair because I knew I was physically very strong and I didn't really want to hurt them, even though in that moment I felt terrible violence was being done to me. I think I loved Mum and Dad very much despite all this, even if all I felt then was absolutely cold furious hatred towards them.

I returned to school and from that moment on my Headmaster never challenged me again, so of course I went back to furiously growing my hair. It was marvellous! I remember the Head Boy (neatly trimmed short hair, pressed uniform, always very clean shiny shoes) saying to me with contempt, "Your hair looks like a floor mop from the back". Cutting: I said nothing.

18 months later, I would be walking down the high street in Chesterfield, still looking like a floor mop, but at least I was an Art College based floor mop, and I saw an apparition walking towards me: long hair (beautifully coiffured), suspiciously clean Levi jeans and expensive looking long afghan coat, carefully scuffed desert boots – the epitome of self-conscious hippy cool in the style of the modern university student. It was the former Head Boy. He smiled nervously as we passed each other in the street. He had swopped one uniform for another!

I applied for Art College when in the Sixth Form, securing a place on the 2 year "Pre-Diploma in Art & Design" at Chesterfield Art College. The Art Teacher at Grammar School, a very human and loving man in my eyes, was one of the few adults I spent any time with in that school of my own volition.

I used to paint and draw in the Art Room during my lunch hour. Laurie the Art Teacher was there too, doing his own water colours and chatting to me very much as an equal, or at least respecting me as an adult with a brain and some nascent powers of discernment. I felt deeply respected by him. After sitting my A Levels, I was in the Art Room one day, when Laurie casually said to me, "It's been rumoured in the Staff Room that you are going to pass all your A Levels out of spite". I did.

School Speech Day arrived. Having ludicrous pretentions to be a mirror of a public school, our Grammar School printed its Speech Day Programme with a list of pupils who had first of all secured places at Oxford or Cambridge; then pupils who had secured places at Red Brick Universities; then pupils who had secured places at the newer Universities; then pupils who had secured places at

Polytechnics; then pupils who had secured places at Teacher Training Colleges. The final category named students who had secured places at "Other Institutions". Of course, I appeared in this section, under "Art Colleges".

As our names were announced, each of us in turn went on stage to be greeted and congratulated by the Headmaster. When it came to my turn, my name was read out, and there were disturbing rumbles from the assembled congregation, especially from teachers lining the side of the school hall like prison guards anticipating a break out. As I walked on stage looking like the Wild Man of Borneo, my Headmaster reached out his right hand towards me, so I reached out my left hand. Obviously no connection possible there; so he then reached out his left hand and I quickly reciprocated by reaching out my right hand. Embarrassed shuffling was rapidly followed by something that seemed a bit like the Heimlich Manoeuvre and I left the stage with a piece of paper with something written on it. To this day I haven't a clue what was written there. All I remember was a feeling of grim satisfaction at the manner of my closure with that institution. I left the school, never to go back and passed silently into the mysterious beyond.

The mysterious beyond was, for me then located in the Chesterfield suburb of Hasland. The day I went for interview, as I approached the Art College a strange long haired figure in a dark cloak was roaming about, shaking people by the hand. He shook my hand. I noticed the lining of his cloak was shimmering with a rainbow of colours and on the back of the cloak in poetic flowing script was written the legend, "It's a Grey, Grey Day". I thought to myself, "Aye aye, this is the place for me", and so it was...

I later found out from my friend Andy, whom I met at the Art College, that this character was not even a student there. In the terminology of Mod culture, he was instead a well-known 'face' in the Chesterfield area, who just liked hanging around outside the Art College looking weird. It didn't matter to me. His presence was enough confirmation I needed that I was in the place I should be.

My authentic Self may well have started the slow journey back from exile at that moment through self-identification with other marginalised but individual characters, although it would take until I was 38 years old before I would begin to fully realise that, and to be increasingly mindful of what was happening to me. In line with the Parsifal story of grace, loss and eventual redemption, I still had at least twenty years roaming in the wilderness before I was led back again to the familiar territory of the forest outside the Grail Castle. Arguably, it then took me a further 20 years, up to the age of 58 to finally re-enter the Grail Castle and begin to recognise that at long last I am now answering the critical question, "Who does the Grail serve?"

***

What was I learning in school and later in my early adulthood? I was learning that fear and intimidation undermines the soul, or makes it stronger when the response is to remind oneself that self-belief, passion, heart and love are the essence of all human meaning. The best human characteristics of local mining communities showed me that true human meaning came through communal action and values supporting a willingness to serve others as well as to defend the self. I remember much of what was good in the people I knew from such a background.

I also "remember 1984" in the words of John Tams, to honour those who are no longer living in the mining communities that once criss-crossed the

County of my birth. Going further back in time, I remember my Great Grandfather, a father of ten, a violent drunk and also a miner, who I was told, attacked my Great Grandmother on Christmas Eve, knocking a Christmas meal off the stove and being confronted by my Grandfather, Heber Holt, who had grown into a strong young man and no longer able to remain a silent witness to domestic violence, stood up to my Great Grandfather, faced him down, physically fought him and then banished him from the house and from our family forever. As far as I know, Great Grandfather disappeared into exile. He was also called John Holt.

I could never understand why my Dad and Mum gave me his name. Yet, perhaps I do understand now: as I look back I am inclined to think that somehow it was always part of my destiny on some kind of metaphysical level, to bring my ancestor Great Granddad Holt back from pain and exile, especially through my involvement in ritual Men's Work, and through a long journey of betrayal, self-hatred, self- forgiveness & the return of love, in order to offer him a place of belonging in spirit from where he could at last move on. I now treasure and honour his memory and the pain that must have caused him to do what he did in his life.

I am in the right place to do it these days – I see the world in very different ways. For example, the next street to my house, just round the corner from where I am sitting writing these words in Silsden, West Yorkshire, is a cul-de-sac called "Heber Close". So bearing that name, it is no longer a cul-de-sac in my eyes. Instead I feel that I am blessed *by the close presence of a much loved Grandfather and ancestor. In contrast, my Great Grandfather John had lost, or quite likely had never learnt the emotional "ability to shudder" as Robert Bly terms it. He was a warrior who was frequently cutting loose within his own community, without the loving containment of a spiritual practice or human holding and sense of belonging. He was wielding a powerful sword of rage, metaphorically beheading all those around him, until he finally beheaded himself.*

What I am now learning is that my job right now is to burst my heart wide open, to live life to the full, to honour and encourage the deepest love I can within the human family of which I am a part. The only reason we are here, and as far as I can see, the only lesson to learn, is to love: to move beyond the poison of what Otto Scharmer calls "Attentional Violence" and instead, as therapists and healers, and co-creators, to hold in trust a deep belief that the person with us, WILL one day manifest all the magnificent potential for personal and spiritual growth that lays dormant within them, as long as we believe in them long enough for them to believe in themselves.

We can see their human value and potential even if they cannot – and I think we are often called to hold the vision until they can finally see it, feel it and live it for themselves, and for all of us.

***

John aged 11 years

John at Art College with Friend

CHAPTER 4:

Early conversations with power

I met Jane in the spring of 1970. She was in the year below me at Grammar School, came from the same part of North East Derbyshire as my best mate Jimmy Antcliffe, known to his friends as Jim. Jane travelled into school with Jim and others on the same school bus, every weekday. By the early summer of 1970, I had become much more aware of her presence.

I had first got to know Jane through Jim, and then she became part of my 6th Form group studying Architecture as part of our Art A Level class with the Art Teacher Laurie. My connection with Jane felt like a big event in my life right from the beginning. Somehow I knew I had been met on a very deep level. Looking back, it is clear that I knew very early on that I had made a profoundly important connection with her. We chatted a lot on our field trips. One day we visited a beautiful old church in Carlton in Lindrick, North Nottinghamshire, with a small school party. Unusually, the church identifiably retained both Anglo-Saxon and Norman features in its architecture, which made it a special place to visit as far as Laurie the Art Teacher was concerned. Jane and I were the last to leave the church, together.

As I closed the ancient church door behind me, I pulled on the iron door handle, shaped in the form of a sacred circle. It came away in my hand. Spontaneously, I gave it to Jane who was staring at me with delight and disbelief in her eyes. I meant it as a joke, but little did I know then, it was no joke. Back then, despite the joke aspect that gesture also felt like a magical moment in time. It must have been as the whole scene including my actions, the eye connections and smiles between us are indelibly printed in my memory to this day. As I gradually got to know Jane and her school mates, I realised I was forming a powerful friendship with a very friendly, open and beautiful person. I was slowly realising I was in the presence not of a girl, but of a real woman.

I was already involved with my 'first love' Sue, whom I had met two years previously at the local dance hall come concert venue in Chesterfield. Sue never seemed to be able to love me the way I loved her. Sue and her family spent summers in Aberdaron, North Wales and by that time I was also visiting Llanfairfechan, North Wales on a regular basis to enjoy weekends and week-long holidays mountaineering and rock climbing, staying at the now sadly defunct Manchester based C.H.A. ("Co-operative Holidays Association") hostel, known as Plas-Heulog.

In the summer of 1970, I was staying at a climbing hut, Tyn-Y-Maes, owned by Plas-Heulog, situated between the small slate quarrying town of Bethesda and the settlement of Ogwen Cottage, in the Ogwen Valley. Sue and I had arranged to meet by the coast, in Caernarvon one day in the middle of the week, to (I hoped) further our relationship. I was very much looking forward to seeing her, but I sensed trouble ahead.

We met on a beautiful sunny day and Sue spent 30 minutes at ease, chatting with me, walking around Caernarvon before she began to carefully explain to me that she had met someone else at Aberdaron, someone she had known before, who came from the same part of the world as herself, Mottram in Longdendale near Manchester. Even though she cared about me she had decided she needed to be with this new lover (she was pretty emotionally and sexually sophisticated for a 17 year old!). As she told me, it began to rain and then she said she had to get the bus in 10 minutes back to Aberdaron. I stood in the rain, disbelieving what I

72

was hearing but at the same time knowing the girl-woman I loved was about to roll out of my life forever on a green Crosville bus.

I had spent time carefully getting ready for meeting Sue that morning, washing my hair and choosing to wear, for me at least, my best clothes. I stood there, somewhat emotionally paralysed, in the pouring rain as she got on the bus. My hair by now was plastered down flat by the rain, and I was soaking wet. The tears began and I could not stop them flowing, no matter how hard I tried. I felt like I was breaking apart, stood there crying my eyes out, feeling anything but a man, lost in pain and feelings of shame and terrible grief, as Sue looked at me from the bus window, I felt at the time, almost with a disdainful pity.

Yes, there I was. I felt broken, crushed and defeated, a little boy, no longer the arsey rebel of my Grammar School, but just revealed for the lonely and lost soul that I was. The bus pulled out and I watched it go all the way down the road until it disappeared. It seemed I was in a broken daze as I wandered aimlessly around Caernarvon until I found the bus stop for the journey back to Bethesda.

I walked back to Tyn-Y-Maes from Bethesda, and stayed very still for some time. To my surprise, before very long I began to notice myself slipping out of grief into a strange sense of peace. Then, I was suddenly really clear. I needed to let Sue go and I needed to write to Jane and ask her if she wanted to be with me, because I very deeply wanted to be with her. I wrote my desire down in a letter and then posted the letter, content that I had said all I could say of my truth.

Two days later I got a letter back. I will never forget the very first word I read, it filled me with one of the deepest experiences of joy I have ever had in my life. I can see the letter now as I stood outside of the climbing hut at Tyn-Y-Maes and pulled it eagerly out of the envelope. The word was

"Yes!" Jane brought a deeply nourishing form of love into my life, which in contrast to the somewhat idealised unrequited love feelings I always experienced around Sue, felt very real. It was a beautiful relationship that the two of us created together. She loved me for who I was. In fact she insisted on me being who I was with her, and it was not hard, it was easy. As we got to know each other I realised I was being taught at a profound level how to be in a loving, intimate relationship. On some level, I was being offered a deeply nourishing replacement for the "missing experience" that the Hakomi method of psychotherapy speaks of, and I was beginning to heal. I distinctly remember getting to a point where I was feeling very laid back and open about the world: too laid back for Jimmy Antcliffe (bless him!!) who often berated me for, "Looking like a pretentious cool twat with your thumbs in the pockets of your Levi's". Naturally, despite Jim's protestations, this was the way the world *was* meant to be – relationships *were* meant to be this easy after all, the world *was* safe again, just as it had been before I met the world through the impact of a house brick.

Small but powerful things happened quite frequently with Jane. I can think of many examples which illustrate just how much I was in love with her. For the sake of communicating the richness of the experience and also somewhat indulgently re-living that magical time, I would like to list them all:

becoming aware that I really disliked a pair of shoes she had bought, but I held my counsel about them because it was so obvious she loved them... then becoming amazed that I began to love Jane's shoes too, and then I was delighted to find that I was now loving her even more deeply; remaining open to Jane's Dad even though he obviously disliked me or felt threatened by me, and even growing to like him despite the things he was clearly continuing to feel (and say!) about

74

me; going through a gate with Jane across the fields from Creswell to Elmton a small rural village where her family lived, where she told me very authoritatively, "This is a kissing gate" and insisted on demonstrating the correct technique to me before we went a step further; spending one magical Christmas evening in a silent snowfall, talking quietly with Jane outside her grandparent's council house in the same pit village of Creswell where my Dad had dealt with bereaved children from the pit disaster around 20 years previously; growing to love her music that I had dismissed judgmentally only a few months before (it wasn't rock music) and I still love it to this day (the hit single "Jimmy Mack" by Martha Reeves and The Vandellas; "Harlem Shuffle" by Bob and Earl; [well, at least some of the music by!] The Equals; and last but not least, the absolute magic and creative genius of Smokey Robinson & The Miracles... "Tears of a Clown" / "Tracks of My Tears" / "Going to a Go-Go")

.... In fact, as I think back, I remember the first time I really met Jane was on the Number 4 bus to Doncaster from Chesterfield, just after Jimmy Antcliffe and I had been to see some progressive rock band on the second floor of the Victoria Ballroom, Chesterfield, and Jane and her friends had been to see The Equals who were performing on the first floor of the same venue. Jim introduced me to her on the bus. She had a pretty face, blond hair, mischievous & shy smile and beautiful big brown eyes. Her face was covered in sparkly sequins which I thought at the time were very endearing. I thought she looked absolutely gorgeous, beautiful and wonderful. "Do you like my sequins?" she said. "No" I said.

It was probably from that moment, the start of a magical love affair with a real soul mate, or someone very close to that, and in retrospect I recognise, using the language of

Robert Johnson, that it was my first visit to "The Grail Castle" (2009).

Those who know the story of Parsifal and The Fisher King may begin to recognise here as I describe how my relationship with Jane unfolded, that she very powerfully represented for me the first visit to the Grail Castle (a symbolic representation of the Kingdom and the Christ presence spoken of in the biblical Gospels, and related to in the story through the mysterious character of the Fisher King). I knew nothing of the Grail Myth back then, so looking back I am left wondering how, in line with tradition, like Parsifal suddenly finding myself inside the Grail Castle, witnessing a cornucopia of spiritual riches I failed to answer the Grail Question, "Who does the Grail serve?", and why I failed to answer it.

I was told much later in life, that the answer to the Grail Question is: the Grail serves the God in each one of us. Had I answered it, I think I would have recognised the inherent goodness in myself and I would not have lost my connection to Jane – but the Myth itself suggests it is an inevitability that I or anyone else in my position back then, would have failed to answer the question.

All I can say now is that, symbolically speaking, I failed to answer the question back then because a subsequent rapid turn of events had turned my idyllic world upside down and consequently I was overcome by doubt at a very low point in my life, when I chose not to believe that the wonderful things happening to me could be true. It seems to me that I then spent almost the next forty years paying for the consequences that flowed from the decisions I made at that time. I did this because in the context of the 'Grail Myth', I failed to see the God in all of us, *especially* in myself as I repeatedly punished myself for being fatally swayed by the sudden re-appearance in my life of Sue, after eighteen months of bliss with Jane.

During those eighteen months, I had most powerfully felt what seemed to me to be the presence of God in my life: in my creative work at Art College as a student and in my relationship with Jane. I am aware a part of me felt this God given love, this state of grace, was perfectly natural and right and I knew its truth intimately, profoundly at 18 years old. Sitting alongside me however was my all too familiar shame-based self. I knew him too, I thought I was him, but in retrospect I was in reality, carrying the shame based patriarchal legacy of at least four generations, given to me by my father – and just to complete the self-hating ideological loop, I conveniently bore the same name as my Great Grandfather. I did not realise it at the time, but because of the persisting presence of this toxic history and internal self-narrative, my subsequent and very personal fall from grace was already well underway, before Sue reappeared in my life.

I had left Chesterfield to be a Diploma in Art & Design student at Leeds Polytechnic, in the autumn of 1971. During the summer before I left for Leeds, Jane and I spent the season working together at Butlin's Holiday Camp, in Skegness, Lincolnshire. The Camp had little to commend it: we worked there on split shifts throughout the day, with one day off every week but not necessarily the same day, which often meant working for ten or more days straight; the deal was full board, a frugal chalet for accommodation and £6 per week.

I went there simply to spend the summer with Jane. Quite frankly I would have cleaned toilets for twelve hours a day for no pay, just to be there. However, enchantingly and touchingly as I see it now, the place became my magical Grail Castle. Mysteriously but very conveniently, Jane's chalet mate went home after 48 hours, claiming that she couldn't stand the working conditions, and suddenly Jane had the place to herself. Well, Jane had the place to herself for an hour before I moved in! We spent a blissful long five summer weeks together, living in sin (ooh and wasn't that good!!) and yes, it was fantastic! My own chalet mate was quite happy to have our place to himself and not tell the authorities that I was living elsewhere. I was absolutely exhausted from the work, but in a state of emotional bliss every night, sharing a single bed with the woman I loved more than anyone or anything in the world. From time to time we had to dodge the morality squad security guards as we made our way back to our secret idyll, but grace certainly smiled upon us, as despite the constant threat of discovery by the morality police, we were not disturbed in all that time.

During the five weeks at Butlin's, I visited heaven on earth and I felt truly blessed. Our love grew stronger, deeper and more intimate than anything I had ever known. By the end of the summer, we knew we wanted to spend our lives together, and we decided to get engaged.

One magical day in September, I used all of my £24 savings to buy an engagement ring for Jane, from Steven Gryska's Jewellery Shop in Worksop, North Nottinghamshire. The Grail Vision was still very powerfully alive. In that context, the worst thing that could have happened to me then was moving away from home and from Jane to Art College in Leeds, but in my mind I felt I had to go. By September I was a Leeds based student. I was in no way emotionally prepared or equipped to make that move. It was also my first time living away from home, so unsurprisingly I was terribly lovesick and homesick in Leeds, without Jane.

The sense of pain and loss was so bad, I decided to drop out of college and went back home, but before I left I at least had the sense to visit the Sociology Department at the

Polytechnic and ask for an interview for a place on the Sociology Degree course the following autumn. The wise adult part of me was in charge of that course of action; the fearful child part of me couldn't wait to get home, but was already feeling the shame of failure at not being tough enough to make it beyond the end of the first term of my Diploma in Art & Design at Leeds.

Back home, my parents had moved away from where we had lived, a relatively short car ride from Jane's family home in Elmton and close to my old school, to a new dwelling ten miles further away on the other side of Chesterfield, close to the Peak District National Park. Even though I was back in my home area, I may as well have been on the moon as I had no money and could only see Jane occasionally by public transport.

In an attempt to salvage some pride, to see Jane more frequently and also to save money for an improbable dream trip with her the following summer to the USA, I had by January got a 'boys from the black stuff' type unofficial job on a building site as a plasterer's mate. I was working on a new housing estate construction next to the council estate where I had grown up. It was a disaster. In my first week, very new to the job, I was standing up to my ankles in thick cloying mud on the building site. I was asked by the plasterer to pick up a bucket of compo, a mixture of sand and cement, and a very heavy load. In so doing I lost my balance. Instead of dropping the bucket as my body was pulled violently to the right with the weight, in a frozen state of shock, my hand involuntarily locked around the handle and I continued to fall but my leg stayed rooted at a 90 degree angle in the mud. I felt my muscles and ligaments tearing and my right leg dislocated at the knee. Then in the aftermath of shock I let go of the handle and shot upright in excruciating pain locking my knee joint back into its socket, tearing my cartilage in half as it did so. Within a minute my knee joint had ballooned out to three times its normal size.

The site foreman saw what happened and sacked me on the spot – no insurance, no health and safety, no job and no help to leave the building site, but he made it very clear in no uncertain terms he wanted me out of there, off site and gone, immediately. Somehow I crawled and hobbled for over two miles to friends of my parents who still lived on the street where we used to live, on the nearby council estate. Having no transport of their own, they took me on the bus back home.

Over the days and weeks, my knee pain gradually subsided but it was obvious I needed surgery. Within a couple more weeks I had undergone a cartilage operation at the hospital, but my cruciate ligament was not operated upon, in my typically stoic way I didn't tell anyone how painful it felt and subsequently the ligaments healed themselves after a fashion. It was only in retrospect that I found out I had torn my cruciate ligament, but that was eight years later when a sports consultant in Leeds told me I had a, "48 year old knee"! I hate to think how old that knee is now.

As a consequence of my operation I was in heavy plaster on my right leg, from my groin to my ankle for six weeks. In all that time I hardly saw Jane at all and we had no telephone, so I could only contact her by letter and the occasional visit she made to my parents' new home. Her Dad, still intensely disliking me, almost pathologically by now, after we had had the temerity to get engaged, was not willing to drive Jane to see me. She could only make it very infrequently on her meagre savings, by difficult and uncoordinated public transport.

So unsurprisingly I became very depressed: my leg was shattered and it seemed my dreams were also. Even after I got rid of the accursed plaster, I was virtually immobile for months, living on £6 per week social security. I felt like a prisoner under house arrest, living back with my parental jailers, gradually succumbing once again to my Dad's by now rather milder but still very toxic, psychological abuse

As I gradually grew physically stronger, but in a deeply depressed state, one day the following Spring, I received a letter from Sue asking to see me. Very unwisely, I agreed to meet her. Yes, Sue was my first and unrequited love: when she suddenly re-entered my life, wanting contact, "To work out who I want to be with", I was once again cast under a powerful spell.

My grace visited Self knew it would end in tears, but I ignored my wiser self- judgment and went ahead to meet her anyway, on a warm sunny day, in the leafy sanctuary of Queen's Park, Chesterfield.

I came across the poem, "Raglan Road" by Irish poet Patrick Kavanagh many years later – I first heard it on a record by the Chieftains and Van Morrison, set to music as a powerful song. It spoke eloquently to me of the power of unrequited love and the absolute dangers of being drawn back into its emotional orbit. The poem describes such reckless actions, *"I saw the danger yet I walked along the enchanted way"*, and their inevitable consequence, *"I loved too much and by such and such, is happiness thrown away"*. It seems clear to me, looking back that I did indeed walk the precarious, enchanted way and as a consequence I fell disastrously into the abyss.

Predictably, Sue reached no useful conclusion for me, which really meant I would never replace her current lover. But it was already too late for my relationship with Jane. I had been absolutely unable to prevent the inexorable surge of emotional energy breaking through my defences and flooding out the sense and memories of my all too brief time of incredible bliss with Jane. This destructive energy

81

surfaced powerfully at the forefront of my consciousness, twisted and entwined in a bleak and archaic sense of longing. It felt like an unstoppable explosive firestorm of very old feelings of desperately unrequited love.

I was by now a very troubled soul, well on the way to self-destruction. I knew ancient and dangerous longings had been stirred again, and in my teenage morality I told myself I had committed some sort of unforgivable emotional adultery. On the infrequent occasions when it was possible to be alone with Jane, I could no longer bring myself to make love with her, as I told myself my actions had proved that I was worthless and that I didn't love her fully enough, that had been proved by my desperate interest in Sue, even though in reality my feelings were powerfully telling me that I still absolutely longed to be with Jane.

By the time this shame haunted version of myself realised how self-deluded this so called morality was, I was already losing Jane. I felt it. She had clearly and unmistakeably felt the distance in me. She said nothing but I knew she was rapidly moving away from me and the idyllic intimacy we had previously known. I frantically tried to pretend that I had pulled myself back from the abyss, but in reality I knew that I was staring desperately up from the bottom of the abyss itself, looking for a way out and away from this madness, back to the deep love I had known with Jane.

It was far too late for me. One day as I rode in the car with my Dad through Chesterfield town centre, I saw Jane walking happily and affectionately arm in arm with an Art College student, a young man from the North East she had casually mentioned to me once or twice. As I saw them walking arm in arm down the street, I could see the loving energy flowing between them. I felt that instant like I had a spear thrust violently right through my guts. Dad didn't notice a thing as I bled to death in silence, sat on the car seat next to him.

Watching Sue's bus pull away from me in Caernarvon had been awful, but this was truly the worst moment of my life - not surpassed until my wife told me she was leaving me for someone else 34 years later. I thought I was going to die from the pain and grief, and I told myself I was entirely to blame for this development.

In the autumn of 1972 Jane moved to London, to Hornsey Art College. She never talked to me directly about her feelings for the student I saw her with that day, but I felt then and now that she had been involved in an intimate relationship with him and in my grief and pain I never told her I had seen her. Instead, in a state of considerable denial, I tried all the ways I could to make things right again, but it was hopeless.

Jane clearly couldn't wait to get away to London. I had already been offered and accepted a place back at Leeds to read Sociology, but in my desperation I also sought an interview at North London Polytechnic for the same University of London External Degree. But my heavy heart knew that Jane didn't want me there and I turned down a place after it was offered to me. By now, even I knew it was all over and I returned to Leeds.

About four weeks into my first term at Leeds, I visited Jane in London and she told me officially that our engagement was over. She gave me back the engagement ring that weekend. I remember catching the train back to Yorkshire. At Kings Cross, in a state of emotional distress, I bought a copy of the book "The Exorcist". I couldn't read it, but I sat in deep depression staring at the book cover all the way back to Leeds.

The next seven years felt to me to be even worse than the nightmare depicted in the film. For those next seven years I was not in any relationship worth the name, apart from a number of painful and desolate one night stands. Emotionally I was completely lost. I spent most of that time longing for Jane and fantasising we would somehow reconnect. God help me, two years into this process, I even wrote to her mother saying how much I missed Jane and asking how she was, which of course fuelled my self-loathing even further. But after five more years of loss and longing even I could stand this no more.

One weekend, I was driving down the M1 Motorway towards Chesterfield, to visit my parents. Near Junction 30, my wise soul took over the steering wheel, and instead drove me down familiar country lanes to Elmton, to Jane's old house. As I pulled up beside the garden wall, I saw what I assumed to be her lover's van outside the house. Whether or not this was an accurate assumption, the spell was simply broken. I felt it profoundly and I finally let go.

Many years later reading about the Grail Myth really helped me to stop punishing myself. In the course of this reflective self-analysis, I think I have also learnt something of considerable value to me as a psychotherapist in my clinical work with clients.

So why did it take me almost forty years to deal with this? I think because at the core of my perception of what happened, there was one major decision: the decision to never forgive myself for throwing away the love of a lifetime! Or from a more fundamentalist religious perspective, I suppose it might be seen as proof of the default presence of what St Augustine referred to as 'original sin', within me, which meant I did not 'deserve' to be so loved, and that the stain of original sin for me, like everyone else, would inexorably lead to unhealthy and grief creating decision making. Also, from such a perspective, apparently neither I nor anyone else has the power or right to remove the existence of this core original sin from myself.

For the sake of self-forgiveness and an attempt at spiritual self-empowerment, I would like to be clear now, with a forgiving heart towards myself, more than that – with a loving and retrospectively compassionate heart, what happened and probably why I did what I did – and perhaps why anyone who ever found themselves in a similar position may have done something very similar. It had nothing to do with me being a 'miserable sinner'. In metaphysical, spiritual and mythical terms the reason things fell apart, was that *they were supposed to do so*. It is enshrined in the Parsifal myth. As I look back now, I recognise the wisdom of Robert Johnson's opinion that *in harmony with the "Grail Myth" the "first soul mate" meeting could never be the "final soul mate meeting". It is only a glimpse of the future, almost certainly with someone else one is yet to meet.*

Probably like everyone else who has ever been at that place in their early adult years: firstly, I failed to see the God in everyone, critically especially myself and secondly to realise that the answer to the Grail Question IS precisely that the "Grail serves the God in everyone". The Grail being the potential for entering the Kingdom of the Christ-Self through realising that the God in each and every one of us is the authentic centre of who we are; whether we are categorised or self-categorise as good people, bad people, sinners, holy men and women, the fallen and the chosen, the people of faith and the people of doubt or no faith or even of outright opposition....

I am reminded of this when listening to the Joan Osborne song, "What if God was one of us" (*"Just a slob like one of us, just a stranger on the bus, just trying to find his way home, like a holy rolling stone"*).

In my view, no-one is excluded in this philosophy, no matter who they appear to be and whatever great good or evil they have done, or appear to have done. Whoever we are and whatever we have done, at the level of the authentic Self, in terms of the 'Grail Myth', God exists within every one of us. We serve each other because God IS in ALL of us and in essence God includes everyone and excludes absolutely no one. And of course, the journey to this truth is an interior one – we find interpersonal, intimate and heart based human love from, and of, God *from* within, not from some external source.

On reflection, it struck me from the therapeutic perspective that this is very similar to saying that the key to therapeutic healing is through the conscious shift within the client, from the external to the internal locus of control. It is often signalled by a significant increase in levels of self-esteem, perception of self-competence and self-acceptance. Consequently it is experienced as a deeper and much more intimate acceptance of the Self and all one's gifts and idiosyncrasies, through growth of love and trust of the Self.

This move towards self-acceptance is sometimes, in effect, held in trust in the counselling relationship by the therapist, sometimes more consciously co-held by therapist and the client, and sometimes held by the therapist simply through mindful identification, honouring and holding of missing experience transference (sometimes expressed as erotic transference), long enough for the client to complete and take back processes of transferential projection and re-integrate them within the Self... or as Jungians might say – reintegration of the "shadow aspects of the Self" towards full individuation.

In my experience, if I can begin to recognise what was the client's primary 'missing experience' from childhood, I can begin to consistently provide at least a basic replication of those missing elements as a present, not absent, part of the therapeutic frame; thus ultimately encouraging and facilitating the emergence of the sort of processes I describe above.

However, it is never possible to fully provide in the here and now, what was missing from childhood. To explain this further, it is illustrative to describe early childhood experiences in clients who endured very significant levels of neglect or loss during their early years.

This can be a particularly difficult process to deal with therapeutically, when such deep childhood grief is involved. If that is the case, there are often strong elements of sadism and masochism present within the relational field, as the client powerfully denies original grief by transferring the bleak and devastating feelings of early loss into an insatiably relentless desire for some kind of fulfilment from the therapist, only to be inevitably disappointed.

One of the best expositions of this process I have read is mapped out by Martha Stark M.D. (2006) in her paper, "Transformation of Relentless Hope: A Relational Approach to Sadomasochism". This paper used to be available on the Internet, but is hard to find now. Her book "Working with Resistance" (2002), is however worth exploring. The paper focuses on the reality that (in effect) the original "missing experience" can never be fully replaced, because it is primary grief about what was not (and now never will be) provided by the primary care-giver or care-givers.

There will always be something missing, that which fuels almost insatiable and yet inevitably unrequited desire in the adult. At some point, the client needs to experience a powerful sense of betrayal or lack of complete support from the therapist. This is necessary in order to come face to face with visceral pain and through so doing, finally accept that they need to go back to deal with the original denied grief from childhood, if they are ever to move on into more adult living, self-empowerment and ultimate self-acceptance.

In part, it also struck me that Otto Scharmer (2008) is exploring very similar territory around facilitating potential change and shift from external to internal locus of control, when he speaks in his Blog of the concept of *"Attentional Violence"*.

Scharmer talks of three different types of violence he has seen and witnessed in the world: War and direct physical violence towards others; Structural violence as experienced by the economically and politically marginalised – whether on the basis of race, gender, ethnic or social minority, disaffected communities or categorisation as an under-class; and what he calls "Attentional Violence", committed consciously or unconsciously against another person by holding a vision of that person's ability or humanity, which is smaller than their true potential.

Scharmer, Peter Senge and Others (2005) have very interesting things to say about authentic communication and by inference attentional violence, in their powerful book, "Presence". Their suggestion is that conscious choice to engage in deeper and deeper levels of listening and learning offer us increasing opportunities to move towards dialogue and co-creation at the level of the authentic Self.

Otto Scharmer (2007) took the ideas first developed in "Presence" further and still deeper, in his book which mapped out his "Theory U" process. Scharmer contends that the deepest levels of listening and learning require a willingness to move beyond habitual *"Downloading"* (repeating patterns of reliance on old mental models), through *"Seeing"* (acknowledging the possibility that more than one level of perceptual reality exists in the world), *"Sensing"* (recognising with empathic awareness some glimpse of what it must be like to live in the world of the

Other) and finally to enter the deep level of *"Presence"*, where one is listening so deeply that a glimpse of a much broader and more resonant future in line with authentic Self-expression, can be potentially co-created. In a delightful phrase, he describes this place of presence and co-creation as an environment where one can enjoy, *"Walking back towards oneself from the future"*. This process is quite possible both at intrapsychic and interpersonal levels.

The book "Presence" suggests that it is indeed also perfectly and powerfully possible at the level of community. There is an intensely moving example of this in the introduction to "Presence", where the authors talk of facilitating a three day leadership workshop in South Africa in 1990. At this workshop participants, "included a black South African and a white South African who were being trained to lead the program on their own future".

At one point during the day, the South African President at the time, F.W. de Klerk made a TV broadcast which, it transpired was to become the famous speech that set in motion the ending of apartheid. Later in the day, the group also watched a video of Martin Luther King Jr.'s, "I have a dream" speech, a broadcast previously banned in South Africa, which as a consequence many participants had never seen before. At the closing check-out the fifth person to speak was a white Afrikaans business executive, who turned to look directly at Anne, a black community leader and said, *"I want you to know that I was raised to think that you were an animal"*, after which he broke down in tears. *"Anne just held him in her gaze and nodded"*. Peter Senge describes in the book how he, *"Saw a huge knot become untied. I don't know how to describe it except to say it was as if a rope simply became untied and broke apart. I knew intuitively that what had been holding him and so many others prisoners of the past was breaking. They were becoming free"* (2005, P4).

I am reminded that M. Scott Peck, in his book on processes of community building, (1987) suggests that the reality of what he calls "true community" is not a recognition that we are all the same and that no differences exist between us, it is instead a recognition and willing acceptance of difference. He maps out a similar four stage process, moving from *"False Community"* (fear of and repeated attempts to deny difference), through *"Evangelising"* (trying to convince others that your reality is the true reality), *"Speaking from the Heart"* (being honest about the pain you are experiencing from others' attempts to evangelise you), into *"True Community"* where heart based realities are communally recognised at the level of the authentic Self, and honoured as they manifest in genuine difference, articulated and if at all possible absolutely celebrated.

Scharmer's concept of "Attentional Violence" hints at the toxic power of attempting to categorise others according to one's own values or prejudices. If we perpetrate this third level of violence, we are effectively pathologising people and given that, according to Stephen Buhner (2004), the heart is a very sensitive "second brain", the recipients of our toxic attention will inevitably feel this, even if they cannot explain it. Certainly, if they know shame, they will also very quickly self-pathologise anyway and lock themselves into a wasteland of lost faith in the Self.

Paradoxically, we are much more likely to visit attentional violence on others if we habitually value others more than we value ourselves, in a misguided (but ultimately toxically emotionally rescuing) attempt to be a self-sacrificing carer, either in professional or personal settings. In reality we are unconsciously visiting attentional violence on ourselves the moment we believe our own needs are less than others' needs. And of course, if we visit attentional violence on ourselves, we render ourselves less than we can be in terms of living out our full potential.

Given what we already know, from Carl Rogers and others, about the impact of congruence or lack of congruence on the therapeutic process, it is clear that to visit attentional violence on the Self, in some misguided thinking about the need to avoid so called selfishness, makes it impossible to do anything than simultaneously visit attentional violence on the Other. When this happens fear continues to spread and love in its truest spiritual sense is blocked or absent from human emotional and intellectual discourse. We thus sabotage and disempower both ourselves and others whilst believing we are doing precisely the opposite.

I hear conscious attempts to practice 'Attentional Non Violence' in the famous, "I have a dream" speech delivered by Martin Luther King Jr., from the steps of the Washington Memorial in Washington DC in August 1963. King was a man who knew the reality of many forms of violence committed against himself and the people he represented. He was also a man who from a position of bestowed power, consciously chose to love rather than to hate. It cost him his life, but he was an enormous catalyst for profound and lasting change within American society. I also hear it in the speech often wrongly attributed to Nelson Mandela, which in fact is a quote from Marrianne Williamson's book (1992).

The direct quote from Williamson frequently attributed to Nelson Mandela is as follows: *"Our deepest fear is not that we are inadequate. Our deepest fear is that we are powerful beyond measure. It is our light, not our darkness, that most frightens us. We ask ourselves, who am I to be brilliant, gorgeous, talented, fabulous? Actually, who are you not to be? You are a child of God. Your playing small doesn't serve the world. There's nothing enlightened about shrinking so that other people won't feel insecure around you. We are all meant to shine, as children do. We were born to make manifest the glory of God that is within us. It's not just in some of us; it's in everyone. And as we let our own light shine, we unconsciously give other people permission to do the same. As we're liberated from our own fear, our presence automatically liberates others".*

Currently, in the Coaching world, particularly in the more recent coaching practice journals, the work of Otto Scharmer and the work of Eric De Haan (2008) is gradually becoming known. Published practitioners seem to recognise the need for more reflective and mindful practice, from a relational rather than an analytically observational base, and their outlined approaches are often linked in such practitioner articles with a concept first developed in the Counselling field known as, "working at relational depth", by Cooper & Mearns (2005).

However, I feel that some of these practitioner articles are all too often written without fully describing or perhaps even understanding the true challenge of developing one's craft as a practitioner and human being, should one truly choose to work from these perspectives. In contrast, I believe Cooper and Mearns and also authors such as Brian Thorne greatly understand this.

Really exploring the true meaning of personal power, choosing to work at a level required to evoke 'Presencing' and relational depth, and to consciously avoid attentional violence, is a lifelong process. Even if the learning develops gradually over time, it will make very great demands on us. The rewards of this hard work are vast, and also in my view, vital to the continued healthy unfolding of individual and collective human potential. In fact any failure to understand the enormity of what we are choosing when we say we wish to work in the professional field in this way, is in my view potentially disastrous and certainly very self-limiting, in the context of our human and spiritual evolution. Making a conscious choice to live and act *without* attentional violence towards the Self and others in our professional (and also personal) lives, requires the re-emergence and sustainability of self-belief, self-forgiveness and self-loving.

From here with the help and presence of grace we can naturally facilitate the client by holding an active vision of their potential for ultimate expansion to become fully manifest in terms of the abundant unfolding of the miracle of what I would regard as their God given and God fulfilled Self, even if they cannot yet see it for themselves. I think this is the true meaning and true reality of the concepts of faith and power as applied to therapeutic work, when seen from a spiritual perspective, whatever religion or philosophy holds meaning for us.

It now seems to me that if we hold true to faith, and as a result faith holds true to us, apparent miracles and synchronicity become a so natural and ever present state of being, that we come to realise we are in reality constantly surrounded by and visited by 'grace', as M Scott Peck suggests in "The Road Less Travelled" (1978). To realise this and to be and act from this place, without or beyond fear, is in my view the true and authentic place of personal and spiritual power. Ultimately, it comes from within, from our own choice to actively live, to really choose to live and to go on choosing life, whatever our current illnesses, fears, trials, grief and tribulations; to continue to believe in ourselves, and to go on believing, whatever the cost, as we simultaneously love through our work, and facilitate and celebrate the emergence of the magnificent human and God given potential within others.

But often, on the rare occasions we are open to receiving and experiencing its nourishment, we may instead mistakenly believe grace only occasionally visits us; and just to compound matters, some spiritual charlatan somewhere has more than likely, already whispered in our fear-attuned ears that we will only receive grace if we are good and prove this by giving our personal power away to a fearful punitive God, or conviction politician, or priestly confessional, or critical parent, or those who profess to teach and educate others through exclusivity and fear, or narcissistically charismatic therapist, or spiritual guru come cult leader, or self-appointed religious scholar... and do what they tell us is right for us, as true followers and believers.

From my perspective, the above processes are frequent reflections of numerous ways in which abdication of personal power and replacement of its previous presence by fear may continue to hold sway in this world. They go some way towards illustrating how we may continue to co-manifest fear and ultimately give solidity to the obscenity of what we visit on ourselves and others as apparent moral correctness, but in reality as some form of human evil. The word 'evil' is 'live' backwards, and to live backwards or to withdraw from truly living, is one powerful way we can unconsciously attempt to create the death of the soul in others and of course ultimately in ourselves. It doesn't have to be this way.

I attended an inspirational workshop at The University of Wales in Wrexham in 2010, hosted by Dave Mearns and Brian Thorne, where amongst other things they explored, "Personal experiences of the power of being human, in Counselling and Psychotherapy". They suggested that to be truly present with clients requires willingness to, *"Endow relationships with the totality of humanity"*, and we can only do this if we are prepared to be properly present within ourselves as well as within the professional relationship.

Brian Thorne contended that each unique person in the form of a client *"Will call on different aspects of your own being. It is when you feel most powerful and vulnerable that if you stay there, new energy is released into the relational dynamic. Your presence for a client is vital"*... ..."A quality of tenderness is what happens for me when I am enabled to be fully present. I also need to prepare in order to be such a channel in the therapeutic relationship".*

Thorne described how he experienced a personal epiphany on Good Friday in 1946, whilst still a boy. *"I felt tenderly embraced and powerfully affirmed without judgment"* (by a loving God), *"I came to know that I am infinitely loved, and not especially favoured above anyone else. The nature of God is an unconditional loving creator; I can rest and relax in this presence. All is well, no matter what I may do or not do, because I am infinitely loved. The implication is that I am linked indissolubly to all creation, and I have a capacity to be infinitely loving; being with my Self and others as authentically as I can be".* For Dave Mearns, this meant *"Going way beneath the superficial in relation to each other".*

It occurs to me now that had I possessed even an inkling of awareness as a young man, of what I have just described in the last seven pages, when I was struggling with the emotional impact of the re-emergence of Sue in my life, things may have turned out very differently. I could have really benefitted from a solid therapeutic relationship with a psychotherapist or counsellor, which may have helped me to let go of years of self-punishment and instead of struggling for decades to forgive myself, I could have been steadily growing and loving myself and others, including Jane.

Maybe I was just destined to learn the hard way!

***

Why does this chapter in my life pre-figure a greater understanding of and relationship with power?

As I reflect back on my early adult experiences, I now realise that the only true power is spiritual power, for the greater good – it only really manifests through the intervention of grace, which is ever present, when we find the courage to live without or beyond fear.

Here in this "Promised Land" as Martin Luther King said, we are equal and magnificent and inclusively choose to live in a communal spirit of mutual respect, appreciation and joy – we taste our birth right which is to be without fear, and wherever fear is absent I believe the God within us, amongst us and around us, naturally and spontaneously creates love and peace from the depths of the heart.

We know we are once more at home, where the heart is truly free and we see each other for the authentic and wondrously creative beings that we are, as we continue to generate and regenerate love and healthy human power.

With the hindsight of adult wisdom, The 'Grail Myth' becomes a guide for me here as I think about what happened to me in relation to Jane.

When we first glimpse this Promised Land, we are neither prepared nor aware enough to move beyond fear and the experience rarely lasts, even though at the time the authentic aspect of the Self knows how natural such a state of being is to our heart at peace. More often than not, we lose the faith that this can be real, and we are all too soon reminded of our wounds – the most toxic of all being shame, often enmeshed in some aspect of unrequited love; a shame which is always projected on to us by other fearful people, even though we may come to regard it as exclusively personal proof of the worthless person we are. So we cannot stay in the light of the Promised Land, we lose faith in ourselves through self-doubt, self-hatred, self-defeat and once again fear gradually or suddenly replaces love. Once again, we are lost, cast out from the Garden of Eden, because someone somewhere taught us that we are the source of original sin. That being so, we obviously don't deserve to truly love or be truly loved, so one way or another, we sabotage ourselves to confirm how bad we are.

In time, if grace blesses us once again and we have the courage to go beyond fear and stay there, to instead, risk reaching out and touch other hearts, we slowly come to realise that original sin is a powerful and possibly ultimate lie. As we open up again from the heart, we take on the biggest challenge of all, we start to genuinely love ourselves, from where we are able to reconnect with the God in ourselves and in others – we learn to really love without fear and we come to power. If I knew all this aged 18, my life would have been very different!

In therapeutic terms I see this as a shift from an external to an internal locus of control. In human terms it seems that we become truly blessed and can now bless others. In humanistic terms we manifest our authentic Selves. In spiritual terms perhaps this is how, in our different ways, we give ourselves and the Earth back to The Tao, to Buddha, to Hindu Deities, to Yahweh, to the Tenth Guru and beyond, to Allah, to Gaia, to God and to the Goddess-Sacred Feminine within.

***

John aged 21

CHAPTER 5:

Glimpses of Freedom

During the lost years after my relationship with Jane ended, I inevitably focused upon my work and naturally unfolding career. My way of continuing to live in some fashion, beyond a state of frozen grief, seemed to involve being active in other areas of my life and focusing on work was a good way of shifting my attention away from my grief enmeshed emotions. I think on some level I just gave up on relationships and decided to focus on work. That seemed a lot less painful.

I discovered a love of working with young people. Initially I thought this should be as a teacher, but instead, my path took me eventually into social work with Young Offenders via initial work as a nursing assistant in an Adolescent Psychiatric Unit.

I was drawn to work with the outcast, the broken and the lost probably because I identified with all three aspects within myself. I met some beautiful young souls in the psychiatric unit, more often than not there because they were carrying the projected shadow of parental or family shame and unexpressed fear.

The unit used mostly young adults, like me, known as 'lay therapists' who worked to befriend and support the children and young people referred there. Looking back, I think most of the soul healing that took place in that Adolescent Psychiatric Unit came about through unconscious application by lay therapists of "Attentional Non Violence".

As much as we could, we treated the kids pretty much as normal and loveable and fun to be with, as well as giving time to be with them in their pain and listen to their articulation of fear and grief. Some young people there however clearly suffered a higher level of disturbance and required more than just being related to as a normal kid, and where that was necessary, more support was offered with close assistance from the Child Psychiatrist, Unit Social Worker and / or Nursing Staff at the Unit. However, in my experience, most of the young people there gradually learned to love and trust us and in so doing began to love and trust themselves.

I worked closely and intimately with children struggling with a variety of identified psychiatric or behavioural difficulties: anorexia, bulimia, encopretic and enuretic disorders, hair pulling and other forms of severe self-mutilation and self-harming, extreme low self-esteem, depression, agoraphobia, school phobia, bullying, anti-social and sociopathic behaviour patterns, hysteria and panic. I think in every case I knew, the child was significantly misunderstood within their family system of origin and very often singled out and scapegoated as the problem within the family, when closer examination, especially from the frame of reference of family systems therapy, would often reveal complex cognitive and behavioural threads of what film director Mike Leigh would probably refer to as "secrets and lies", either locked within failing marriages or passed down the generational line through decade upon decade of shame and guilt projection.

The worst cases where children were the most disturbed seemed to carry both elements within the family history. Frequently, the child or young person was the convenient focus for projective identification of family and/or parental trauma. They appeared on one hand to take a lot of this toxicity on board, because it seems that children are often quick to try and make things better, because they love their parents and siblings and feel responsible for repeatedly launching (inevitably futile) attempts to heal the family sickness (often pushing themselves deeper into trauma and self-pathologising as a result); and on the other hand, fighting for psychological survival and attempts to love themselves via disturbed behaviour patterns, which were calling out for someone with compassion, wisdom understanding and power to help them back from the frozen wastelands they stumbled through, alone, day after day, month after month and sometimes year after year. If they were lucky they didn't pick up too many diagnostic labels; if they were not then they often became very lost in psychiatric and child care social work systems or institutions.

The children we worked with would often find that compassion and understanding in a 1:1 relationship with one of the young adult lay therapists within the unit. Unfortunately, nursing assistants with low status in the NHS, earning £1,770 per year (my wage at the time), didn't have much in the way of power. Also most were in transit to other jobs or further education. I was a typical example: a graduate aware I could not stay in such a low paid job forever, much as I loved the children and young people with whom I worked.

I left after 18 months, to move away to the West Midlands, to take up an unqualified social worker post in the newly developing field of *Intermediate Treatment*, an area of work I had been introduced to by Mary, the social worker at the psychiatric unit. I was employed by Birmingham Social Services Department, to work with Young Offenders in the community, who would otherwise have been sent to Secure Community Homes, Detention Centres or Borstal as a result of their offending behaviour.

We were located in an old school in the All Saints area of Birmingham, in a very run-down part of the inner city, close to Winson Green Prison. The run-down nature of the place symbolised the way most decision makers in social policy dealt with so called 'problem children' – dump them somewhere where they can do minimal damage and forget about them. The evidence of that was all too clear by the nature of referrals we received and the laboured excuses social workers and others employed to attempt to gain a place for a young person at the Centre. In my experience, once a referrer succeeded in securing a place they soon disappeared and were never very available or interested to talk about the young people they had referred. We as a staff group felt pretty insulted by such attitudes; for the young people referred it must have been even worse but sadly, probably all too familiar an experience for them. We had other ideas: the Centre was called the 'BAY Centre' which stood for 'Birmingham Action for Youth'. We did our best to work with young people, respect them and act as advocates on their behalf in terms of visioning a better future for them.

Most of the kids at the BAY Centre were either poor White working class or poor African Caribbean. Given the popularity at the time of Bob Marley and the Wailers and Jamaican reggae, almost all the kids, white or black, spoke in a curious and to me, fascinating Brummie-Caribbean patois...., "Me kyaaan believe it, yous is bloody yampy youse are, yer raass claat". It made communication attempts very interesting.

Five years later, after post qualifying from my CQSW (Social Work Training) Course and Post Graduate Diploma in Applied Social Studies at Leeds University, I studied at Keele University for an M.A. in Criminology, where I learned what I already knew from first hand lived experience working in Birmingham, and later in inner city Wakefield and Bradford: that inevitably the first to be criminalised in our society are the poorest, the most economically and socially marginalised and the most socially alienated and disenfranchised. No one values them, many are afraid of them, no one listens to them, and very few people are prepared to help them without heavy judgment or moralising.

Being somewhat of an outcast myself, and in particular very estranged from my own father, I felt a lot of empathy for those kids and enjoyed sometimes turbulent, and often humour filled moments with them. At times it is true to say that I was fearful and afraid, but I chose as best I could to stay open to them despite my fear, as kids acted out their frustration, rage and pain.

I remember once, "Big D.", a loveable enormous and muscular 15 year old African Caribbean lad, lost it in the back of the Centre transit van, stirred to anger by a random racist insult from one of the White kids, and I had the job of attempting to physically restrain him as we drove through the streets of Coventry. He landed a spectacular kung fu leg kick on my left eye socket almost knocking me out. Fortunately I was eventually able to restrain him, as I was anxious at the time that the van would crash with the sudden turbulent movement. After he calmed down he was full of genuine remorse and concern for my welfare. I carried a magnificent black-eye for a couple of weeks after that. Strangely, or maybe not so strangely, I got a lot closer to Big D. as a result of what happened.

I and my rugby playing colleague (ex-army man and inner city youth worker) Chalky White, were natural targets for the kids' favourite ball game known as "murder ball", which consisted of fifteen or more kids using the excuse of a game vaguely based on the rules of Association Football, to kick the shit out of us in an enclosed gym, at every available opportunity within a thirty minute period. Assuming we didn't get genuinely angry and violent in return, they were very open and connected to us after such, er... challenging work-outs.

The periods after murder ball were often when the kids could be reached the easiest, and where I think they often began to heal or rebuild their broken self-esteem as their authentic Selves were seen and connected with those of our own. I often wonder what happened to many of those young people.

I had a glimpse of the unfolding and somewhat inevitable future for some, one day when I was queuing for an F.A. Cup ticket at Bradford City Football Club. I heard this voice behind me say, "Hello John, how are you doing mate?" I turned round to see a very large muscular man smiling at me. It took me quite a while to recognise him. I had worked with him around six years previously in Wakefield, a likeable lad and somewhat of a career offender. The last time I had seen him he was about a third of the size he was that day. "Hi Paul, I'm fine. What have you been up to since I last saw you?" Daft question I think. He replied, "I've been in Armley Jail".

When I recall my work with Young Offenders, I often remember the good times of connection, humour and empathy with the kids, some of whom had done some very destructive things (arson, ABH and GBH, cruelty to horses, common assault or threatening behaviour), but most of whom were simply socially alienated repeat petty offenders, without much love in their lives or any sense of being blessed or cherished by adult carers. They were mostly male and almost to a person, as far as I could see, had received no blessing from older men in their lives. They often responded well to being offered such vital missing experiences, growing visibly in self-confidence, self-belief, self-esteem and care for their fellow inmates.

There were exceptions to the rule however: I remember one occasion co-facilitating a group work session, where a particularly irritating youth was provoking and winding everybody up. Suddenly Sean (age fifteen and recently responsible for stealing a double decker bus after he ran out of money for a taxi fare, taking the top of the bus clean off attempting to negotiate a low bridge near Wakefield......

.....fortunately, he was the only one on the bus at the time) leapt out of his chair, hauled the irritating youth robustly into the air pinning him to the wall by the throat and uttered the immortal words, "What tha needs son is instant fuckin' treatment". We eventually managed to calm Sean down and save the irritating little bastard's life. Some other inmates sitting there that evening certainly didn't thank us for doing so.

I was also at that time, spectacularly declared (and I have it in writing!) a "persona non grata" by a local somewhat fascist headmaster, because I had the temerity to turn up at his school, according to him, "Dressed in a scruffy jumper and no trousers". In reality however, I was simply wearing a new pair of Levi's, and my mum's best knitted jumper from the previous Christmas, but it conjured up amusing images for my boss, Ron, the local Social Services Area Manager. Between bouts of almost uncontrollable laughter, he succeeded in writing back to the headmaster, promising to reprimand me most severely. He hadn't succeeded in doing so before I managed to magnificently publically humiliate one of Ron's colleagues.

Isobel W. was a refined, sophisticated and very professional Scottish lady, who spoke with great authority and gravitas. She was the Social Services Area Manager in the adjoining locality and was responsible one evening for chairing a case conference for one of our lads, attended by ourselves, the young person in question, his parents and social worker. I and my colleagues Steve and Dave arrived early at the Area Office, and Isobel was kind enough to let us set up the chairs in her own office prior to the meeting. I noticed she had a nameplate on her desk bearing her name, in letters made out of something akin to Lego. Before the meeting, in a mood of mischievous creativity, I managed to re-arrange the letters. Isobel conducted the entire meeting extremely professionally with great dignity, and utmost seriousness, whilst totally unaware that everyone in the room was being led to believe that they were being chaired by Boseli Arkwel. Luckily after the event, she quickly saw the funny side. Isobel was a very good sport and I respected her greatly despite what I had done.

A year or so after the 'persona non grata' drama, the headmaster became a cause celebre on the local regional news, as they reported his growing public unpopularity with staff and students alike. He was firstly suspended by the local education authority and then finally sacked, after his staff simply refused to work with him any longer.

I greatly missed working in Wakefield when I moved to an 'Intermediate Treatment Officer' post in Bradford, yet the kids I met there were essentially no different to the ones I had left behind in Wakefield. I was also blessed to work with some wise and loving people, no more so than my colleague Mike who helped me develop my ideas around working with Young Offenders.

The leading practitioner in my previous local authority in Wakefield had pioneered an approach to working with Young Offenders which was very creative but centred on key aspects of behaviour modification. This didn't ring true for me as the best way to work with young people. I wasn't interested in modifying anybody's behaviour unless they were in full agreement with the idea – anyway, nothing sustainable was likely to come from attempting to modify someone else. In my experience, it has to be a self-determined decision if it is going to have any meaning or ultimate chance of success.

I found the approach of my Wakefield colleague far too controlling, in some parts very manipulative and very much in the territory of wielding what I would call "power over" young people. I felt sure there was a need to treat Young Offenders more as equals if we were going to affect any fundamental long term change in their offending behaviour. Mike agreed with me and helped me to put into practice a different approach to the work, based more on genuine attempts to work in dialogical partnership with young people.

By that time, I had also embarked on a part time M.A. in Criminology at Keele University, which was very Marxist in approach and very aware of the damaging effects of pathologising young people through non mindful, or sometimes very deliberate, use of 'power over' approaches. I was drawn to the more dialogical forms of intervention, which offered opportunities to Young Offenders to engage in partnership work towards the goal of reducing offending behaviour, from the perspective of a relational dynamic of adult to adult dialogue and social interaction, in terms familiar to practitioners of *Transactional Analysis*. Mike and I were convinced that this would accelerate the growth of emotional maturity in young people, the singular factor known from research to reduce offending behaviour as young people psychologically matured.

We also felt that young people deserved transparency from us (in contrast to significant elements of the Wakefield behaviour modification programme which utilised hidden agendas of control, and which was both manipulative and also anything but transparent in its approach). For example one of the group work exercises was called 'The Sting' based on a popular film of the time about con artists. It set up a young person to react in a scenario of temptation, to steal from another and then the group leader would expose the wrong doing, thus highlighting the claimed 'habitual tendency' of the young person towards dishonesty and theft. So what was that all about if it was not a crude attempt to shame a young person into changing his ways?

For the life of me, I cannot believe that anything good in therapeutic terms could ever come from shaming a young person as a form of education. All I know of shaming and manipulation is that it is toxic and destructive in the extreme. Clearly I was not operating in the same world of professional values as my Wakefield colleague.

So in contrast, Mike and I went to considerable lengths to explain to the young people, in plain language, why we were working in the way we were, what the research showed, what we were aiming to achieve and how best we felt we could do that, through working as far as we could in partnership with them.

However, we were still taught a sobering lesson by the young people, which helped lift us out of naiveté, as they vociferously pointed out that nothing much would have changed if we didn't acknowledge we still held power. They wanted us to be totally transparent. Clearly, we still held power given that we had the legal recourse to return any young person we worked with, back to court for a breach of Supervision Order, if we didn't like their behaviour or wanted to impose authority over those who challenged us or made us angry with their specific behaviour or attitude towards us. Once we admitted that and also accepted that we had a legitimate right given our role, to exercise ultimate authority if necessary, the kids were very enthusiastic and supportive of our efforts to pioneer this new approach.

We did not have the research facilities to conduct any kind of thorough study of results but we saw young people maturing quicker than we had previously experienced and rates of offending behaviour certainly diminished. Also, during all the time we worked using this style of intervention, I cannot recall that we ever returned any Young Offender to court for breach of a Supervision Order (something I had done on quite a few occasions in the past).

When I left Bradford Social Services Department in 1984, it was to take up a post as Training and Development Officer with Save the Children, UK Child Care Department. In this role, I trained social workers, probation officers and youth workers to work 1:1 with, or run group work sessions for Young Offenders.

During this time I wrote my first book, 'No Holiday Camps' (1985), published by the Association for Juvenile Justice, an exploration of the political and ideological constructs surrounding much of the contemporary law and order debate at the time.

Two years after taking up my post with SCF, I was promoted to Deputy Director of the consultancy and training project which employed me. The post also carried the role of Director of the newly established 'Practice Development and Publications Unit'.

I was given the task of establishing the value base, philosophy and working practice of the Unit and decided I wanted it to offer opportunities to experienced practitioners, many of whom did not have formal qualifications, to publish write ups of their direct work with Young Offenders. I thought it was important to honour and bless skilled practitioners who had never bothered or never had the previous self-confidence to publish their work.

During my tenure, we published seven books and articles on direct work with Young Offenders, or models of effective systems management of young person and Young Adult Justice Systems.

I felt the most satisfied with a book entitled, 'Worth The Risk' (1987), written jointly by myself, Steve and Mandy, two young group workers employed by the Halifax Office of the West Yorkshire Probation Service. Steve and Mandy had a naturally 'Power-With' style of intervention and applied it with enthusiasm and self-belief. But they would have been the last people in the world to seek to publish their work.

My writing at this stage, in terms of my contribution to 'Worth The Risk' also included references to the work of M. Scott Peck on the development of mental health and spiritual growth in individuals (1978), Jimmy Boyle on the rehabilitation of violent offenders through the use of creative arts (1977) and (1984), and Eric Fromm on the authoritarian impulse in society (1942).

As I reflect back now, I can see that my focus was beginning to broaden out from the perspective of a predominantly political practitioner, to a wider interest in a more holistic approach to working with marginalised and disenfranchised individuals and groups. The focus was no longer solely on a structural perspective (political, economic and ideological) and its relationship to social policy and criminology; it was now encompassing personal values, individual meaning and the existence of soul focused concerns of the authentic Self.... To some extent this was mirroring my own personal journey.

The synchronistic and possibly metaphysical also put in an appearance one weekend when I was on a hill-walking break in the Lake District with my friend from my social work training, Jim, who hailed originally from Dundee. It was the weekend of the international celebration of Nelson Mandela's release from prison on Robben Island, in South

Africa. We had been sitting in Zefferreli's restaurant in Ambleside.

At that time, before the restaurant was redesigned, a set of French windows led out on to the street. I was sitting at a table, facing the French windows; Jim was sitting with his back to them. We had been talking in an animated fashion for over an hour and a half when the conversation gradually turned to Glasgow gang culture of the 1960s and the fate of Jimmy Boyle, imprisoned, wrongly he always claimed, for murder and later reaching a personal epiphany whilst still in prison, through discovery of a natural talent as a sculptor.

Jim said, "Aye, I understand he's immigrated to Australia". "No he's not", I said, "He's just walked through the door". Jim could not believe what I was saying, "You're kidding me". But I was not kidding him. At the precise moment his name was mentioned, he did walk through the entrance into Zefferreli's, with his wife and their two children!

The above was for me a fantastic example of what Jungians term 'synchronicity': an occurrence or range of occurrences which seem to go beyond mere coincidence. According to a Jungian perspective, when synchronicitous events begin to happen in one's life, it is a sign that one's archetypal energies have been activated. So something was stirring deep within my own soul.

The future was starting to look very interesting!

Further reflections on what we developed in our group work with Young Offenders in Bradford

Years later, through further research and synthesis of other theoreticians' ideas, I recognised that in our thinking and ideas around more effective and relevant forms of group work with Young Offenders in Bradford, we had pragmatically developed and applied what we termed a

113

'Power-With' approach, which drew on work done elsewhere that we had not previously known of:

- Steven Karpman's development of the Transactional Analysis based theory of the 'Drama Triangle' (1968);
- Will Schutz' work on human interaction as mapped out in his book 'Profound Simplicity' (1979) and
- Joanna Macy's radical direct action work within the anti-nuclear movement which (honouring the earlier 1920's work of Mary Parker Follett) she had named 'Power-With' (2005).

Will Schutz claimed that human interaction centred around three elements of behaviour between human beings: 'inclusion, affection and control'. He suggested that in order to be psychologically healthy, human beings needed to be balanced around these three elements, and that any one element, or combinations of them, could easily fall out of balance into under or over expressed forms. In the case of the control element, under expressed behaviour was Victim focused, abdicratic in nature and often manifested as sullen silence or vociferous blaming of others. Over expressed behaviour was Persecutor focused, autocratic in nature and often manifested as bullying and severely judging others.

Karpman's 'Drama Triangle' consists of 'Victim–Persecutor–Rescuer' behaviours. The Rescuer element was what we initially displayed in our work with young people, when we were naively attempting to deny the fact that control elements would still remain, no matter how much we were able to manifest a sense of working in partnership with Young Offenders.

I later learnt from Will Schutz, that the root fear behind all the abdicratic and autocratic positions is a hidden belief that, 'I am not competent'. The same could clearly be said for rescuing behaviour. Transparency, on the other hand, offers

114

a golden opportunity to move out of and beyond fear, into healthier, more democratic and "power-with" forms of interaction.

I think what we initially feared was that we were not competent to deal with serious conflict with young people if we insisted on exercising our legal authority over them should circumstances require us to do so. Once we accepted the challenge of using occasional "power-over" if required, and in context use it legitimately, we were freed up from fear and much more able to engage in robust, and at time extremely challenging, dialogue with young people, which helped them mature and helped us believe in what we were doing.

The *"Power-With Approach and"* (see diagram p.123) suggests that whether mapping communication styles between Young Offenders and social workers, or staff and management in organisational settings (no direct comparisons implied!), or even relational dynamics between two people in therapeutic – non therapeutic or coaching settings, there is a distinct tendency for people to avoid direct and transparent dialogue and instead engage in the manipulative dynamics of Stephen Karpman's 'Drama Triangle', of 'Victim-Rescuer-Persecutor'. This is represented in the diagram by the inverted lower triangle.

The reason why this happens is more often than not the presence of fear. As previously indicated, according to Will Schutz, whether we or others engage in autocratic or abdicratic behaviour, the root fear (sometimes not even admitted to the Self) is that "we are not competent". I would also strongly suggest that this similarly pertains for us when we choose to respond to others from the place of the rescuer. This is so because we may well fear that we do not have the ability to deal with direct conflict if we insist on putting our cards on the table around a particular control issue. This would have certainly often been the case for me and social work colleagues working with Young Offenders, before we developed the 'Power-With Approach and Model'.

Characteristically, the Power-With Approach and Model seeks to:

- Encourage open sharing of professional-personal values;

- Invite partnership working on the basis of seeking and identifying common ground within the range of disclosed values;

- Engage in open negotiation over areas of potential collaboration especially where there initially appears to be lack of common ground in relation to those declared professional-personal values;

- Achieve clarity about potentially shared strategies or ways forwards;

- Uphold the vital need for both assertiveness and flexibility to be present in relational dialogue. On the surface assertiveness and flexibility may appear to be somewhat contradictory positions, but if viewed from a 'both-and paradigm' rather than an 'either-or paradigm', it is easier to see that what is required here is both assertiveness about expressing professional-personal values in the context of what may or may not be negotiable, and also flexibility in terms of a willingness to genuinely engage in dialogue. By definition, no one can know beforehand what the eventual outcome of any dialogue will be - so to engage with it, encourages flexibility of outcomes.

- It is also imperative that all parties are willing to, 'Value Self and Others Equally'. If we value the Other above the Self, we are likely to slide inexorably back into a rescuing position, and immediately restimulate "Drama Triangle" relational dynamics. If we egotistically or narcissistically value the Self as a priority, then we cannot be open to genuine dialogue because ultimately, we will not be willing to listen at deeper and deeper levels to what other parties have to say, or more importantly feel from a heart space.

- The box surrounding the diamond shape represents the boundary between what may be negotiable and what may not be negotiable. If one is entering this relational field from a position of given power over the Other (as we were with our relational engagement with Young Offenders), then effectively it is a matter of choice whether we seek to engage in the process fundamentally from a place of 'Power-With', or toxically, from a place constantly within the 'Drama Triangle'. It is up to us – and in my experience, allowing fear to gain the upper hand in our internal self-dialogue will inevitably pitch us into the 'Drama Triangle' as a virtual default position.

In the context of the whole diamond shape outlined in the Diagram, the only healthy place in communication terms is the "Power-With" position. In contrast to the "Drama Triangle" dynamics, it is transparent and open; it directly seeks dialogue and does so from a willingness to clearly state what may be negotiable and also non-negotiable for each party.

In my experience, it takes courage to occupy and honour the 'Power-With' position. It requires sustained belief in the

Self and an outcome for the greater good, whilst being willing to be exposed to the potential turbulence of conflict before a place of genuine partnership can be secured within the relational field.

In Transactional Analysis terms, it is an 'adult to adult' position which promotes total self-responsibility and is essentially a non-adversarial paradigm. In contrast, the "Drama Triangle" positions are all essentially adversarial and promote manipulation. They are variations on 'parent-child' / 'child-child' / 'parent-parent' ego states.

The challenge for the helper working from a "Power-With" position is to facilitate and engage in dialogue:

- without fear and defensiveness;

- without justifying oneself;

- without appeasement (especially in the presence of attempted bullying behaviour from other parties);

- with clarity, compassion and assertiveness without being pulled into "Persecutor'"

- with openness and appropriate limited disclosure without being pulled into "Victim"; and

- to create relational and environmental safety for others without being pulled into "Rescuer", *whilst*
- recognising one's own old stories (archaic relational self-narratives and habitual defensive positions) which could pull one in a collusive way directly into "Drama Triangle" relational dynamics.

For those who have knowledge of other models (often derived from Humanistic Psychology) and are familiar with the model of the 'Conflict Management Grid', it is also worth pointing out that the "Power-With" position also has strong links to the "Collaborative" stance in the 'Conflict Management Grid' model. Similarly, in the context of the 'Grid', the "Rescuer" position equates with the "Avoidant" stance; the "Power Over / Autocrat" position equates with the "Competing" stance and the "Powerless / Abdicrat" position equate with the "Accommodating" stance.

In relation to the 'Power-With Approach and Model', it is reasonable to ask, how might one encourage and facilitate the other party to move away from 'Rescuing - Abdicating – Power Over' behaviour (which in 'Conflict Management Grid' terms is also 'avoidant' behaviour)?

Will Schutz offers a strong steer when he asserts that the 'Abdicrat' and the 'Autocrat' (and in my view, also the 'Rescuer') have a hidden fear that they are not competent, which is why in their different ways they avoid transparency and open honest dialogue. If this is the case, and I believe it to be so, then it implies that the helper-facilitator must pay attention to creating as much relational safety in the working environment as possible. Having done so, it may then be easier for the other party to begin to talk more openly about their vulnerabilities.

This will provide an opportunity to the helper to both hold an attentionally non-violent stance in terms of encouraging further personal and professional development (possibly in the form of further training and - or additional support), and also to listen at deeper and deeper levels to what the other person may be sharing in terms of not only vulnerabilities, but possibly also aspirations, hopes, inherent strengths and already developed skills.

Whilst working for The Open University as a Tutor on the 'Voluntary Sector Management and Leadership Programme', I came across the "Change Equation".

I am not entirely sure of its origins but it has been attributed to Richard Beckhard (1969) and it reads as follows:-

(A) plus (B) plus (C) being greater than (D) = CHANGE

(A) Represents a "significant degree of dissatisfaction with the current situation"

(B) Represents "some level of shared vision about the future"

(C) Represents "the existence of a safe first step"

(D) Represents "the perceived cost of change".

If the helper is fully present, with a non-confrontational stance, holding a positive and attentionally non-violent vision of the other person's potential, then critically it may in itself be enough to create the existence of a safe first step. From this position, it may be much easier for the other person to begin to talk from a deeper place about what might feel unhealthy or uncomfortable for them in their current situation, and may also provide a basic platform for creating helpful dialogue about a possibly better personal and professional vision for the future.

Most contemporary research into the effectiveness of psychotherapeutic interventions with clients shows that the single biggest factor influencing positive behaviour change and development of self-empowered mental health is the client's perception that the therapist *believes* in their own form of intervention and its application, and that includes the expectation of positive outcomes. Eric de Haan [2008] suggests that this research is equally applicable to the profession and practice of Coaching.

***

What 'freedom' was I beginning to sense in my early career in youth social work?

I sensed a freedom from received wisdom ("Young Offenders only respond to discipline. We know best; we've always done it this way. You give them an inch and they will take a mile").

I took the freedom of clear seeing to recognise the unblessed child beyond the evidence based details of a criminal case history or family defined projection of individual neurosis;

I accepted my freedom to choose to see the authentic presence of a young person's soul and spirit despite them being labelled as representatives of feral so called "troublesome youth" from tough backgrounds;

I chose the freedom to see their identified "acting out behaviours" as both unprocessed grief, rage and lack of early nourishment and also an awareness of their refusal to be defined or categorized by others;

I claimed the freedom to see beyond the simplistic notions of crime and punishment from an authoritarian law and order perspective, by choosing instead to develop a broader ideological and structural understanding of the way society often works and defines its participants;

I sought freedom from prejudice to accept that those labelled 'criminals'
are not born evil or hopeless cases, but instead are most often drawn from the most marginalized and disadvantaged groups in society, and invariably are the first to be criminalised.

I decided wherever I could, to acknowledge the damage done to the young person by their upbringing and life chances, and the damage they also visited upon others – most often perpetrated within the same communities from which they originated – and then to do my best to treat them as people with intelligence, and the power of discernment; through which they could choose instead to develop their potential for transformation, growth and change, with encouragement from my honest dialogue and support.

I recognised the need to bless young people wherever possible, and the ultimate pointlessness of choosing to condemn and judge them.

***

THE POWER-WITH APPROACH AND MODEL

Power & Communication Issues in Organisations

Power With
(Democrat/*Dialogue*)

- Partnership
- Negotiation
- Common Ground
- Clarity
- Valuing Self & Others Equally
- Assertive & Flexible

Power Over (Persecutor)
Autocrat/*Monologue*

Negotiable
(inside the box):

Negotiate with abdicrats and autocrats to move towards 'power-with' by creating safety for them to talk about their vulnerabilities

The Drama Triangle

Shadow aspects in organisations

Non-negotiable
(outside the box)

Powerlessness
(Victim)
Abdicrat/*Silence*

Adapted and synthesised from:
Schutz, W.
(Control issues for individuals & groups)
Macy, J. & Follett, M.P.
(Aspects of power in human relationships)
Karpman, S
(The drama triangle' in Transactional Analysis)

Rescuer

(False image of Power-With: Help them see this is false & identify 'pay-off' for them in rescuing)

THE PHOENIX PARTNERSHIP
Creative Change Management
www.phoenixpartnership.co.uk 01535-658800

CHAPTER 6:

Grace & Illness Part 1 -where the road of starvation meets the water of life

However well I was doing in following my bliss in my career, my emotional life was suffering. Joseph Campbell said, *"The purpose of life is to find your bliss and then follow it"* (2004). I should have known I was not fully following my bliss as the emotional side of my life was still trapped in frozen grief. The references I made, in my contributions to 'Worth The Risk', to the work of Peck, Boyle and Fromm were a precursor of a profound change in me that would be triggered by a serious illness.

The illness developed a couple of months after I was promoted again to Director of the Consultancy & Training Project following the sudden resignation of my boss, who could no longer stand the conflict created and repeatedly manifested in his relationship with his line manager, the Divisional Director (the previous and original Director of the Project). My promotion also meant my previous Deputy Director post was advertised, although I retained responsibility as Director for the Practice Development and Publications Unit.

Even though the post attracted three internal candidates, we appointed an outside applicant, Deirdre. Despite the appointability of other applicants, I simply felt Deirdre was the right person for the job: she was smart, street-wise (perhaps as a result of being a native of West Belfast), intelligent and personable. The Selection Panel agreed with me. She had a tough time initially, learning the ropes and dealing with the emotional and energetic turbulence from the other disappointed candidates working at the Project.

Out of a technical team of three (we had additional support staff), all three had applied for the post as internal candidates, so it was a tough choice to appoint Deirdre, but I knew in my bones that it was the right choice. But I felt I paid a high price for it in terms of relational dynamics and feelings of stress.

During this period, covering around eight weeks: my work in the field of Juvenile Justice was as intense as ever; we were a staff member short as my previous post was vacant; we appointed Deirdre who had to work hard in the face of a fair amount of resistance, to find her feet and my colleague Peter was driven into deep trauma by his wife's sudden allergic reaction to food at a Friday evening family meal. Within 48 hours she had slipped into a coma and devastatingly, died on the Sunday, leaving Peter alone with two young sons to care for, bereaved and stricken with grief. We remained short staffed as Peter went off on long term sick leave and we were unable to find an immediate temporary replacement.

I held things together as long as I could, but a mere four weeks after Deirdre's appointment I went into physical, emotional and it felt like mental collapse. I went off sick and went home where, apart for struggling out of bed to use the toilet or make myself some simple food, I slept solidly for three weeks. I was in a state of complete exhaustion. As those weeks went on and my sense of duty coupled with what Hakomi would term my "burdened and enduring" strategy kicked in, I attempted to pull myself together in an attempt to prepare myself to go back to work. But every time I pushed myself further I got more ill. A few weeks later in the middle of the night, it began to dawn upon me what was happening with my internal process. I had to let go of my habitual patterns of self-reliance, stoicism and endurance. I sat up in bed and said, "Alright, I accept I will never work again". From that point of complete surrender and despair, I slowly began to heal. As I was to learn again many years later, the moment of complete surrender to greater forces is almost always a turning point in healing, especially if done mindfully and with awareness.

My GP diagnosed Myalgic Encephalomyelitis, more commonly known as "M.E." Rest of itself didn't seem to help much, as my brain was still exhausted and still wouldn't function in the way it had previously done so. I was aware I could do nothing that would tax my brain in any way whatsoever: reading; dialogue; watching TV; reading newspapers or magazines. If I even attempted any of those things I quickly went into relapse. In my continuing exhausted state, I began as best I could, despite the experience of frequent relapse, to explore other possible treatment options. This included finding my way slowly towards exploring homeopathy and especially its connection to medical dowsing, in the form of 'Radionics', with healer Dorothy Lewis who lived in Reeth, North Yorkshire. Dorothy was the person who identified I had been severely traumatised at the age of 4½ years when I was assaulted by a teenager who threw a house brick at my head.

The first day after intensive healing with Dorothy, I felt totally energised. I was so elated that I went for a five mile walk by the River Swale around Reeth. The very fact that I could do this was amazing, as prior to the sessions with Dorothy I could barely walk twenty yards without a feeling of complete physical and mental exhaustion. I felt like I had been released from prison, but it was very premature. The walk was an extremely unwise thing to do, as I suffered a powerful physical collapse again soon after.

However over time with repeated visits, Dorothy helped me a great deal, and furthermore suggested I needed to expand my treatment with a practitioner of 'Psionic

Medicine', which was a deeper and more intensive form of Radionics.

I found such a practitioner in Chorley, near Blackburn, in the person of G.P., Dr. Vincent Mainey (or 'Big Vince' as I fondly came to think of him when describing his considerable sense of presence to others). Dr. Mainey also helped me greatly, and over a five year period from first diagnosis of 'M.E.' I regained around 80% of my previous physical functioning and a good 95% of my mental health functioning, although I had a lot more work and grief resolution to complete around my emotional life.

During the time I worked with Dorothy, I had a few intense dreams, including a dream of driving up the Yorkshire Dales towards Reeth and pulling in to a lay-by at the side of the road. I got out of the car in an exhausted state and noticed that a canal ran alongside the road. As I stood there a brightly painted traditional barge came into view, briefly moored alongside the lay-by and waited until I stepped on board, then moved on down the canal. Very shortly afterwards I began to realise that the boat and canal were veering off away from the road, with me still on board the boat. I made no attempt to get off the boat, and I left the car way behind, without any sense of loss or distress, never to return.

The above dream turned out to be a vision of the future, but it took quite a while for the journey to unfold. I returned to work on a phased basis, and spent a lot of time doing my best to help Deirdre with her severely interrupted induction, as well as dealing with a disciplinary process for one of the previous internal candidates, whom I guessed, in a spirit of extreme non-cooperation and resistance to recognising my authority in my new Director role, had badly sabotaged a major consultancy contract with one of our main purchasers, losing the Project a £12,000 contract, which at that time was one of our biggest contracts in monetary terms – and somewhat damaging our professional reputation.

I was fortunate in receiving excellent and solid support from my line manager Annie, also recently appointed to a new post, as our parent body was re-organised. It was hard dealing with an angry and traumatised member of staff, undergoing a disciplinary hearing, but made worse by frequent even more angry and accusatory phone calls from their spouse.

I began to feel that my bliss had changed, or somehow I had lost contact with it as my career appeared to lose its allure for me. Also, emotionally, quite frankly, I was lost. I had pretty much spent seven years on my own after my relationship fell apart with Jane. I just couldn't face opening my heart again, it felt far too raw and emotionally I felt burnt away, spent, and empty, standing in the centre of a wasteland of grief which was very frozen.

I had taken a risk and chosen to thaw out just a little, a few years before when I met Shoshanna, a fellow student on my social work training course. Bearing in mind I was essentially a rather naïve working class lad from an educationally socially mobile family, but moving into the rarefied world of the professional middle class, Shoshanna seemed an exotic creature to me. She fascinated me. She was pretty, sophisticated, Jewish, with refined tastes and spoke with a beautifully modulated voice that sounded just like Julie Andrews. Her parents lived in a very prosperous part of North London. Her Dad was a property developer and her mum was a very intelligent, also sophisticated and refined lady, in a very upper middle class kind of way.

I really liked Shoshanna's mum, she was kind and caring, intelligent and personable and a delight to converse with, but in contrast I was socially inept, gauche and lacking severely in confidence. To me, at that time, the class divide was so big

I could not see the other side of the canyon. I felt I stood often alone, looking over at what some people might regard as the Promised Land and feeling very unsophisticated and disempowered. What Shoshanna saw in me I will never know; although a clue might be that she had once joked that her boyfriend before me was a black Arab (he wasn't, he was a Greek Cypriot) and after me she definitely did marry a nice Jewish doctor.

We got on pretty well really in the five years we spent in an on-off relationship, which became long distance after our Course ended and Shoshanna returned to work for Waltham Forest Social Services in London. She was kind, sensitive and when she wanted to be, very assertive.

One summer we holidayed in Crete and Shoshanna refused to walk on the beach with me in Chania on the northern coast of Crete, because I refused to remove my scruffy old Chesterfield FC football socks that were crumpled around my ankles above a pair of battered trainers. She wasn't too impressed either, that I took a copy of 'The New Criminology' on holiday with us!

Whilst I was immersing myself in radical Marxist criminology, Shoshanna was probably dreaming of her lost world of sophistication and wondering how the hell she had ended up with me. We weren't exactly compatible; we were genuinely the odd couple. In time we both recognised there was no future in our relationship, but it still hurt greatly to let go. Looking back now, I'm really pleased she met Barry and continued on with the life to which she was clearly accustomed.

I then embarked on a passionate but short lived and ill-starred affair with a married woman who showed a very powerful interest in me. I met her as a colleague and peer through my work as a social worker. I had not felt such feelings of intensity for many years, but despite the

130

overpowering passion I felt for her, I let go when it was clear to me she had no intention of ending her marriage, and decided to set off with her partner, on a yearlong trek to the Far East and Australia. Although she wanted to reconnect on her return, my heart was really not in it anymore.

I then met Muireann, a wonderful loving soul from East Belfast who was a student on placement at the social work office where I worked. She was fun, full of energy and enthusiasm, very kind hearted, but much younger than me. In the end, that was the key issue which convinced me we had to part. It was very painful. I grew to love her very much but would not admit it to myself nor for that matter, to Muireann. She was much more open with her feelings and even came to live with me for a while, before she moved to the Greater Manchester area for work. I was left in no doubt about Muireann's feelings for me but it seemed I was unable to reciprocate in the way she needed me to do so.

I attempted to end the relationship one emotionally exhausting weekend but Muireann could not take on board what I was saying. When we parted on the Sunday however, I was convinced she understood and had very tearfully accepted the reality. I had to end the relationship all over again a few days later when Muireann came back saying she never wanted to go through such a weekend again, and I realised she was still in denial about what had happened, or perhaps was simply refusing to accept the so called wisdom of my decision. The final parting was so much harder after that realisation, as it would have been so easy for me to collude with the denial / refusal. But despite this, I chose to go through with the final ending. I felt terrible for what I had done to her, but I knew in my heart of hearts, at that time given the state I was in, that I had no other choice.

The following poem gives some idea of how deeply it all affected me at the time:

SEPTEMBER '86 / FOR MUIREANN

O.K. so where to now?

What do I expect from this mechanical exorcism?

After the pain
And the rising panic
I find myself
Still holding on for grim death
As the compass point swings
Inexorably away from the past
I hang over the edge
Fingernails beginning to crack
With every reminder
Of the hand I let go

Yes it seemed so wrong when we were together
Giving nothing to someone who gave me so much
And yet it seems so wrong now we are apart
This place haunts me
Her face reveals itself with every memory
Once the circuit connects
Images tumble into place

Her smile that December morning

Watching my eyes

Feeling my resistance melt

As I slowly removed each present

From the parcel she gave me

How could anyone love me so much

And still leave me distant and afraid?

How could I care so much

Yet offer so little?

If we live on this earth

To find the truth

Why is the truth so empty

So graceless

So unrelenting?

There is no magic anymore

Her vain hopes and torn dreams

Have lain in the gutter outside my door

These past six weeks

Tonight the rain washed them away.

John Holt

A number of difficult short term, often very painful, relationships followed and it was not until I met Pam a good few years later that I genuinely fell in love again.

My relationship with Pam was a confusing mixture of deep love, powerful sexual attraction and on too many occasions deep jealousy from her, which in the end destroyed the relationship for me. Pam had had a very difficult and in the worst possible way, sexually abusive childhood. She had been deeply scarred by the experience and saw my sexual betrayal of her everywhere. She convinced herself on a number of occasions that I was seeing other women and yet I was not. The sadly ironic reality was that I felt enormous passion for her alone and had absolutely no interest in looking at other women.

I also found it hard being a step parent to young Alana, Pam's daughter, who was seven when Pam and I got together. Alana was a loving child but also very insecure: when Pam and I were emotionally close Alana was very negative towards me; when Pam and I struggled Alana was close and needy around me, desperately fearful that I would leave. Pam and I were together for three years before I finally gave up and ended the relationship. At that time, Alana was 10 years old. I missed both Pam and Alana terribly when we parted, but knew I could not go back.

I was very sad last year to receive an E-mail out of the blue from Alana, now a young woman in her twenties, telling me that Pam had died in her early 40s of a massive cerebral haemorrhage. Although I wrote back to Alana hoping we would reconnect, I have not heard from her since.

Pam was a very beautiful, intelligent, funny and mischievous soul, battered by life and the cruel things human beings do to each other as a result of receiving cruelty from those that went before them. Her loving energy was profoundly deep, I felt the power of it on many occasions, but hard to hold as the wounds and trauma took their toll. God bless you Pam, I don't think you ever knew just how much I loved you.

The same year my relationship ended with Pam, I met Lis, a woman I felt instantly attracted to, and who was a friend of my dear friend Julia. She moved in with me after a year and some years later in 1999 we were married.

My love for Lis ran, and still runs very deep. But after a number of years, we were fated to part. There had been very difficult emotional histories in both our families, and although I was initially very open to working through stuff, in time we both grew very untrusting of each other. It seemed a case of, "I'll commit to you if you commit to me". Lis got involved with someone else before we lived together, and working through that was excruciatingly painful, but it did eventually bring us a lot closer together. However, it was never close enough, despite, for me, our honeymoon near Loch Morar and Arisaig and the months that followed, being a magical blessed time together.

We had been married a few years when I became ill again. I was diagnosed originally with lymphoma based on CT and MRI scans of my liver, where it appeared there were cancerous lesions. I lived with this news for seven weeks over the summer, until I had a liver biopsy and was told that the lesions were only "fatty liver deposits", caused by a too sedentary lifestyle. It came as a great relief at the time, but ten years down the line, it was clear that post-biopsy diagnosis had been dangerously incorrect.

Despite two or three separate attempts to get help via couple counselling, Lis and I eventually parted in 2003 although thankfully we remained good friends. We were finally divorced in 2010. Although we had obtained a Decree Nisi some years previously, it took me that long to finally let go. I couldn't face the final stage of the Divorce process; I was still emotionally much attached to Lis. But in the end, especially given the reoccurrence of serious health difficulties, and the need for Lis to be financially free of me, it seemed irresponsible to hang on and I finally acted to end the marriage.

I have never been able to turn off the love I feel for Lis. To me it is a truth that once married; two souls are forever entwined in some way. (I can hear Paul Simon's song, "Hearts and Bones" echoing in my head: *You take two bodies and you twirl them into one, their hearts and their bones, and they won't come undone, no they won't come undone, hearts and bones, hearts and bones*"). This is a blessing to me. I don't know if this is a man thing, but I feel a deep river of love for Lis which will always flow strongly in me. I suppose without knowing it, by 2011, I had at last emotionally begun to profoundly heal.

Today, Lis is with her partner Dan. I like him very much; he is a good man with much sensitivity and integrity. I am so delighted they have found each other and I can now love Lis the way I wanted to, as I said in a text to her on Christmas Eve last year, "Lissie and Dan, have a great Christmas and New Year. It's so wonderful to be able to love you and appreciate you at last, without all the old crap. Thank you for being you and for being a very treasured and dear person in my life and heart". I felt very blessed by Lis' reply which felt deeply reciprocal.

***

What did I learn from my journey through 'starvation' towards a greater promise of life?

I learnt that the human heart cannot sustain a long term choice to live without love or the potential of intimate relationships. If we starve the heart we also starve the body and ultimately we starve the soul. My illness seemed to me at the time to be a disaster, but in retrospect I can see it was a powerful intervention of grace in my life. It forced me to look at my emptiness and disconnection from the essential and authentic Self within me. Yes, I was expressing a vital part of myself in my work and it did reflect some aspects of my authentic Self, but it was only a partial glimpse of who I was, who I am and who I can be.

I did 'love' through my work, but I was starving myself of opportunities to really risk intimate love as a form of essential reciprocal nourishment, especially essential as I was choosing to be of service in the world in my career. Without being open to risk and intimacy at a very personal level, I would simply eventually starve, burn out and collapse; which is precisely what happened to me when I contracted M.E.

Earlier that summer, I had ended my relationship with Muireann. I went on holiday to the Isle of Jura with friends Andy, Julia and Sue. I became ill on holiday – worse than I had felt for some time, but not at that point full blown M.E. There were signs of doom all around me that holiday: A caravan full of angry young men trashed their own accommodation one drunken evening and threatened to trash the caravan we were staying in which was standing next door to them; I was alone on the beach feeling lost and saw an old wooden box used for fish storage washed up on the beach – as I looked at it I saw it had a name stencilled on the side, which turned out to be Muireann's surname.

I went off alone for the day to the neighbouring Island of Islay and made my way down to the Mull of Oa at the southern tip of the Island. It was a beautiful day and I gazed out to sea below a blue cloudless sky, resting next to a war memorial to American soldiers who had died in a U-boat torpedo attack near there during the First World War. I felt troubled but was unsure why.

As I looked up into the sky I saw what looked like an intercontinental ballistic nuclear missile falling down out of the sky towards Islay and the sea. It was the 1980s and the threat of nuclear war was often in the news, at least according to Ronald Reagan who spent much time talking of Russia as an 'evil empire'. I was absolutely convinced I was watching the Bomb dropping on me and thought, "Oh well, this is the way it ends then. Well at least it's a sunny day". The missile fell through the blue sky and at the last minute turned through 45 degrees, to shoot upwards. I could then see the outline of a jet plane, where there had previously been simply the shape of a missile.

Nuclear War did not happen after all – but a deeper war was beginning to break out within my soul as it fought to bring me back to life.

***

CHAPTER 7:

Showing the Self in the world

My experience of illness with M.E. and subsequent healing opened me up to the existence of other worlds than the one I had previously known. Others have referred to this space as the 'liminal world', beyond the everyday experience where mythos and logos meet, I suspect as they always have done, despite some conclusions and ideas within the broad philosophy of the Enlightenment!

Here, both allopathic and complementary medicine have a place; here there are greater things than, "are dreamt of in our philosophy"; here many if not all things are possible should we choose to live in and be open to the presence of faith alongside a commitment to balanced scientific reason. Yes, I believe from both a somatic-physiological and also a metaphysical perspective, there is a time to live and a time to die, but I also believe we have much greater choice over the latter than we are often prepared to admit.

I have seen people choose death. Some, metaphorically, choose death in unconscious ways of addiction, fear of life and loss of faith in anything good in the world. Others choose it literally, with great wisdom.

I saw my Mum do the latter. Shortly after her 81st birthday and after at least three very debilitating strokes in the previous few years, she spent a long time with my Dad's cousin Enid, who is quite a family historian, asking her how long various people in our family had lived. At the end of the conversation she apparently said, "Enid, I don't want to see my 82nd birthday". Despite the fact that Mum's health was settled, her condition was very stable, and she was relatively very comfortable, within three weeks she had died of renal failure. I believe that this was the result of a very conscious choice.

I was with Mum the night before she died and stayed until 9.30pm, as did other members of my family. I recall that I was the last to leave, a few minutes after the others. I had a very heavy heart, it was hard for me to let Mum go, but I knew this was the end. She was clearly embarking on a journey out of this physical world. It must have been very similar for Glyn, Chris and my niece Kerry, who were all nearby and all loved my Mum dearly, as did nephew Liam who at that time was living and working abroad. I went to a local off-licence to buy a bottle of wine for the evening meal with Glyn and Chris. I remember sitting in my car outside the store for a long time, quietly, just taking in that I didn't expect to see my Mum alive again. It was a tough evening.

Mum died around 9am the next morning, thirty minutes before normal visiting hours at the Nursing Home. I think she knew the only way she could leave us all was when we were not there. I was the first to arrive around 9.30am and I was given time to be alone with her. Mum's body was still very warm; I also sensed her presence in the room but she was unmistakeably and clearly moving away to another place. I talked to her as much as I felt able, before Glyn and Kerry arrived a while later at the Nursing home.

If anyone has taught me not to fear death, it is my Mum, Joan Holt, spiritualist and humanist. She always taught me that death is not the end; it is a mere gateway into an unfolding and potentially magnificent future which we can begin to create and consolidate here on earth, long before we take our final 'Dance with death'.

She never claimed to be much of an intellectual, in fact she often referred to herself as 'daft', but she was far from it. She had the gift of a strange mixture of deep wisdom and occasional social faux pas. The way she re-told stories of what happened to her in various social situations, showed me clearly that in the moment of living her humorous naiveté she knew exactly what she was doing. I believe it was a practised art.

I think on some level it was true that Mum was always an innocent abroad in the world, but she had some inner steel too, which I saw from time to time, and she knew how to use it when she decided she had to – not often, admittedly, but when she revealed that "witch" energy as Robert Bly would call it, there was no messing with her. My Dad's difficult moods could absolutely dominate the emotional and energetic climate in our house and Mum seemed to put up with a lot of this, but when she decided she had had enough, she could speak with a tangible ferocity that was perfectly capable of stopping my Dad in his tracks, which I certainly witnessed on a number of occasions.

Mum and Dad once had neighbours two doors away who reckoned to be sophisticated and no doubt impressed that they were living close by a local head teacher and his wife. The lady of the household was a bit of a social climber, and a curtain twitcher. One day Mum was getting out of the car after Dad had pulled into the driveway in front of their bungalow; unfortunately as she attempted to get out of the car she got her leg tangled in the seat-belt and fell half out of the car rather ungainly on to the driveway. Noticing in her peripheral vision, the curtain twitching two doors away, she described to me how she gave a very gracious regal wave, dusted herself down and with as much dignity as she could muster, and made her way into our house.

A couple of days later she was engaged in conversation with the same lady about husbands and D-I-Y. The lady's husband was, of course, an expert. She asked Mum if Dad did any D-I-Y, "Ah yes", Mum replied, "Only yesterday, Harold was poly-urinating the doors". As Mum said, "After that day she never bothered putting any airs and graces on with me again, in fact when I see her these days she often swears a lot when talking to me". Mum delivered the final 'coup de gras' with a twinkle in her eye, "That says just about everything about the way she sees me now". To this day I don't know whether Mum's comment had been a delightful Malapropism or subtle tactics designed to distance herself from a petty bourgeois social climber.

Just as Mum taught me not to be afraid in the world, in a strange way, my M.E. illness also began to show me there is nothing to be afraid of in this life. I learnt that at the moment of total surrender, "Alright, I accept I will never work again", this is where healing can begin, unless God already has plans for you to move on into the life beyond physical death. M.E. also showed me a new way of life: beyond my familiar reliance on old character strategies, I also had the opportunity to expand my awareness from the social and political into the spiritual and eventually deeply intimate world of sacred partnership in my work.

In reality, it was never a case of 'either/or' because there was no need for me to choose between the political and the spiritual; it can always be 'both/and' if I chose it to be. And I did choose that, slowly at first without really knowing it, then increasingly over the years until my terminal diagnosis and my response to it, after a titanic struggle to let go of old singular ways, finally catapulted me into joyous life, as I know now, with my life partner, and I'm sure, on some level, my twin soul Carol. I still had political awareness, but alongside this radical pragmatism, more mysterious and other worldly manifestations began to create a presence in my life.

Here and now, I have just entered liminal space yet again, or perhaps I never left it behind. Having just written the words in the paragraphs above, the VDU computer screen has suddenly shifted without me pressing any keys, to show me the title of the next chapter in this book. This kind of somewhat inexplicable happening has not been an isolated phenomenon since Carol and I have been together. For me, it is a sense of a heart feeling deeply welcome and at peace in the presence of another, blessed by the watchful presence of grace.

Another mysterious process occurred in relation to the genesis of this book. All the chapter headings and the book title revealed themselves to me in their precise entirety, on a Mandorla Men's Work Weekend in North Wales, at 4am in the morning in late May 2011.

Cae Mabon has always had its own special energy for me – often as I arrive at the place, parking my car above the site in the woods and walking down through the trees to the encampment area, I sense the living trees and earth and their silent disincarnate human ancestral companions, move energetically with love and warmth to greet me. I have felt this so many times over the years that I can relate to it as no less than coming home to a place of love, support and communal fellowship, where everything in the living environment seems absolutely committed to welcoming me, helping me and validating me whilst I am there.

It is especially profound since walking on the path down to the encampment I pass the natural graveside of an ex-client and ex-men's work participant, Steve. The last time I saw Steve alive was in an IKEA Store just off the M62, where I bumped into him and his son Lyle at the checkout. I had bought a load of furniture including bookcases in order to reshape my living environment at home. The last thing Steve said to me, with a twinkle in his eye, when he saw all the stuff I'd bought was, "Enjoy!" That word is a great one to remember him by.

This is especially so when I think of all the crap things that happened to Steve in his life. I recall vividly how upset he was at an incident that had happened to him in a trendy city centre bookstore in Leeds. Steve suffered from lots of ailments, not least breathing and nasal problems. He tended to snuffle a lot. He also dressed as a rather bohemian type. Whilst in the... 'oh so trendy aren't' we liberal.... bookstore, he was spotted by the bookstore manager and asked to leave because his appearance and demeanour, "might upset the customers". Steve was very well read and my guess is that over the years he was one of that store's best customers. But he didn't look right for them, so he was humiliated and shown the exit door.

Steve was taken ill on a Men's event at Cae Mabon which I didn't attend. My colleague Simon was there and knew Steve well. Simon and others were so concerned at Steve's health they felt he should go back home to Leeds. As I recall, his wife had paid for his attendance at the event as a birthday present, knowing how much Steve loved Cae Mabon and the Men's Work. Steve was accompanied back home and became very ill very quickly. He was admitted into hospital and had fallen into a coma. He died a few days later and I recall Simon was with him through this.

It was the wish of Steve's wife that Steve be buried at Cae Mabon, which duly took place. Steve's body is now buried there in the grave beside the path amongst the beautiful trees.

My personal revelation at Cae Mabon was not the first time I had experienced strange and mysterious happenings there. This time, in May 2011 at the Mandorla Event, it seemed to me to be tinged with metaphysical resonance. The fact that the revelation actually happened, was a major surprise to me at the time of 4am, as I had been hoping around six hours earlier that the group ritual we did on the theme of 'Emerging', would show me the most appropriate title for the book I knew I must write.

Collectively, we had come to expect within Mandorla, that the planned or emerging ritual part of any event (usually around three days in), would coalesce and consolidate some kind of internal shift, that would certainly show itself to the person in question, and often also to other men there. But nothing happened in the ritual space as I had hoped.

I felt sad and disappointed, but accepted it, and went to bed around midnight. At 4am however, I awoke, not only with the book title clear as day, but with all seventeen chapter headings quite obviously formed within my internal field of vision, in my mind's eye. Wherever these chapter headings and book title came from, they have shown me what to write and in what order – a roadmap for the soul given to me from way beyond my conscious awareness at the time. I have followed that route without deviation throughout the whole process of writing the book.

And right now, something else has revealed itself to my conscious awareness in relation to my still unfolding and developing connection with Carol and how it might link with the book blueprint given to me on that earlier occasion in North Wales. Because, it is only now, as I sit at a table in a cottage near Ballycastle in County Mayo, in March 2012, with Carol ten feet away from me doing her own sacred writing, knowing what I know now about me, Carol and the journey we have been on together so very powerfully since July last year, that I understand why the next chapter heading, which suddenly appeared on my VDU screen, is entitled 'Bridging and integration of the split Self'.

This isn't the way I had anticipated writing the book, or even this chapter, when I thought about the chapters to be. But I am certainly not complaining!! Carol is for me a manifestation of my decision to go beyond fear and stay open to loving and being loved. As I am able to reflect now, realisation of the power of love, including how much I am truly loved, has healed the split Self deep within me, I am sure of it.

However, at the time of my M.E., Carol was over 20 years in the future. All I knew then was that I would not be staying in the world I had known up to the point of my illness. The change started in small ways. I had been profoundly influenced and guided by M. Scott Peck's book, "The Road Less Travelled", especially his chapters on 'love' and 'grace'. The book came to me at a point in my life, prior to the serious onset of my M.E. illness, where I did not want to learn the life lessons being shown to me.

I remember being in Bath, with my friend Julia, visiting her childhood home for the weekend. I was starting to get increasingly concerned about my flagging health, but deeply wary of the pain of relationships, spiritual seeking and the path of love. We were in Waterstone's Bookstore, and Julia had asked me if I wanted to look in the personal development and spirituality section. I was probably standing fifteen feet away from her and the spirituality section at the time, and I said, "No, I'm sick of spirituality". At the instant I said it, I became an observer and witness of my own actions – I noticed my right arm and hand reaching out to the bookshelf which was next to me, I watched as I pulled out a book from the shelf, and then watched my two hands open it. The book was, 'The Road Less Travelled', a book I had no previous knowledge of whatsoever, and it opened at the beginning of the chapter entitled, "The Miracle of Health". My instant reaction at the time was to feel angry then I spontaneously began to laugh. I did not know it then, but at the point of laughter I think my journey towards soul liberation had actually begun.

A few years later, after the worst point of my M.E., I was facilitating a residential training event in St, Anne's, Lancashire, with a Team from West Yorkshire Probation Service. At an early afternoon session, I had been chatting to participants in the break about my interest in more spiritual aspects of personal development. I remember feeling almost embarrassed that such a side to my way of being even existed – I was known at the time for being very thorough and very theoretical as a pragmatically focused practitioner, in the field of Adult and Juvenile Justice. I may have been regarded by some as obviously political and at times philosophical and reflective, but I don't think anyone saw me at that time as being a particularly spiritual person.

However, it seemed that this somewhat hidden aspect of my authentic Self really intrigued people. So much so that four people, separately, asked me if I would run an extra session on these ideas that evening. I said yes, if the majority wanted to do so. It was quickly checked out with the rest of the Team and they all showed considerable enthusiasm for the suggestion. (I was once told that the word enthusiasm is derived from the phrase 'En Theo', which apparently means 'filled with God').

Before the session, resting alone in my hotel bedroom, I remember initially wondering what on earth I would talk about, but the predominant feeling I had was curiosity about what might happen at the evening session. It was one of those situations where I knew at some internal level that all would be well and I actually had no anxiety whatsoever about what I might say or do in a two hour evening session.

At the appointed hour, we all gathered together in the training room downstairs, and as I remember it, I simply opened my mouth and began talking – I can't remember what I said or did except to say I spoke absolutely spontaneously from the heart, and we all joined in what turned out to be a fabulously stimulating and engaging group dialogue, where people shared a range of out of the ordinary experiences they had previously known.

Later that evening, I walked on the beach at St Anne's with two of the participants, Terry and his Probation Officer colleague. I vividly remember the experience as one Abraham Maslow would describe as a 'peak experience'. I would describe it as a profound sense of being (definitely 'being') in the right place, at the right time, with the right people, and also doing what was absolutely right for me in a way that seemed to strongly nourish others. I suppose for Joseph Campbell this would be an example of someone knowing that they had touched something profound both intra-psychically, interpersonally and possibly communally, which demonstrated that they were clearly, if only for a while, 'following their bliss'.

I decided after the session that wherever appropriate I should widen the context of my training events to include the possibility of the spiritual or transpersonal. It was clear to me then that those aspects were just as much part of me as the aspects that were the more publically known in terms of my professional profile. Those elements became increasingly part of my work from that time onwards, to this day, whether I am working 1:1 or with groups.

Further reflections on more spontaneous approaches to group work

I have noticed over the years that even though I will do detailed planning of events, and in a much more relaxed fashion than I used to do this, by now I will often simply use the prepared material as a base point for open dialogue and experimentation in the moment.

On many occasions I have been aware of reflecting that this feels somewhat like the process of Jazz improvisation as I understand the process experienced and enjoyed by musicians, where after a while they return the music to the baseline theme before concluding: in my case, before concluding our group discussions. All I have to do to tap into this process in a useful way is to be without fear and to trust. If I do that it always seems to work, even when, especially when, the initial responses from participants can be challenging or occasionally hostile.

By contrast however, if I let such fears get the better of me, it tends to fall apart very quickly and I have to revert to the official curriculum or programme. It seems to me that if I make such fear based choices, participants gain much less from the experience.

This awareness has been around me now for over twenty years, by now it is much more obvious to me as I become very familiar with witnessing my own process, and it has been a gentle and persistent matter of encouraging myself to accept and show more and more of my authentic Self to others in the context of my work.

In so doing, I am clearly encouraging others to reveal more and more of their authentic Selves and the collective wisdom we uncover can at times be astonishing: both deeply synchronistic and also profoundly healing, particularly for those participants with low self-esteem issues.

In my mind, it is another way of realising that, as Julian of Norwich said, "All shall be well and all manner of things shall be well"(1978). We are and always have been blessed, each and every one of us. We just need to be who we are and who we have always been. It's just that most of the time we don't realise that neither are we encouraged to believe it. In not realising it, I feel we often deeply wound ourselves and others. We can repeat the maxim, "We have nothing to fear but fear itself", but even that is only half the story, because 'fear' is still there in the equation.

I think, it is much better to simply say and live the truth that, "We have nothing to fear". I think that is the true meaning of 'blessing the self and others'. The world needs us to show our true Selves to ourselves and to others and in so doing to know we are blessed and loved.

This for me is the path of life. I believe it also reflects some of the deepest longings of every human heart and we can only truly love others if we first and then equally love ourselves. As we give and receive, so we heal.

***

It seems that there is a deeper rhythm to our own being and to life, if we can step away from fear and relax into the organic pace of the authentic Self as it opens up its presence to the world around us.

At this deeper level, we begin to connect naturally with others who have also risked stepping away from fear. I feel the human family knows and resonates with a more natural state of being. That is evident when we speak and express ourselves from the heart, because it is clear that others hear it and naturally respond to it. The more those others respond, the less we and they feel alone in the world.

At the times in my life when I have stepped beyond fear, it seems that I have also trusted that I am of enough value to know that if I say something with heart and with honest intent, it will have a resonance and meaning that can be a strong source of nourishment for others.

These days, I also anticipate and often receive an equal measure of nourishment from others in return as they respond to me from a similarly open hearted level.

This was certainly the case in relation to the evening sessions I ran for the group at the Probation Service Residential in Lancashire. I had to get beyond my anxieties about the way I may have been viewed by others, but once I did that there was very little anxiety or fear around, despite the fact that I really had little clue of what I was going to say, or how things might turn out at the evening training session I ran for the group.

I also feel God has a definite sense of humour, because invariably the times I have stepped beyond fear into authentic Self-expression, I have done it with a light heart and a sense of fun which has been almost instantly reciprocated. It was there in powerful measure at the Probation Service group training event.

I tend to think that when I speak with sincerity and from the heart, that before long, as I get into my rhythm, I will soon be doing so with humour – and as the humour begins to show itself, I often reflect that when laughter is around then God is never very far away.

In the place without fear, even death has less power – of course we are human to feel deep grief and sadness in the midst of a sense of loss, and yet we can also do this without fear, if in the moment of saying goodbye to a loved one we also take time to remember and celebrate that person's life with gratitude and a sense of respect. As my brother Glyn said about my Mum when she died, "It was a life very well lived".

As I have done the above things, I have often felt the presence of unseen hands helping me to stay grounded and true to myself, in the various ways that are appropriate to a particular moment or combination of circumstances.

It may not be easy, but all I have to do is to choose wherever I can not to be afraid.

***

Mum aged 75 on holiday

Above: Llyn Padarn below Yr Wyddfa
Below:Llyn Padarn

154

CHAPTER 8:

Bridging and integration of the split Self

Before I could open to receiving love into my life and truly follow my bliss, I had to learn to love myself. I would be the first to acknowledge this has taken a lot of doing and eventually being. On one level it is simple, but our collectively created world can often make the journey seem to be a profoundly tough one.

I think that I began to really love and trust myself when I started to reveal my authentic Self to others somewhere around the mid to late 1980s: firstly in my training events, the event with the Probation Service being a very good example; teaching work including tutoring for The Open University where I could bring out much more of my authentic voice at residential Summer Schools; then gradually but consistently over time, in my 1:1 work as a counsellor, psychotherapist, clinical supervisor, coach and coach supervisor.

Here and now reflections

I have been greatly helped by the core trainings I have chosen: Humanistic Psychology in the late 1980s via the Institute for the Development of Human Potential (IDHP); the Hakomi Method of psychotherapy in the early 1990s, via the US based Hakomi Institute and through lived experience over the next twenty years or so, the 'Integrative-Relational Model' (Holmes, Paul & Pelham, 1996) as it has come to be known – a synthesis and balance of both person centred and psychodynamic approaches, which I find to be applicable to both psychotherapy and coaching. The space where all those disciplines can meet would potentially embrace: a deepening understanding of the effects and workings of unconscious process within the therapeutic and where appropriate, coaching relationship; the importance of creating safe environments to encourage client self-development and self-sustainability; and an understanding of the intrapsychic impact of personal perception and processes, on the way an individual sees themselves in relation to life's opportunities and challenges.

I now have the hindsight of many more years in this world, and especially so in the aftermath of my illness journey. From this place, I now think that the predominately common experience for many of us, is to live within the confines and restrictions of a deeply fearful paradigm of life. We go against the usual flow when we choose to live beyond fear. I believe it is for this reason that M. Scott Peck (1978) defines "love" as, *"The will to extend one's self for the purpose of nurturing one's own or another's spiritual growth"*. Love is, *"not a feeling"*, (Page 81). For him, it is consciously chosen action.

The predominant paradigm in our world is a scarcity and fear based one, referred to by Matthew Fox in his book, "Original Blessing" (1987), as the 'Via Negativa', and by writer and theologian James Allison, (1996) as the 'Apocalyptic Imagination'. Amongst other things, the apocalyptic place of experiencing the world is: dramatic, bloody, painful, judgmental, accusatory, toxically power dominated, exclusive, suffering based, shaming, arrogant, patronising, guilt inducing and unforgiving.

It occurs to me that this seems to be the ideological construct within which much of our social and political discourse is undertaken; or in other words, the subtle or not so subtle hidden agenda behind most current affairs debates and commonly accepted ways of seeing and experiencing the world in our post-industrial western culture. What Matthew Fox calls the 'Via Positiva' and what James Allison refers to as the 'Eschatological Imagination' is the stage that follows, or even sometimes precedes the 'Via Negativa' when life's depths have not yet been fully experienced; it is much more of an abundance based and non-fearful paradigm. I understand eschatological to mean the end of things but also, in reality, the beginning of other things. In this sense, it is rather more natural, organic, developmental and incremental than is the 'apocalyptic'.

Amongst other qualities, the eschatological, or potentially transformational as I would describe it, includes the: non-dramatic, gentle, pain free, non-judgmental, accepting and empathic, dialogical and power sharing, inclusive, joy and often fun and laughter based, blessing and cherishing, humbly assertive, encouraging, self-accepting and forgiving. Matthew Fox implies that in order to move from the 'Via Negativa' to the 'Via Positiva' a, *kind of death* is always required. This of course could be read as a tautological statement of the apocalyptic, but in reality means the giving up of habitual and self-restricting belief systems, in order to embrace and live life, in my opinion, as it is meant to be lived. As Fox describes it, it is clear that the 'Via Negativa' needs to exist in order to encourage a shift into the 'Via Positiva'. The real problem is becoming stuck in the 'Via Negativa' stage with all its challenges and its attendant tendency to invite apocalyptic thinking almost as a life choice.

For Fox, the 'Via Negativa' is an absolutely necessary stage to bring human experience towards a sense of cosmic consciousness through descent into grief and suffering. Emergence into the space of the 'Via Positiva' can then set up an oscillation of lived experience through comparison of those two different states of existence, which merge over time into the 'Via Creativa' where possibilities exist to apply human creativity, but in the context of a required

157

internalised sense of personal responsibility. Fox's view is that the 'Via Creativa' is morally neutral and can be used for good or ill, but if used with human compassion can lead to a further stage he terms the 'Via Transformativa'. This represents for me, a deepened awareness and a possibility of revisiting the whole cycle as one's journey takes on even deeper levels of meaning and personal awareness. Indeed the 'journey' appears to be of a cyclical or spiral nature, it is not a simple linear model.

Depending on the level of fear we are used to living with in life, the moment before we act and move from the 'Via Negativa' into the realms of the 'Via Positiva', (or the days, weeks, months and sometimes even years leading up to some form of decisive action) can be deeply troubling. To experience thoughts of the anticipated action itself, the imagined impact of subsequent change, or the potential anticipated details of required change, can often feel deeply apocalyptic and terrifying. I have come to believe we are talking here about the matter of faith and the reality of faith (and therefore love) in action. As spiritual adolescents we look for virtual guarantees before we act, but in the world of adult spirituality there simply are no guarantees other than the active engagement in and lived experience of faith in action. I have come to realise that to love the Self and others requires us to act without any guarantees, in a lived expression of total faith in our own self-worth.

What I mean by this is that we choose to live out an active and affirmative response to the question, "Do you love yourself or another-others enough, to risk losing everything you have, in order to create positive change?" And to choose this in the belief that to do so will make possible what would otherwise have remained impossible, because you would not have loved and trusted as much as you could have done?

As David Whyte expresses it in his poem "The Truelove" (1996), this is ultimately the choice to stop 'drowning', and instead to embrace life. An act or series of acts, of faith seem to be the only way to achieve this transformation beyond the apocalyptic, and to escape a living death locked in to place in the psyche by the all too familiar toxic presence of fear.

For Whyte, for that matter also for me based on what I have felt and lived, there are times when all doubt about reaching out to a more powerful and loving future, vanishes and the choice to act is in reality the only path to take. Yet, metaphorically speaking, to 'step out of the boat' to walk on the water towards the person or place holding that energy, seems like a choice of certain death. It is a choice of death unless it is done with openness to faith as an active presence within oneself and surrounding oneself in the very act of stepping out of the boat. Half choices in the past would have led to a process of drowning in pain and indecision. But as Whyte says, a time will come when, "if you wanted to drown you could", but this time there is no desire left to drown in indecision and the power to act pulls you out onto the water, where you make the journey you always knew you would eventually make.

When I think about all this in relation to my work as a counsellor and psychotherapist, I would be the first to acknowledge the dangers of imposing one's own value system on others; but I don't believe a person-centred humanistic approach means to be so non directive that one does not show one's unique authentic Self in dialogical processes with clients. I have in fact come to the conclusion after many years of 1:1 work that the deepest growth and healing for clients is found in helping them recognise, express, love and through that, eventually bless their own unique and authentic Selves.

This is difficult to do, if we see ourselves through apocalyptic perspectives. Generally in our western post-industrial and post-Christian culture, that is what we are encouraged to do. Matthew Fox (2006), says it becomes very clear very quickly, in contemporary American society, that *"two Christianities exist"* (P19): one loyal to a Punitive Father God and one reflecting a loving compassionate God, and that the former not only dominates ecclesiastical discourse, but more generally pervades largely right wing fundamentalist and populist American culture.

To some extent one could also argue it is woven in to some interpretations of the American Psychiatric Association's Dialogical and Statistical Manual ("DSM") medical symptom categorisations of mental health issues and difficulties as identifiable illnesses. I think it could reasonably be argued that as we receive and adapt so many cultural references in this country from the United States, particularly in the field of psychiatry and mental health, that post-Christian or not, much of those cultural signifiers are likely to carry a similar apocalyptic and punitive God message in our own culture.

Fox describes the influence of the punitive God as creating a 'bad relationship' with itself, *"Those espousing the theology of the Punitive Father who seeks obedience at all costs, harbour a bad relationship with their own faith tradition. They know Original Sin but not Original Blessing"* (P17). The Punitive Father God, as the term implies, is patriarchal in nature, has close links to fascistic forms of control and, *"Demonises women, the earth, other species, science and gays and lesbians. It builds on fear and supports empire building"* (P19).

In contrast, the 'other Christianity' recognises that all derives from Original Blessing and takes as its starting point awe, rather than sin and guilt, *"As the starting point of true religion"* (P19). Its perspective is, as James Alison would describe, eschatological: gentle, developmental, inclusive, blessing, accepting and celebrating.

I would contend that whatever the client's cultural or religious background in our society, there is often an all pervading sense of the apocalyptic which seeps into relational discourse and dynamics as much in the therapy room as elsewhere. As much of it is internally embedded within the client, it does not even need to be reflected in the energetic and attitudinal presence of the therapist. It is already part of the internal narrative for many clients who are starting out on the therapeutic journey.

I know, for example, the pain and anguish of traumatised clients and how far removed they frequently are from an understanding of and conscious connection to the authentic Self – mostly I sense instead, the presence of the traumatised child within who was frozen many years ago, and in hopelessly emotionally ill-resourced ways, still attempts to act as an adult carer to the adult Self, and gets very frightened and overwhelmed, sometimes to the point of suicide, other extremely self-destructive acts, and/or abuse of others.

I feel that at the absolute core of much transformative psychotherapeutic work the client's path to healing is through eventually being prepared to trust: firstly to trust the adult Self in the therapist, then through the vehicle of partnership work between the therapist and the client's own adult aspect, to trust the adult Self in the client.

The final and transformative stages require the further extension of trust, from the client's child-self to an acceptance of the skill and good intentions of their own adult Self, and the adult Self's ability to independently look after the child aspect and release the child from years of inappropriate adult caring, by taking over responsibility for the emotional management of the client's life.

This effectively offers freedom to the child aspect, to enable that part of the unique Self to gently grow up in the way they always had a birth-right to expect, but unfortunately never experienced as a child. This may well require the adult Self being prepared to revisit and reintegrate as much as possible from original childhood states of grief, at least in terms of understanding what must be grieved and eventually let go of.

In the Hakomi approach, I recognise that whatever the child's missing experience was, will be both the root of their child-based trauma and development of what Hakomi refers to as 'character strategies', *(see Appendix One, p.357)* to shield themselves from immediate and overwhelming psychic pain, and also the potential therapeutic frame for healing, if offered mindfully by the therapist in the context of a therapeutic contract.

If this contract also includes a commitment from the therapist to nurture and honour the emergence of the authentic Self and also the emergence of self-love in the client, then healing and personal-spiritual growth can be deep, profound and often deeply transformative; through acceptance of what cannot be changed but must be grieved and through courage to change that which is in the power of the self-responsible adult to change.... And as the old prayer, attributed to St. Francis of Assisi, says, "The wisdom to know the difference" between the two! This can happen in powerful ways if the therapist is firstly able to bless themselves and through that process and internal shift, to consciously and genuinely bless the client.

As I have previously stated, I sense a distinct energetic shift when the client moves from an external ("please fix me or cure me") locus of control, to an internal one ("I believe I can access my own internalised resources to heal myself").

Otto Scharmer highlights the potentially transformative role the professional helper or therapist can play in this process, by consciously avoiding the imposition on the client of what he calls 'Attentional Violence' *(www.blog.ottoscharmer.com* August 24th, 2008).

One would be indulging in attentional violence if one held a vision of the client's ability to eventually realise their own potential through full expression of the authentic Self, as being less than the client is capable of developing. By holding a vision of the unfolding of the client's Self which is less than their full authentic Self is capable of manifesting, is in effect to impose a reductive act of pathologising the client.

So, to offer the opposite of this reductive impulse, by holding a powerfully complete vision of great potential within the client, is to encourage them over time to believe in and aspire towards, their own full expression of the authentic Self. This is so, even if in the immediate situation the client is unable to feel so positive about their self-potential. Over time the client is nevertheless, very likely to come to accept this therapeutically held vision of the potential unfolding Self, and move towards co-creation and the emergence and consolidation of that vision.

However, this cannot be achieved if the therapist is unable to offer the same depth of nourishment and attentionally non-violent caring, to the unfolding potential of their own authentic Self. So, to offer deep empathic respect and nourishing attentional non-violence to the client, whilst at the same time regarding the Self as in some way flawed, incomplete, lacking or inadequate, will simply result in the client receiving this therapist's self-belief as a reflection and mirror of their own unacceptability.

Consequently the client will remain wounded, traumatised and frozen. This highlights the vital importance of the therapist's need to do their own self-loving and self-healing before they can hope to really help clients, or for that matter, to attract the type of intimate intrapsychic and sometimes also interpersonal relationship that will help them bridge, heal and integrate the split Self within themselves.

I am frequently amazed and somewhat disturbed when I come across counselling or psychotherapy training courses that do not require their participants to undergo their own experience of structured counselling or psychotherapy as a client. I fail to see how anyone can really develop in the appropriate way for this level of work without opportunities to experience this deepening awareness of personal process and self-reflection. Such attitudes within the training world seem to reflect an over preoccupation with so called 'technique' at the expense of what I would advocate and describe as 'developing a craft'. I think there are three absolute essentials for both trainees and also qualified practitioners: time as a client whilst undergoing training; regular clinical supervision, and finally easy access to counselling or psychotherapy in order to process counter-transferential material that is a reflection of some unfinished business in their own process. Without the presence of those professional safeguards I wonder what kind of practitioners we are creating.

At times I reflect that to work consistently with responsible intent, at the level of relational depth, whether 1:1 as a therapist, or perhaps as a writer recalling their own journey through the dark night of the soul towards the new dawn of liberation and life without fear, requires something very much out of the ordinary.

It seems that sooner or later, one is often called on a journey to heal the split aspects of the authentic Self. I am reminded of Joseph Campbell's work in relation to the archetypal process he describes as the 'Hero's Journey' (1990

& Centennial Edition, 2003), where he asserts there is a long tradition of the individual and often isolated pilgrim going far beyond his or her community, in search of a 'diamond' to bring back to the community. It is in effect a deeply shamanic process, which at the level of the collective unconscious would be instantly understood across many cultures, because it is an archetypal journey.

'The Therapeutic Use of Self' as advocated by writers such as Val Wosket (1999), is what is encouraged here, but I am doing so, borrowing the language of Joseph Campbell, in the context of a chosen 'shamanic journey'. To work intentionally, using aspects of the therapeutic Self, at the profound level of relational depth will require that kind of challenging 'Hero's Journey' if one's aim is to provide and eventually co-create transformational therapeutic environments for clients.

Ultimately, we have to come to believe and accept in relation to our own selves and what we bring back to the therapeutic community from our soul or shamanic journeys, that in Julian of Norwich's words "All shall be well and all manner of things shall be well" (1978), because in the context of the permanently present accessibility of grace, it always has been well and always will be, simply because we are and always have been blessed. But in my case, because of my early life experiences, acquired internal narratives and the challenge of dealing with the impact of a potentially terminal diagnosis, I feel that I had to go on a very long and arduous journey to realise it.

In reality, as I have come to know, there is no separation between ourselves and God, it just takes the majority of us an awful long time to understand this, and for most of that time it seems we, and many of our clients, choose to live within the toxic confines of what Alison terms the apocalyptic imagination, simultaneously deeply hurting and damaging ourselves and others – it is the polar opposite of "the eschatological imagination" (1998; P212).

In my own experience, a shamanic journey can give us a greater range of internal awareness and vision – we see ourselves in deeper ways than ever before. By way of example, I will reflect for a moment on my process of writing this book.

As I completed the first phase of writing the book, I was reminded by my own process of internal reflection that the bulk of it had been written from a very spontaneous place. That was the right thing to do in my mind – it was central to my process and this chosen act of creation.

Around a year later, I then began a second phase of drafting the book and quickly came to recognise that this next stage was asking me to expand and further develop certain sections – in order to create what I felt I was being asked to do (by my authentic Self, or God, I'm not sure there is a difference), in order to be of service to the wider human community.

The first phase was necessarily spontaneous, I am absolutely sure about that; I was very aware that it demanded to be written that way. I recognise that this second phase is in a way, accessing and mining the gold seam of what I was preparing for all along – to hopefully bring out the best of who I am and how I can express myself, in order to offer something that I hope will be of real value to people. I hope this turns out to be my way of 'bringing back the diamond' as Campbell describes it (1990), to my own human community.

It is, from this place of expanded vision, a very deliberate weaving together of autobiographical narrative; description of a journey through ill health and near death to an extension and fuller expression of life; and a cumulative reflection and illustration of how my craft skills have developed over a lifetime of work.

By way of illustrating why I think I am hitting this gold seam now, I would make reference to an approach which has proved very useful for me and also I think, for many people with whom I have worked over the years, especially as a coach or external supervisor.

I have been strongly influenced in my professional work by the 'Strengths Approach' advocated by Marcus Buckingham and Donald Clifton (2001). The book offers an opportunity firstly to undertake an on line psychometric test, to identify what Buckingham and Clifton regard as one's 'talent profile'. This is drawn from 34 possible 'ways of being' *("The thirty four themes of strengths-finder in the world")* (P73). The psychometric test results prioritise five 'themes' or ways of being.

With an increased awareness of these potential strengths, it is possible in a much more mindful way, both through retrospective review and also in the here and now, to apply reflection and action in order to embed one's 'talent profile' in everyday action, and thus eventually turn the potentiality of a talent profile into a range of consciously consolidated 'strengths'.

I found through doing the on-line psychometric test that the five 'themes' constituting my own *'talent profile'* were, in order of priority, as follows:

- **"Connectedness":** Amongst other things, this position sees connection between all things and that things happen for a reason. The authors suggest this perspective holds that, "Certain of the unity of humankind, you are a bridge builder for people of different cultures (P87)."

- **"Strategic":** Seeing a way through where other people are likely to see confusion and chaos.

- **"Learner":** Loving to learn and always drawn to the process of learning.

- **"Individualisation":** Being intrigued by the qualities of each person and focusing on the differences between individuals.

- **"Achiever":** A constant need for achievement – possessing an internal fire which pushes you to achieve more.

When I first completed this exercise, I had a powerful reaction and realisation. I was very strongly reminded that what Buckingham and Clifton are identifying here as a 'strength', I used to unhelpfully regard very much, would you believe, as my 'cowardice', and if I am honest, I know at the time that I felt some sense of shame around this.

I had been aware for a long time, in the spirit of learning to witness my own process, that prior to starting to deliver or facilitate any training event, particularly with strangers, I would almost habitually engage as many people as possible in dialogue, one to one, before the start of the event, where I would carefully listen to what they said in order to identify a possible common area of interest. I always thought I was doing this to get them on my side, (a kind of tactic similar to *heading them off at the pass'* talked of as a psychological 'game' by Alfred Kadushin in the field of Transactional Analysis) so hopefully, they wouldn't give me a hard time as a facilitator when proceedings commenced!

After I completed the 'strengths profile', I recognised that, far from being a coward in my actions, I was instead being very much true to my authentic Self in my actions by, in particular, linking together *"Connectedness"* with *"Individualisation"*. The strategy was always very powerful when I did find a personal connection – and I often did. I remember my biggest challenge, in terms of individualisation, was talking to a group participant who turned out to be from Belgium. The only thing I could remember about Belgium (apart from great beer), was the Belgian road racing cyclist Eddie Merckx. As soon as I mentioned Eddie's name the participant Yves' eyes lit up and he remained very attentive throughout the whole day!

So, in writing the book, I feel I am in particular drawing upon my 'strength' of being a "Bridge builder for people of different cultures". I recognise I have always done this in my work, alongside strong elements of holding an "individualisation" perspective in relation to the needs of each person I work with. A fairly constant maxim in my work, whether in the role of therapist, clinical supervisor, coach, coach supervisor or facilitator is to ask myself at frequent junctures, ***"What is needed here right now"***, (at this time, at this point in the relational process, with this person or groups of people?)

I think my particular strength, especially as a trainer, facilitator, coach and clinical supervisor, and perhaps also as a writer, is to juxtapose different elements and often already existing theories of human experience and re-order them in such a way that they potentially offer a new way of seeing to people. I think the Power-With Approach and Model referred to in a previous chapter, is a good example of this. Hopefully, this approach also has the potential for offering (in strategic terms) a way through, and away from previous chaos or at the least, a possibly previous lack of clarity.

Certainly, the 'Strengths-Finder' approach at least helped me to bless myself where previously I had harshly judged myself. It also helps me now, when I consider judgment from others, of what I am doing and writing about.

If I have had any particularly challenging criticism to date in writing this book, it has been from people who tell me which audience I should be writing for. Sometimes this has also extended into including vociferous comments on the sort of language I should leave out. Some have suggested I should most certainly leave out references to "God" or to "grace" or to "faith" because it will, "really put people off". Well, that may be so but I have to consider other aspects of my experience, if I am going to honour a 'both-and approach' rather than stick rigidly to a more apocalyptically flavoured 'either-or approach'.

My response now would be to say, I have been profoundly changed in writing the book and I think the potential audience has changed with me. At some level I felt from the start that I was potentially addressing a wider readership than fellow professionals. I am now sure that is the case – I think there is a lot here that could also be of relevance to many other people: not least those 'riding the rapids' as Hakomi describes it; or going through some kind of 'dark night of the soul' as described by Thomas Moore (2004), in relation to their own illness, the illness of a relative and loved one; or those simply dealing with the formidable trials and tribulations of everyday life. In such places, even if one does not have a religious or spiritual frame of reference, I think it highly likely at the very least that major existential questions will arise for those facing such uncertain futures.

As for my language, I am quite clear that it is entirely authentic to my own experience – it may be challenging to some, or off putting to others, but I am being faithful to the soul or shamanic journey and bringing back what I can to the human community in a voice that is as close to my authentic Self-expression as it can be. People will make of this what they will – I do hope it is helpful, whatever people's response to the language, because whatever my language contains, I am speaking very much from the heart. After all I have been through, there seems to me to be no point in doing anything else.

Further reflection has also moved me to revise the depth of detail I have included here, especially in relation to my journey through illness. I had recently been reading Philip Gould's very harrowing autobiography, (2012). Gould's book, finally completed by his wife after his death, is powerfully written and is not at all sparing about the ordeals he went through. I sensed his frame of reference was largely personal and political, and there was not a good ending. He wrote with considerable courage, right up until the end of his life. Philip Gould died in 2011 at the age of sixty one, the age I am now.

Reading Philip's book motivated me to think again about what I was doing in writing this, and why. I am changed and my reasons have changed. When I started I was writing with some sense of urgency hoping I could share something of what I had learnt about myself and about living life without fear, before death overtook me.

Yet I am still here and furthermore, I am now motivated to say, it IS possible to live again, if you are very fortunate and if grace smiles on you, and if you actively choose to do your best to be without fear. You may just do something, with the help of known and unknown sources, to change what appears to be an inevitable end.

But even if changing the end is not possible, you can still walk the path with some semblance of equanimity, with trust in the natural unfolding of things and remain open to faith in the ultimate meaning of life, and death. For me that means that what I describe as the "split Self" within me, has been healed, whatever the final outcome of my journey through cancer and heart failure. Much as I do not want my life to end now, or leave loved ones behind me, if I had to die tomorrow I would be doing so in the full knowledge that something fundamental in me at a soul level, has been absolutely healed.

I think my 'soul journey' or 'shamanic journey' has been to visit places of deep darkness and despair and return to life - to both convey what that journey has demanded and to also show it is indeed possible to return to life, from places of complete bleakness and despair where no hope appeared to remain.

As a consequence of reappraising what I had produced so far, and reflecting on Philip Gould's work, I decided to include in particular, much more of the painful details of what happened to me around various medical procedures and my emotional and psychological responses to them.

So what is here now is different to how it originally was. I am a changed person and I hope what I can bring back from this soul or shamanic journey will help those in despair and those with fading hopes – whether on a journey themselves, or witnessing friends and family going through such ordeals.

Healing the split Self is a *'diamond'* beyond value for anyone – however long or short their life turns out to be. It is a diamond that can and should be shared with our fellow human beings, to bring as much meaning to the human experience as possible. I understand from Viktor Frankl, concentration camp survivor, psychiatrist and author, that the key to enduring and then transforming circumstance and life opportunities is through a process of 'metanoia' in the midst of suffering, in order to create the ability to derive *meaning* from the experience.

I believe that and I also believe in myself and what I have attempted to do in writing this book.

***

If we don't believe in ourselves, who will? And can we do it from a place of peace and relaxation? That might just be our biggest challenge: to live and be from such a perspective, exercising healthy power in the world and holding an open heart towards ourselves & others.

However, our culture seems to be frequently locked into fearful ways of being – where self-belief is rarely a relaxed matter. We may over emphasise our so called 'self-belief' to mask inner insecurities, or to guard against anticipated attack, and thus come across in the eyes of others as brittle, patronising, ruthless or arrogant – or we may hide ourselves away, fearful of the responsibilities of exercising adult choice and a commitment to living in an adult way in the world.

We will go against that 'flow' if we choose to live without fear, and it will often threaten and disturb others. Some may try to invalidate us through use of dismissive or apocalyptic language; they may do all they can to keep us from growing and changing.

Our over concern with other people's opinions or threats will not take us from the 'Via Negativa' to the 'Via Positiva'. We may need to accept that the part of us that "rescues" or appeases, has to die if we are to be open to life as it should be lived. This emotional and attitudinal shift cannot be supported by guarantees – no outcome may yet be clear, yet the only thing certain is that if we do not accept that call, we will drown. One way or another we WILL drown.

Do we believe in ourselves enough to 'Step out of the boat and walk'? Courage is a reality when we

173

act without guarantees but with love for ourselves, and thus ultimately love for others. We may need to protect our own younger frightened 'inner self' in order to make such moves, but the reality is that any act of 'trust' is always accompanied by potential betrayal, whether we are aware of it or not. If we 'let ourselves down' in some way, we will be challenged to forgive ourselves and to "try again". I would encourage that.

We may need to journey a long way before we can find the authentic Self and trust its wisdom will heal us and guide us back to the human community. Whatever 'treasure' we discover along the way, is likely to show us we are truly blessed in some way – for example, we may come to realise how loved we are after all. That was certainly the case for me when my terminal diagnosis opened me up to realising how much I was and am loved by others. I can tell you that the power of such love and 'prayers' is tangible and awe inspiring – it changes things and it certainly changed me. I hope, and believe that it changed me for the better.

To realise just how much I was and am loved by my family and friends has healed the 'split Self' within me. I know that things are possible now that were not possible before. I see the beauty and love in my friends on a regular basis - mixed in from time to time with all the usual irritating stuff that can occasionally come up with people you know well - but absolutely irrelevant in the overwhelming healing presence and power of human love.

We are all powerful beyond measure when we love and allow ourselves to be loved – all we have to do is believe that, and it is there. Believe me, it is there!!

***

CHAPTER 9:

Healing spirals - risk taking, competency and confidence

Like begets like. This is an evident truth to anyone who takes time to observe the way of things. If we feel negative about ourselves or others we frequently create and often co-create further negativity in the world. Alternatively, if we feel positive we create and often co-create further positivity in the world. In my view, we are very powerful creators and co-creators of our own individual and collective experience.

What we believe we see and what we see we live and experience; what we live and experience is also what we tend to believe to be 'the truth'. That is fine if we choose to see and experience what, National Geographic Magazine photographer, Dewitt Jones refers to as, *"What is right with the world"*, (2010) but it is deeply problematic if we predominantly choose to see *and* experience "what is wrong with the world". We are talking here of the spiral nature of things: we can either spiral upwards or downwards, it is our choice and whatever we choose, one thing will tend to lead to another. Hence like begets like and hence the nature and reality of spirals in our experiences of the world's we create and co-create.

This is not a complacent plea for feeling comfortable with a status quo of naiveté about the world, nor a demand to be in denial of the pain and conscious or unconscious acts of human evil which are daily perpetrated in the world. It is a deliberate call to be both fully conscious of such realities *and* at the same time, to also choose as a conscious act of love, to see, experience and to live out, "what is right with the world". This is not an act of abdicracy; it is an act of power.

I think I began to experience the reality of this during the 1980's, as I was making a gradual but inexorable transition from the purely political towards the personal, relational, emotionally present, spiritual **and** political in my work.

My M.A. in Criminology was taught from a Marxist perspective in terms of a structural and ideological analysis of social and political systems and populist discourse in the media. I am very clear, even twenty nine or so years later, that it was a highly valid, intellectually coherent and accurate view of the way power structures operate in our society.

In particular it opened my eyes to the ever present influence of the ideology of the ruling "hegemony" as Gramsci (1971) described it, in any society. Opinion makers and influencers have a profound effect on what the man and woman in the street regard or are encouraged to regard as a so called 'common sense' perspective, which is often nothing of the sort.

Such perspectives are in reality, often deliberate ideological constructs, persuading us that opinions and perspectives which offer alternative interpretations to the authoritarian populist view, should be regarded as "mad", 'bad' 'dangerous' or combinations of such descriptors. This was clearly the case in terms of predominant media analyses of the Miner's Strike in 1984, or the authoritarian impulse behind the populist concept 'law and order' media interpretations of how to develop aspects of social policy in relation to so called 'troublesome youth'.

A broader view of such distorted ideological positions is much more possible over twenty five years later, and is visible now in the context of cumulative revelations of the corrupt influence of such ideologies on the conduct of the South Yorkshire Police in relation to both the Hillsborough Disaster and the policing of the Miner's Strike, including the

"Battle of Orgreave" and also contemporary media interpretations of such conduct.

Much as this approach helped me to see a broader picture in relation to politics, social policy, and influence of the media, it did not however, particularly provide me with an understanding of the personal, the emotional nor the intimate world of relationships, where it might be possible to move beyond the more adversarial paradigms into a more inclusive world of emotional and spiritual co-creation.

Through a growing interest in Taoism, I became familiar with the paradigm of 'both/and' that can exist as an alternative to an 'either/or' view of the world. It is a paradigm which not only tolerates but at its best, actively welcomes apparent contradictions and holds them in dynamic tension alongside each other until a deeper truth which is capable of embracing both perspectives, begins to emerge.

This is the realm of potential inclusivity and partnership, where common ground can be identified and built upon in service of a positive and mutually rewarding shared vision of the present and future. An alignment of shared values and shared goals releases "generative energy" according to Peter Senge (1990), which can greatly boost the potential success of any co-creative project.

The 'both/and' perspective also underpins my own "Power-With" approach, which can work as effectively with individuals as it can with groups, teams and organisations. It is a model which seeks to create the foundations for transparent and inclusive partnership work, far beyond the toxicity of the rather more apocalyptic territory of the "Drama Triangle" (as stated previously, revolving around the interplay, and often rapid switching, from "Victim" to "Rescuer" to "Persecutor" and back again), as first described and mapped out by Stephen Karpman [1968]. The different combinations of the Drama Triangle are all variations on the often hidden and manipulative 'parent – child' relational dynamic. Whereas, *"Power-With"* is at root, transparent, dialogical and also 'adult to adult' in its relational context.

Taking the, "What is right with the world" perspective, I began to move as far as I could into more dialogical and partnership methods of working with individuals and groups.

The first book I published, via the Association for Juvenile Justice, (1985) was largely a political analysis of the law and order debate as applied to the UK Juvenile Justice System in the early to mid-1980s. The book, "Worth the Risk: Creative group-work with Young Offenders" (1987) which I co-wrote with Mandy Davill and Steve Eastwood, was much more focused on the personal and potentially transformational, through use of dialogical forms of intervention and co-creation with young people, which encouraged them to recognise and nurture their own considerable potential for positive change in their lives.

I was interested in the very natural way that Mandy and Steve interacted with Young Offenders, to considerable success, and reflecting now on their approach I can see it was much closer to the 'eschatological' (developmental and potentially transformative), than it was to the 'apocalyptic'.

It is also fair to say that my initial counselling work in the mid to late 1980s (as a volunteer at a Leeds MIND self-help project) was strongly influenced by the more eschatologically minded self-help and co-counselling models. In effect these models encouraged gradual Self and mutual transformation through self-education, and a cumulative acceptance of the need (and possibility) to move more centrally into exercising one's own personal power in the world. Co-counselling itself (both in its American form as developed by Harvey Jackins, and in its UK form as further developed by John Heron) was a humanistic approach very mindful of power issues and seeking to create a more accessible and egalitarian form of therapy. The self-help movement within mental health mirrored this.

By the time I began my psychotherapy career, following on from completion of my Diploma in Humanistic Psychology, in the early 1990s, I was deeply influenced by democratic and dialogical models which sought to uphold principles of transparency and partnership working wherever possible.

My Hakomi training in the early to mid - 1990's further deepened my interest in natural and co-creative forms of relational work, strongly influenced as Hakomi was by both Taoism and Buddhism. Hakomi also acknowledges the need for a systemic understanding of social and relational discourse, and the systems approach is both compatible with a more political and ideological structural analysis and also with an understanding of relational and unconscious psychological processes between clients and therapists.

It is interesting to see that the way I chose to move forwards from a career dilemma point in my life (whether to be an 'organisational consultant' or a 'psychotherapist'), was resolved by holding both potential paths in dynamic tension alongside each other, and living with the discomfort of not knowing, long enough until it became possible for me to realise that at root I was in fact a humanistic psychologist, whatever role I was undertaking.

This realisation helped me to see that I could therefore apply humanistic values to a range of roles: group facilitator, organisational consultant, management consultant, lecturer, counsellor, psychotherapist, clinical supervisor, and in later years, as a coach and coach supervisor. The catalyst for this was being invited to run a modular undergraduate course at the University of Bradford Centre for Continuing and Adult

Education, on the topic of, "The Psychology of Everyday Life", which was in fact a study and application of the principles of Humanistic Psychology.

I also managed to persuade the University authorities to conduct the examination part of the module using the approach and principles of 'Self, Peer and Tutor Assessment' (SPTA) as promoted by John Heron and others in the UK, rather than some external form of examination.

A form of SPTA was I believe originally developed by John Heron at the University of Surrey, and also reflected the aspirations, values and practice of the IDHP ("Institute for the Development of Human Potential") which sponsored my own Leeds based Diploma in Humanistic Psychology in the early 1990s.

SPTA places great emphasis on encouraging the student to take a high degree of personal and collective responsibility for deciding whether each student should pass a module.

The student selects a minimum of three self-chosen criteria on which to be assessed, then writes a personal statement which maps out how they feel they have met the chosen criteria. This is done in front of their peers and the tutor.

On the basis of relational awareness and knowledge of the student throughout the module, these joint assessors give feedback on the following:

- Whether the three criteria are appropriate to constitute a sound basis for assessment of potential success in the module;

- Whether the personal statement is a sufficiently accurate and authentic analysis of progress based on the chosen criteria;

- Whether both the criteria and the statement reflect an accurate picture of the student in the eyes of their peers and the tutor.

If all elements are met, then the student is able to award themselves the qualification contained in the successful completion of the module.

However, if the joint assessors are not satisfied with any aspect of the student's chosen approach, they can request a partial or full re-write and run the process again until the student reaches a satisfactory standard to self and peer award the qualification.

I found that in the case of my work with Young Offenders using the "Power-With" approach, and also in the use of 'Self, Peer and Tutor Assessment' processes with return to learning University Students attending adult and continuing education courses, that certain themes were consistently present:

- the majority of these participants came from economically, socially and culturally marginalised groups;

- the majority struggled with issues of low self-esteem (for Young Offenders their experience was often one of being disaffected at school and consistently under achieving academically, often being told - or telling themselves - they were "stupid" - I know that scenario!!; for University Students their experience was typically a return to learning after many years away from education, with low self-confidence and low expectations of success);

- the majority expected to be criticised, shown up, put down or punished by us as authority figures;

- the majority were initially wary, untrusting, suspicious, rebellious or subservient in attitude and responses.

The approach I and (where I worked with colleagues) we took, was to:

1. Consistently focus on evident or emerging strengths of our participants;

2. Encourage genuine dialogue, which by its very nature has unknown outcomes and is therefore sympathetic with *"Power-With"* rather than "power-over" dynamics around control ;

3. Encourage partnership and co-creative forms of interaction wherever possible;

4. Praise and support rather than judge or criticise, celebrating the unique aspects of each individual's emerging authentic Self;

5. Model 'both/and' rather than 'either/or' paradigms in our explanations, experiential exercises and analysis;

6. Reward engagement and enthusiasm through praise and attention and discourage disruption by offering very little attention or response other than re-clarification of what is or is not negotiable, especially where that disruption mirrors relational aspects of the "Drama Triangle";

7. Be as transparent and straightforward as possible in our interactions;

8. Emphasise a positive reframing of initially depressive or negative ways of seeing the world (in effect encouraging a shift from paranoia to metanoia);

9. Facilitate appropriate risk taking and feedback what we are noticing about emerging competencies to encourage increase in self-confidence, whilst blessing rather than judging or criticising participants.

In relation to that approach, and in relation to the existence of 'spirals' in our known world, this is what I have discovered:

If we recognise and encourage emerging strengths, praise others and ourselves, develop relational dynamics based on *"Power-With"* approaches: we go a long way towards creating and co-creating the optimum environment for relational safety and positive development and emergence of the authentic Self both in others and also in ourselves.

This facilitates a relational, self-perceptive and behavioural pattern which:

- starts with an increase in appropriate level risk taking (beyond initial fear responses);

- leads inevitably to an increase in levels of competence over time (if the student persists with appropriate risk taking until they begin to experience some level of success in areas where they had not previously known such experiences);

- which in turn leads to an increase in self-confidence which can form the basis for choosing to extend appropriate risk taking into new territories, further increasing the possibility of developing even greater competencies in areas previously unknown to the student.

One way or another, I felt this was what I (and others) sought to contribute towards individual and collective learning in the various settings of the University of Everyday Life!

***

What are we risking really, when we decide to truly live as life beckons us to do?

We risk being bigger in the world than we might otherwise have been: as we begin to open up to the potential within our authentic Selves to grow in confidence and competence as fully functioning responsible adults; as we recognize our indissoluble connection to others and the possibility of co-creating a better future for all through the way we think, perceive and choose to be in relation to ourselves and to others; as we move from fear and restriction to a sense of safety in the world by trusting that the natural rhythms and processes which exist at our core, are enough to provide sufficient support and nourishment for living enjoyably and creatively in life, no matter how uncertain the future appears to be.

Choice is a powerful thing – in emotional and perceptual terms it can take us on an upward or downward trajectory. It can also influence others to mirror our own perceptions and choices.

We can choose to see others as rivals and a threat, or as potential partners; we can choose to live within apocalyptic or developmental and potentially transformational paradigms; we can choose to insist on certainties and pre-determined roles, responsibilities and mental models, or we can choose to find a sense of Self within a lived experience of not knowing what is happening or what the future might hold.

If we trust our inherent wisdom, we can live with uncertainty long enough to wait until a deeper truth emerges about us, about others and about the possibilities before us. This is also a place of hope and trust: hope of transformation and trust in a better future – sometimes in this place things begin to manifest that we could not have previously imagined. They manifest precisely because we have chosen to risk cutting through the impossible and because we have chosen not to give up on ourselves or others.

Sometimes this change and decision to act with openness to risk and uncertainty comes to us gradually after periods of reflection and mindful witnessing of our own internal narratives, in the form of deeper insights about the way we choose to be in the world. Sometimes this change comes suddenly in the form of personal metanoia and self-realisation, when we are offered places of safety from which to begin to view the world anew, as our insight barriers spontaneously dissolve because we don't need such psychological defences anymore.

If we are criticized and judged, we come to harshly judge both ourselves and others and we also lose that sense of connection to our Self and to others.

However, if we are praised, supported, encouraged and blessed by others, we will find our confidence and through that find our authentic voice in the world. From this development, we can in turn learn how to bless and encourage others. As "like begets like", this makes it possible to create and co-create a better future, because through these processes we can become a source of self-belief for ourselves and others in the world.

***

CHAPTER 10:

"Following your bliss", or not

THE PAST

Summer 2002, a sunny afternoon, sitting in a quiet wood panelled bar in Tobermory, Isle of Mull, sipping malt whisky, overlooking the harbour. I was talking in depth with Rod for the first time on our motor biking trip to Mull, sharing thoughts and feelings about my health. I just had not wanted to say anything before now about what was going on for me – partly, I did not want to face it, partly I just wanted to enjoy life as long as I could before I turned to look at what I felt was likely to be a very bleak future.

Four weeks previously I had been told by a Hospital Consultant that he was, "99% sure" I had lymphoma, evidenced by a number of lesions in the liver. This had been preceded by months of unexplained discomforts including a sense of being very unwell with a deep internal chill and a subsequent series of medical tests at the local Airedale Hospital. I had spent days sitting in front of the full-on gas fire in our living room at home, wearing a thick duvet coat and shivering uncontrollably. Whatever I did, I just could not get warm. I had contacted Dr Mainey who advised me to get a blood test for the liver as soon as possible, which I did. The test revealed unclear abnormalities in the liver. Subsequently my own GP referred me to a Hospital Consultant who conducted further tests and then eventually pronounced his, for me, unexpected and dramatic diagnosis.

I remember sitting in the waiting area at the hospital after receiving this news, somewhat in a state of shock. I was waiting to give a final blood test. After I left the hospital, I was in a kind of trance – but in those moments I was also basically observing some part of myself which was determined to choose life. I watched as it took over and drove me to Keighley town centre, where I found myself buying a leather jacket and booking a ticket to the Isle of Man TT Races. Two things I had thought about doing a number of times before that day. Then I went home and told Lis, my wife, of the shock news of my diagnosis and we tried to figure out what we were going to do. I think the leather jacket and the TT ticket was a kind of striving for life in the midst of experiencing the roaring noise of confusion in my head.

It was during an interim period when I was awaiting a final liver biopsy that, with Lis' blessing, I planned and then undertook a motorcycle journey with Rod, from Yorkshire, up the west of Scotland to Oban and then by ferry to the Isle of Mull.

This was for me, a taste of freedom whilst it was still possible. It had been a good trip so far and I had chosen to put thoughts of illness out of my mind until now. Instead I had focused on the companionship and shared joys of a long motorcycle trip. Rod was riding his sparkling new Harley, which he was proud to notice, got lots of admiring glances. I was riding my Triumph Trophy 1200, which (being built like a bus and rather dour looking) didn't.

I shared my doubts and confusion about the future, I really didn't know what I was going to do to deal with this and I felt ill prepared to do so. If I was honest, I would have to admit that my future looked bleakly empty and possibly short. I thought it best for now to enjoy the sunshine and feel comfort from Rod's willingness to listen and really be there

190

when I needed to talk. Rod was a big guy in many senses of the word and I felt, for now at least, safe and witnessed in his company. The whisky helped too.

The sunshine didn't last of course. As they say in Scotland, if you want a change in the weather just wait an hour or two. Unfortunately it soon changed for the worse. We explored the west coast of Mull in driving rain and stopped to take a photograph of ourselves on a time delayed camera, in some apparently God forsaken spot. I showed the photo to a friend, John, a week after our return and asked him to guess where we were, "the west coast of Mull" he immediately said. This didn't surprise me, as John knew the weather on the west coast of Scotland only too well. I think John and I have quite an intuitive link anyway. Years earlier, we had shared a car trip to the Isle of Skye. He was driving and at the same time eating from a bag of pink and white marshmallows, he took one out and manipulated it with his fingers to reveal a thin and closed undulating mouth. "Who's that" he said, I replied immediately, "Harry Carpenter". (The famous BBC Boxing Commentator was amongst other things, renowned for appearing to speak without ever opening his mouth). John laughed so much at the accuracy of my reply he almost choked on the marshmallow he was eating and narrowly avoided crashing the car.

So, as I once heard someone say on the radio during a sports broadcast, "And now over to Harry Commentator in the Carpentry Box"....

Rod and I left Mull the next day and headed back down south towards Inverary. The rain was still with us and getting heavier. We rode on towards Dunoon: good steady speeds, little traffic, flowing along straights and round long sweeping bends, through woodland areas and past lochs. The roads were awash with rain, we seemed to be riding through rivers. We rode in good formation, swopping leads from time to time. It was an exhilarating experience of high average speed across country, teamwork, balance and being at one with each other, the road, the bikes and the rain.

When I remember this journey, I instantly understand what Mihaly Czikszentmihalyi meant when he talked of "finding flow" in his book (1990), a lived experience of balance between high challenge and high skill. This was really living, and living at the edge. The last few miles and on the road into Dunoon, the rain was horizontal, driving hard into our faces. We found a hotel near the sea front and booked in, flooding the entrance hall with pools of water. We were met with hospitality, help and kindness – able to store our wet clothes and motorcycle gear in the drying room, and then we headed for our rooms for a well-earned rest.

Later that evening we moved into the bar, sharing the space with a delightful bus load of older ladies on a weekend boat trip from Glasgow, and a sprightly older guy in his mid-seventies who knew about bikes and had ridden at the Isle of Man TT in his youth. Naturally, for those who knew Rod it would not surprise you to hear that he spent a happy half hour (or more!) talking to our new friend about motorcycle part numbers, and every now and again I got a question in about his experience of the TT. A pub quiz was duly announced by the barman and we were invited to choose names and take part. Rod chose the name "The Undampened Spirits" for our team of two – we played with vigour and came last. The women were much too good for us. But we were still smiling. It was a 'magic' evening as they say in that part of the world.

Three weeks later I had the liver biopsy. I remember coming to on the hospital trolley after the procedure and listening on the hospital sound system to David Beckham taking a penalty against Argentina in the World Cup. He scored; we won the game but as usual didn't go on to win the

World Cup. However, the results of the biopsy were much more to my liking. They subsequently appeared to show that I did not have lymphoma; instead the lesions in the liver were diagnosed as "non-alcoholic liver fat deposits". The relief was very tangible, yet I felt I had to change my sedentary lifestyle somewhat in the face of this news. I started to pay more attention to exercise eventually deciding to attend a gym on a regular basis to improve my general fitness. Strangely, because in the end this turned out to be a disastrously wrong diagnosis, the periods of severe chill and shivering ceased.

A year later, Rod and I rode from West Yorkshire to Barcelona, with a group of Rod's Harley Davidson owning friends, to attend the Harley Davidson Festival. I went on my new Triumph Sprint ST to fly the flag for Britain. It was a good trip – Keighley, Halifax, Hull, Zebrugge, through France to the border near Carcassonne, then over the border through the Pyrenees to Gerona and Barcelona. On the Peage approaching Carcassonne, realising there were no gendarmes in sight and that I was on a foreign motorway, I opened up the bike "to see how fast it would go". I was fully laden but the bike cruised smoothly up to 143 mph, with Rod not far behind me. A naughty but very nice example of what Rod referred to as, "Nietzsche's first order experience": it's just you and the bike and the road in close proximity, not the "so much more TV" experience of driving a car and looking through the windscreen, as described by Robert Pirsig in *"Zen and the Art of Motorcycle Maintenance"* (1974 & 1999). But things went very bad soon after my return from Barcelona, with the sudden beginning of an unexpected parting of the ways between Lis and I, and the subsequent end of our marriage.

Rod, a photographer Andy and I went on a bike trip a couple of years later to the Dordogne area of France. By this time Rod was editor of *"Classic Motorcycle Mechanics"*, having moved from Hebden Bridge to Tetford in Lincolnshire with his wife Angie. He was on an assignment to write about an English guy who was starting up a Classic Motorcycle Touring business in the area. I tagged along for the ride as a helper (not as hairy an experience I have to say, as Rod "blagging" me in, as he put it, to the Hell's Angels run "Bulldog Bash" for free, as a fellow journalist a year previously, where I spent an anxious weekend hoping I wasn't going to be rumbled).

On the French trip, Rod sensed and I began to feel that he was becoming unwell, with the first gastro-intestinal signs of what eventually turned out to be pancreatic cancer. We had planned to make a bike trip the following year to the iconic Millau Bridge Viaduct in France, but in the end were unable to make it due to Rod's work commitments.

By late summer 2008 Rod's health had run into major complications. I went to see him at the Queen's Medical Centre in Nottingham, where he had just emerged from the Intensive Care Unit after a complicated operation to remove a massive blood clot from the entrance to his lung; apparently the biggest blood clot anyone in the Intensive Care Unit had ever seen. I tried to be optimistic, but it didn't look at all good for Rod. He had lost a great deal of weight, and (rather than "but") still seemed in good spirits. At this stage he had not received any clear diagnosis. He later returned home.

On the 29th May 2009, Rod sent me a text after another phase of deterioration, by which time he had been diagnosed with pancreatic cancer. I was shocked and very upset to read what I saw on the mobile phone screen in front of me; "Cancer advancing. Now lost all mobility and they move me around on wheels. Morphine good though, Rod".

I visited Rod and Angie in Tetford in June, when I saw him for the very last time. He was much, much thinner and clearly close to death. He reclined in bed facing the TV and his beloved Hi-Fi equipment. We chatted from time to time until Rod drifted off to sleep and then chatted again a while later, once he had regained consciousness. In this fashion, he moved in and out of consciousness a number of times that afternoon.

The last memory I have is of Rod, Angie and I sat in the front room eating ice lollies (one of the few things Rod could eat by this stage). I left soon after. Rod seemed surprised and disappointed I had to go, but despite the poignancy of the situation and my desire to stay, I knew it was time for Rod and Angie to be together alone. They needed in these last few days, to share the deep love and affection they clearly still had for each other without me being around.

As I rode the bike back through the beautiful Lincolnshire Wolds towards Yorkshire, my memory flickered to and fro through all my memories of biking with Rod. I thought of all the adventures Rod and I had shared, and knew it was the end of these particular roads for Rod and I – we would not be riding here or anywhere else together again.

Rod died a few days later aged 54. I attended his Memorial Service and Celebration of a Life in July 2009. These are the words I wrote for Rod which, thankfully as I could not have done it myself, were read out at the gathering by the very supportive and understanding female vicar:

WORDS FOR ROD, FROM JOHN

"I have known Rod mostly as a friend and for a while as a work colleague. Rod was around in the early days of The Phoenix Partnership and typically gave a great deal of

enthusiasm and encouragement to what we were hoping to create in our organisation.

He's gone far too soon for me, but Rod will live on in my memory, in all that he contributed and also all the fun we had, especially on our great and mad biking expeditions, which included journeys to Wales, the West Coast of Scotland, the South of France and to Barcelona.

We made a trip to the west coast of the Isle of Mull after I had, wrongly, as it later turned out, been diagnosed myself with lymphoma. Rod was a great support to me on that trip. On the way back, we had the wettest, and most exhilarating, ride ever from Inverary to Dunoon, fast and focused, horizontal rain most of the way, roads like rivers. We booked in to a hotel where the only other guests were O.A.P's. on a Boat Cruise trip from Glasgow. We entered a pub quiz with them that night, Rod insisted we should go under the team name of "The Undampened Spirits", which was just as well as apart from being soaking wet when we arrived, we also came last every time.

On the day that eventually became known as 9/11, during a biking trip around North Wales, we even broke into Portmeirion Village together (the Italianate Village designed by Welsh Architect Clough-Ellis, where "The Prisoner" cult TV Series was filmed) by climbing over the wall, because we convinced ourselves that we couldn't afford the entrance fee. Obviously, we did it for an ironic laugh really, and because we were not numbers, we were free men... free of cash too!

After annoying Rod in Spain, by suggesting his photo on his business card made him look like Father Abraham from The Smurfs ("we all live in smoky holes", said Rod later) I remember ending up sitting on a beach with him near Barcelona, drinking numerous jugs of sangria and he was telling me all about Schrödinger's Cat - fascinating, *although it didn't make much sense at the time, but it was great sangria and I had great company…. and there was a cat in a box somewhere…*

Rod is the only bloke who has ever ridden alongside me at over 140mph, whilst I was seeing how fast I could go without something falling off, on that occasion on a French Peage just outside Carcassonne, bound for Barcelona. Some might think that kind of behaviour is a death wish. All I can tell you is that it is the very opposite, it is a celebration of life lived to the full, which every now and again I did especially when Rod and I were biking somewhere.

I knew from my last visit to see Rod in Tetford, and from phone conversations with Angie, that he kept that enthusiasm for life right to the end. I'd just like to celebrate that zest for life that I always saw in Rod. Even if our political views seemed to go in opposite directions at times, our wheels went very much in the same direction.

Many thanks for everything Rod. Go in peace brother, ride on….

My own health began to deteriorate again in the late summer of 2009. I felt exhausted most of the time and unable to walk any real distance without perspiring profusely and needing to sit down. I was on quite a short walk with my relatively new friend 'K', and I remember saying, "I just know there is something really wrong with me. This doesn't feel very good at all".

A few days later I was on the cross-trainer at the gym. Normally, if I really pushed myself on the machine, the heart rate monitor showed around 135. On this occasion I was not exerting myself at all; I glanced down and the heart rate monitor showed 160. Shocked, I ensured that the next day I was at the GP's Surgery. An initial stethoscope examination suggested I had a heart murmur or some sound of regurgitation of blood from the heart valves, a possible sign of heart valve failure. My GP arranged for me to see a Cardiologist at Airedale, who henceforth shall be known as "Dr. Hobnail", as this was the name that came up on the spell-checker when I initially typed his name and it seemed to fit him very well.

After a long series of preliminary tests I saw the Consultant Dr. Hobnail for the first time in early December 2009. He explained that he would be doing a further series of tests to determine the problem (CT scan, angiogram, MRI heart scan and if necessary a heart biopsy). I told the Cardiologist that since I had started taking diuretics in September, to reduce oedema in the legs, I had been in some considerable but unspecific abdominal pain. I was hoping he would do something to alleviate this, but instead my sense was that now his chosen strategy was only to address the pain after I had completed all the series of complex hospital tests.

I think this state of affairs came about for two reasons: because I insisted on talking to him as an equal, and not defer to him as some kind of medical god and also; because I refused to go into hospital for Christmas when my oedema was very bad. He seemed to think I had defied him, when all I felt was that I would be in a considerably worse state sat on my own in a hospital bed away from my friends and family for 5 days. I regarded his new strategy as some kind of punishment. Whether he saw it that way I will never know.

I thought that I would cope for a week or so, but unfortunately I did not know then that after my CT scan on the 22nd December, that I would not receive each of the next tests until separate intervals of approximately two months per test. Subsequently I had to wait until the 22nd February the following year before I was able to have the angiogram and until the 20th April, before I was given an MRI test. During all that time my abdominal pain got increasingly worse, to the point where by April I could not sleep at night for its severity.

I was at my lowest ebb after the angiogram, an excruciating procedure simply because I had to lie on my back for three hours without moving, in a body position where the pain was always the most acute. Due to severe heart problems (as I discovered later), to lie on my back created excruciating pain after around five minutes. Three hours was the worst kind of torture I had ever known. Dr Hobnail told me after the procedure, as I attempted to recover from this ordeal, that there was no faulty functioning of the heart valves and also that the abdominal pain was not connected to the heart condition (both inaccurate diagnoses as it turned out), and I needed to request a further series of consultations with another Consultant; I felt close to despair.

It looked like the relatively simple, but still daunting, procedure of heart valve replacement that I had been desperately hoping for, was not going to make everything alright again, and I had something more mysterious and worrying to contend with now. At the very least I had to consider accepting the reality that I was a very disabled person. I think I had held out some hope that there would be a relatively quick solution, albeit through the discomfort of a heart operation. Looking back I realised that I was not at a place of wise surrender to the inevitable reality, that what I had to deal with would be long and very arduous and complicated. I was instead in a place of considerable denial, which gradually eroded as the pain got worse.

Psychologically it was a relentless process – a big part of me hoped and believed in some kind of confused way, that the pain would mercifully leave me alone when I slept – but I hardly ever slept; or I desperately hoped that the pain would

199

be gone in the morning if I was able to sleep and wake again the next day. But every time I regained consciousness, the pain was there and was as acute as ever, day after day. I came to slowly accept there would indeed be no relief from this nightmare, day after day, week after week, month after month - forever. At the thought of that I noticed a small part of me for the very first time, and that part of me simply wanted to die.

Around this time, doing my best to attempt to look after myself, I woke yet again, around 3am and in a fog of depression and exhaustion I turned on the TV to distract myself from the acute pain. The first image that came up on the screen was of all people, Rod in a purple boiler suit, talking to camera, in his role as "special consultant" to a team of wrestlers on the Channel 4 TV Programme *"Scrapheap Challenge"*. The wrestlers were building a mono-wheel cycle, and Rod was their specialist consultant. I had seen the programme before of course when it came out a few years previously; round at Rod and Angie's house where Lis and I enjoyed a happy and amusing evening with our hosts, watching the birth of a new TV Star. Rod had also appeared regularly as "Doctor Rod" on the Granada Men and Motors Channel.

I took deep comfort from this synchronistic experience – "Doctor Rod" was there for me again, and I knew instantly that I was both being witnessed with care and love from somewhere and also that I was really facing something very, very big that was going to demand an awful lot from me in the weeks and months to come.

Around that time, many friends and colleagues had asked me to keep them in touch with health developments. In my deteriorating state the previous November and December I just could not face making a series of phone calls, so I decided to send emails to all instead.

The first email in December mapped out the situation, the second 'Update' on the 26th February 2010 talked of further 'non-developments'. It read as follows:

Dear Colleagues

I promised to keep people informed of my updated health situation, so I felt it was time to write again following my hospital heart test on Monday this week. Not sure how much detail to give, but being the thorough analytical chap I am, most of the gory details are in there, so apologies to those of you with a delicate disposition!

The test was a 'right and left ventricle catheterisation', done under local anesthetic, which consisted of incisions in the groin to enter two metal tubes (one for the main artery & one for the main vein) which are then threaded up to the heart on either side of the body and dyed fluid is flushed in, during and after which x-rays are taken of the heart from many different angles. I think there were over 60 or so x-rays, although I lost count eventually.

The test itself was slightly uncomfortable, but not really a problem. The major challenge was laying on my back in one position without moving for 3.5 hours (1.5 for the procedure and 2 hours afterwards in the recovery room), given my ever constant abdominal pain (worse when I lay down). Good job I'm an expert in being 'burdened and enduring', it was an enormous trial and I'm glad it's over at least for now.

Unfortunately the outcome is not what I wanted as the Consultant is no nearer confirming any diagnosis. He now intends to book me in for a "special heart MRI test" and if necessary after that, a right and left ventricle heart biopsy over the next few weeks / month - months. All that's definite at the moment is what I already knew from previous x-rays, which is that the right side of the heart remains grossly enlarged and I continue to have all the symptoms of heart failure, plus very uncomfortable side effects of something or other (possibly medication)... low energy, breathlessness, abdominal and back pain, swollen legs, extreme false heat in lower legs and ankles / feet, with stagnant blood flow, dry skin that flakes and bleeds. Apart from those minor irritations, this is the best time I've ever had! Nevertheless my reserves of 'stoic fortitude' are running rather low right now as you might imagine.

I'm not happy with lack of diagnosis but need to continue with the plan in the hope that something becomes clearer. At the same time I'm pursuing complementary medicine in the form of acupuncture, Chinese herbal remedies and homeopathy, as a way of at least being active in a process where it's all too easy to feel a passive object having things done to oneself. If I just sat there and did nothing I think I would probably go slightly mad.

The next stage with the cardiologist's process is the MRI scan, but as yet I've had no date set. He did say that he didn't feel the abdominal and back pain was to do with the heart condition or use of diuretics, and that I should talk to the GP about further referral (presumably to another type of consultant) to have that explored. If nothing definitive from the MRI scan, then I'll be having a right and left ventricle biopsy. After that, if there's still no clarity, I will be using any assertive 'kick-ass' energy I have left, for a full assault on the GP and Consultant to do all they can to sort all this out or at least tell me definitively what I might have to live with for the rest of my life. One way or another I'm resolved to get an answer.

In the meantime, I'm carrying on at work as usual to the best of my ability, whilst doing my best to conserve my vital energies as much as I can. I find I am able to do all the work I was doing before, as long as I rest up in between, and I am able to do that. The situation does pray on my mind somewhat from time to time, but work and the support of friends and colleagues offers welcome relief and respite from brooding too much on the whole business.

Your interest and support is very much appreciated.

Love & best wishes to all

John

By this time, my relationship with Dr Hobnail, such as it was, had deteriorated considerably. I had via the GP, asked his opinion on the possibility of a heart transplant and the reply, without any further details was, "out of the question". My GP took further consultation with a colleague on the same team as Dr Hobnail, who seemed to think that a transplant might well be a possibility. But as far as Dr Hobnail was concerned, I was going nowhere fast.

Shortly after my email, in discussion with my facilitated peer group of psychotherapists and other therapists, I decided the time had come to let my clients, supervisees and work colleagues know about my illness. It was clear to me, given Dr Hobnail's pace of work, that it would be a long time before I got a final diagnosis of anything and I was not getting any better.

By and large, people took the news very well, although a couple of my clients were, and remained, convinced that I was going to die. I knew that this was more a reflection of their internal narrative and life outlook than anything else. Instead of trying to tell them I wasn't going to die, I had enough presence of mind to take the opportunities available to work with them on long standing fears of abandonment or on frozen bereavement processes, where they had not had the previous opportunity to say goodbye to a loved one in their lives.

As for myself, despite my twilight zone existence, I felt able to be present and connected in these sessions although from time to time, the abdominal pain dominated all else. Still, I was able to carry on working after a fashion, in a way that still felt appropriate to me in terms of what I could offer people.

In terms of the impact of my health on my work, the very worst time was when I undertook a considerably complex organisational and inter-agency consultancy with the local "Mind The Gap" theatre company and two other local voluntary sector organisations doing community based art development work in the Bradford area. I was co-ordinating a team approach of three of us, plus doing my own not inconsiderable inputs. As I look back on this now, I feel an involuntary shudder at the desperate pain of it all. I endured hour after hour of severe abdominal pain whilst undertaking the consultancy. I did not know what was wrong with me but it felt like I was dying. I said nothing: perhaps because, with my back well and truly against the wall, I was reverting to my self-reliant and burdened and enduring character strategies; or perhaps it was because I didn't want anyone at the theatre company or within "Phoenix" to think I was incapable of doing the work.

Whatever my motivation (and looking back, none of this is really clear to me) I was not incapable anyway, but the pain was so bad I had to draw on all my resources of self-encouragement and stoicism to just get me through every day of the work. It was a big challenge to say the least, to successfully complete that particular contract.

However, I was receiving a lot of verbal, written and practical support from friends, throughout this time which gave me strength and purpose in the midst of a frighteningly unknown world.

Not least was my spiritual connection with Brenda, a spiritual director I had been seeing regularly since 1990. I asked Brenda a few years ago, "What's it all about then Brenda?" and she replied, "Well I think it's a lifelong process of gradually letting go of fear". Well I was certainly living out what all of that meant!

I had been fortunate to find a connection with a spiritual adult, with whom I shared much in the way of thoughts and feelings over the years. Sometime around 2005, I was introduced through Brenda, to Judith, a Quaker, who was interviewing people about their spiritual philosophy. Judith subsequently interviewed me about my beliefs and approach to life. I found it a stimulating and rewarding discussion.

In April 2010, Judith sent me a transcript of that discussion, for review and feedback, which she was hoping to publish as part of a book about individual spiritual journeys. On reading the text, I was aware that my thoughts and feelings had not changed much in the following five years, although they were really beginning to be tested now.

Her transcript read as follows:

JOHN HOLT [KEIGHLEY]

JH is working out his own spiritual path, based on his experience of a wide variety of religions and philosophies, but doesn't see himself as belonging to any particular one, and resists labels, "being in a box": "I'd never describe myself as anything, but I do think the spiritual path is really important."

His parents came from apparently very different religious traditions – his father was a Methodist, his mother a Spiritualist, though they seemed to be moving "side by side", rather than in different directions, in their commitment to left-wing politics and trade unionism: for both families, and for many in his local (mining) community, "politics and religion were one and the same thing".

From a very early age, he accepted this blend of different religious attitudes and politics as "natural": "it all exists and it all makes sense". His mother in particular was keen for him to make up his own mind, and had a very tolerant attitude to different religions and philosophies, so that he never felt he was indoctrinated. He picked up his religion informally from seeing how his family lived their lives, from going to church sometimes with his father's parents, and from talking about Spiritualism and other views of life with his mother and aunt.

He felt no worries about what happens after you die, and had no idea of a wrathful God – though did perhaps have some concept of a God of justice as part of this "very humanitarian sort of religion" which focused very much on this life and "what we're doing here".

As he grew older he encountered and explored many spiritual paths, his only "yardstick" being "following my heart I think and what really intrigued and interested me." He has had a lot of Roman Catholic friends and has found himself drawn to the "symbolic and mystical aspects of Catholicism". His connection with Quakers was also "quite strong for a while", but has rather faded, but it was through Alex Wildwood, a Friend, that he came to men's spiritual work and its links with myth and story, moving on from there to fairy tales like the work of the Brothers Grimm, and to Jungian archetypes and mysticism.

He has a mixed attitude to New Age beliefs, seeing some as "a bit flaky", but others as having "some substance"; and he is interested in healing and has visited a healer in North Yorkshire. He has stayed at the Findhorn Community, which in some ways he finds too "esoteric" for him, though he likes its sense of inclusiveness and community. The small retreat house [i.e. Foster Place] mentioned at the beginning of this section is one of the few spiritual constants in his life – he has attended courses, events and one-to-one retreats there, and sees the woman who runs it regularly as his "spiritual director", though their relationship is more of a "dialogue" than this suggests.

Eastern religions are also of particular interest to him – Hinduism, Buddhism, above all Taoism, which appeals to him with its emphasis on natural processes ("if you create the right environment, things will work themselves out"), on the balance between polarities, "paradox" and "holding things in dynamic tension", a sense of "both/and" rather than "either/or". He feels it is nearer to the world as we experience it than some other religions.

He is constantly seeing connections in different areas of experience and knowledge: for instance he is still interested in Christian Socialism; sees links between the focus on natural processes in Taoism and ecology, creation-centred spirituality and some New Age beliefs. He sees connections, too, between Spiritualism and Hinduism, and Spiritualist - and spiritual – principles in the humanistic psychology in which he has trained.

One particularly vivid experience when he was ill some years ago brought home to him many unexpected connections. He had a powerful dream of a Christ-figure, and as he awoke saw shapes at the side of his bed, and felt as if "confronting the shadow aspect of myself." He then opened at random a book by Alan Watts – a Buddhist writing about Taoism – and found a passage describing how Christ confronted the shadow side of himself during his forty days of temptation, and asserting its central place in Christianity. This experience made him convinced of the importance of facing his own "shadow material" as well as following his spiritual path, and of integrating the two - a very Jungian concept —which in turn opened the way to bringing more "spiritual stuff" into the work he had already been doing for a while.

As mentioned, his work in counselling and psychotherapy links the "value-base" of humanistic, individual psychology with the transpersonal and spiritual. It is about "creating safe places" for people where they can "experience who they are", and "make sense of how they are who they are", helping them to develop their sense of where they're going in life and what life means to them, and their ability to make choices and face the consequences of those choices.

He also works with managers who want to give their businesses an ethical and spiritual value-base. He does a lot of work with people who have been bereaved, which he finds easier than many others might, because he has had many experiences of bereavement, and through Spiritualism and Taoism sees life and death as closely intertwined. He is able to "hold that space", he hopes not in a "judgmental" or "patronising" way.

Asked what he sees happening after death, he replies that reincarnation as making sense, a constant evolving, though in a cyclical rather than a linear sense: he has a "hunch" that if we ever reach nirvana, "we just start all over again."
He sees the human and divine as closely intertwined too, and Jesus as both human and divine. Prayer for him is very much "personal dialogue", and he doesn't need to be in a special place for it, though perhaps in a special part of himself —yet our physical surroundings can help: he sees the Dales as a "natural cathedral", and a "powerful atmosphere" in some churches.

He sees "being in that kind of circle" (for instance among Quakers, or in a men's group) as "quite a profound experience."

One of the most important things for him is a constant open-mindedness and integrity, not feeling we have exclusive access to the only truth, nor feeling we can stop searching because we have found it: he would always say, "That's the way it appears to me at the moment." He likes "communities where you can come and go as you please" and hopes the rigidity and exclusivity often currently found in belief are "just a phase."

Much of this still rang true for me in 2009 and 2010. I still believed in the power of community, and particularly as experienced in Men's Gatherings, whether in a Men's Group or at Men's Events.

It seems however, that fear was still very much around for me as I prepared for the Mandorla Event in May 2010, and my abdominal pains and heart failure symptoms continued to increase in impact and severity.

On the 5th April I emailed my Colleagues in Mandorla with the following message:

Easter Monday 7pm:

Dear Lads

I am not in a good place. I need to write to let you know what's going on and ask you to reflect on my ability or otherwise to be at the forthcoming Mandorla Event at Cae Mabon. I've been on a break from work now for 3 days, and in the absence of having to drag myself to work I'm really impacted by how ill I feel.

I am now in constant abdominal pain, I was before, but the level of pain I have now is stronger and doesn't fade into the background like it once did. I had been able to get to sleep by consuming paracetamol and lying on my side (somewhat fitfully as I usually woke up again an hour later), but this now seems more difficult and the paracetamol isn't having much effect. 3 nights ago I couldn't sleep lying down at all and had to sit up all night downstairs and just doze off when I could. The last 2 nights I just forced myself to lay in pain until exhaustion took over, but this is no way to carry on. Consequently, I have been pushing my GP hard for an abdominal scan and I now have a scan date for Monday 12th April. I don't know what, if anything, they will find, but I'm sure anxiety is contributing to the overall discomfort.

The other symptoms that are almost intolerable are as follows: underlying feeling of illness - just a sense of something being really wrong and a deep internal chill (sometimes I look grey in the face, sometimes - annoyingly - due to blood pressure I suppose, I look very healthy but feel absolutely shit at the same time); my oedema persists despite now using 3 diuretics a day which cause me to pee very frequently over a period of up to 8 hours at a time - my legs are often red raw looking and bleed easily if I accidentally catch them on something, the feeling is best described as like constant scalding water on the legs or walking through a field of stinging nettles when I move, and the water retention bloats the legs so that it's hard to walk at times or move the joints; I fall asleep very unpredictably and / or feel exhausted much of the time; I am breathless with a palpitating heart and nausea if I walk any distance at all, certainly up any incline whatsoever, and steps are an ordeal. Going to work in Skipton is an expedition: I have to walk from my car up two or three inclines and 41 steps to get to the Psychotherapy Centre, which feels like it burns up the same amount of energy I used to put in walking the Aonach Eagach ridge in Scotland, and when I get in the Centre I collapse breathless and feel nauseous for 5 minutes or so before things settle down); oh yes, the diuretics dry you out and increase the possibility of constipation which of course brings on piles if you are not too careful.

So what has Consultant Dr Hobnail said about the above? Well, very little. Dr Hobnail, my Consultant Cardiologit (no spelling error) claims the abdominal pain has nothing to do with the heart condition and in any event he is not inclined to offer any symptom management nor pain reduction until he has completed all the tests. This might be bearable if I didn't have to wait 2 months between each fucking test. So far, I had a scan on December 22nd, a left and right ventricle catheterisation on February 22nd and now I have an appointment for an MRI scan of the heart for Tuesday April 20th at LGI in Leeds. I asked him to let me know how quickly I would get the last test (left and right ventricle heart biopsy) if it was needed after the MRI scan, and instead of reassuring me it would follow quickly he simply said, "You might not need a biopsy". But if I do, it seems to me that might not happen until June at this rate, which is precisely what I am trying to avoid.

I have been in frequent dialogue with my GP who does appear very frustrated with the Cardiologit, and has consulted his friend another cardiologist, Dr Z who works on the same team as the Cardiologit. He has looked at all my results so far, and what he has said doesn't sound good: It appears I have an extremely rare condition, a "pure right ventricle heart failure" - apparently with the level of deterioration I have in the right ventricle this would only happen if I had severe lung disease and the left ventricle was also severely affected. I have neither of those things, nor any damage to any arteries. The 2nd opinion man feels it is as a result of a heart virus last summer and possibly also a long standing but slowly developing genetic condition.

211

Dr Z said, "it will be very difficult to treat". This of course is prior to the final 2 tests, but it raises real worries for me: Is my right ventricle continuing to deteriorate or can the decline be halted by medication? If not, the implication is that one day the heart will give out entirely - and if so, I don't know how soon that will be. Some days it doesn't feel very far away, and I imagine I can sense ol' Death sitting somewhere near my shoulder, breathing heavily in my ear. Secondly, if the above is true then it seems the only eventual recourse would be a heart transplant - I don't know how ill I would have to be before they would consider putting me on a list, but if the current hypothetical prognosis is accurate I would take the risk and go for a transplant tomorrow. I'd rather take my chances in a bid for a quality life, than live like this until the final "Dance with Death" as Mr. Castaneda says.

What does this all mean for me living some kind of life right now, and what I am able to do? Well, to be honest I feel like doing nothing, it's all too exhausting and all too much to bear. But if I give in to that, it seems I'm slipping away from the world. So, I do what I can. I keep visiting friends when I can, or go to a music gig or football match if I can - sometimes I can do it with not much after effect, sometimes it feels I pay hard for it afterwards, but sometimes I just have to say no to things I want to do. I have still missed a lot of things recently. I can feel OK - ish at 11am or early afternoon, but exhausted by 5pm. It's very unpredictable.

With all the above in mind, I don't know if I'm going to be able to get through the Planning Weekend here, but I still want to go ahead with it. But I seriously doubt my ability to make it through the Cae Mabon event. You may have to write me out of the picture this time round, I just don't know. The thought of trying to sleep there, or get up and down hills is at the moment a nightmare to me and I don't want to visit that on the Team or the Participants. On the other hand it's real and it's raw and it's uncompromisingly life, or death, and maybe that is a gift to people there if I honour it and myself by turning up. But I might be a ghost at the feast. I just don't know compadres - I really don't know what to do.

I just needed to let you all know where I'm at and put it out there.

Love, John

The response from the Mandorla Team was tremendous. I received Emails, phone calls and words of great encouragement. This message from Patrick was typical of the response:

Christ John

I'm so sorry to hear about your problems. I'm not clear: have you got support from friends nearby? How isolated are you? The worst thing sounds like dealing with all this to all intents and purposes, on your own, without the support to make meals, look after your house etc. And what about work? Are you carrying on with it through this?
   I'm so sorry John. Wish I could do something to help.

All my love

Patrick xxx

In the event, we did meet after all at my house on the weekend of the 17th to 18th April. The guys in the Team really looked after me: making all the meals; insisting I sat down to rest whenever possible; vacuuming the house and cutting the jungle (euphemistically known as the 'lawn') out the back. They also said they could arrange for me to be driven down onto the site at Cae Mabon in a Four Wheeled Vehicle, where my gear could be unloaded and also brought back up again at the end of the Event. I started to get into the spirit of things and suggested they could build a litter to transport me regally around the site from one location to the other. "Fuck off", they all replied in unison. Ah, so I had found the outer limits of their support!

Despite the love and care of my co-leaders at the planning meeting, I just couldn't envisage how I was going to find the energy and focus to complete the weekend Event. However, as it turned out I was prescribed painkillers at the last moment before the Event, following much assertive lobbying on my part to get an active response from the Consultant Cardiologist. After six months or so of considerable pain, without any prescribed painkillers, I was suddenly virtually free of pain and my participation in the Event went ahead as planned.

The best thing I could have done at that Event was what I eventually did: I told all the participants about my health condition and that I was seriously considering giving up my Mandorla work.

Men I had worked with previously were visibly upset and one or two simply said, "You can't give this up; it's too important for us and for you to let go of it". I resolved after reflection to redouble my commitment to Mandorla; I simply chose not to give up. It was the wisest thing I could have done and I'm delighted I stayed with it through all that was to follow.

We need a vision and meaning in our lives in order to continue to dream and to follow our bliss. Without it we can often become lost.

I recalled a powerful print I saw years previously at the Bradford Printmaking Biennale. It was an image of a hand letting go and giving flight to a dove. The print was celebrating the work of the African-American poet Langston Hughes. Words from his poetry were printed below the image.

The words read:

"Hold fast to dreams

For if dreams die

Life is a broken winged bird

That cannot fly".

THE RECENT PAST

Receiving a terminal diagnosis is a very challenging experience. It wasn't communicated to me in plain black and white terms; it sunk in gradually and powerfully over a week after talking to my Consultant Oncologist in early summer 2010. Instead of offering a stark diagnosis, he told me I would "have no major problem" in living long enough to see my next milestone birthday, at that time 18 months or so ahead, "But let's say anything more after that is a very long way off".

The future didn't sound too promising at all, especially as a few weeks previously the same Oncologist had told me with enthusiasm in his voice, "We are definitely looking at the possibility of a cure". This no longer sounded like a cure and was communicated now in much more sombre tones, after he had just received a long letter and further diagnosis from a Consultant Surgeon in Leeds.

I had an instant reaction when I heard the news from my Oncologist which I could only describe as "defiant", however I also explored a great deal of information on the Internet in the days following, and it became very clear that my life expectancy could be measured in a few years at most, probably around three.

This was in the light of information about the stage my cancer had reached with secondary tumours spreading to the liver. There are variations on Carcinoid Syndrome but with 'Gastrointestinal Carcinoid Tumours' when the original tumours have metastasised and produced secondary tumours in the liver, as in my case, this is one of the worst prognoses. Without surgery, the only treatment left is usually Hormone Therapy, given by injection on a regular basis, using either Octreotide or Lanreotide drugs. They block the flow of harmful hormones (in my case an absolute excess of Serotonin) and may have a small effect on stopping tumour growth, but will not reduce existing tumours.

It had been a tough journey until this point, including what seemed like an endless round of CT and MRI scans. The worst experience I had was what I remembered as a full body 'nuclear scan'+ at St James Hospital. I already knew that lying on my back would be an ordeal after at most 5 minutes and that the full scan would take around 1.5 hours. So, I let the radiologists and nursing staff know before the start that the pain would probably be acute for me after five minutes and that if it got unbearable I would just have to shout and moan to get through it. I asked them not to stop under any circumstances, no matter how much noise I was making, because I could not stand the thought of going through the ordeal again if the MRI scan was aborted. As it turned out, I kept silent for around forty five minutes, in acute pain and then just had to let the pain out through making a noise – I did so for the remaining forty five minutes, mostly at full volume from the bottom of my lungs, and the staff were clearly upset by it all but, bless them, did indeed continue the full scan whilst repeatedly asking me over the intercom if I wanted to stop. I insisted on carrying on and thankfully made it through to the end.

I had a further scan a couple of weeks later when my heart pain was not so acute, and the scan was a shorter one, but on this occasion the liquid going into a vein in my arm, used for reading the scan, came loose and instead of flowing into my vein the liquid went into the muscle. I didn't notice for ten minutes – I felt the pain, but thought that was just what I had to put up with, until I saw my hand out of the corner of my eye had expanded into an enormous balloon. The process was stopped but it took a long time for the pain and swelling to subside.

So on the day that I heard my Oncologist's "diagnosis – prognosis", I was aware of what I had already been through. I was also acutely aware of a previous dialogue with the Consultant Surgeon, Professor Lodge at St James, Leeds, who until a fateful meeting with myself and my ex-wife Lis (who despite our earlier parting of the ways in terms of marriage, was offering me tremendous and unwavering support), had been in the preceding weeks (through clinical correspondence with my Oncologist and others), encouragingly intent on a liver operation to remove my secondary tumours.

However, on that difficult day when Lis and I met with him at St James Hospital Cancer Unit in Leeds, he had explained that since the latest in-depth MRI nuclear and other scans had revealed my liver was 80% covered in tumours, any major surgery would almost certainly kill me and that he could no longer risk considering carrying out an operation. So the dialogue that followed soon after, with my Consultant Oncologist gave me news that I was certainly dreading but also stoically expecting.

Since an operation on the liver was now out of the question and it appeared that no one much survived carcinoid syndrome when it had advanced to the stage mine had reached, I recognised any treatment I would be given by the Airedale Hospital Team would essentially be palliative care. I was offered and accepted regular Lanreotide injections at the Haematology & Oncology Day Unit (HODU), which were given to counteract the worst effects on my heart of massive doses of the hormone '5HIAA' (Serotonin). The Serotonin levels were 40 times the 'normal' level, and were attacking the functioning of my heart, leading to two faulty heart valves and a severely extended muscle wall in the right ventricle, otherwise described as 'pure right ventricle heart failure'. The Oncologist had no real expectation that the Lanreotide would have anything other than a palliative effect on my tumours. It just seemed a matter of time before the end.

Nevertheless, my authentic Self had other ideas. I distinctly recall hearing a voice in side me say emphatically, "fuck that!" when I heard the Consultant Oncologist giving me his views on my future and though I was fearful as I explored the Internet for information, I was still very much alive. I had not given up and I was still on some deep level, continuing in my determination to follow my Bliss in life and work, no matter what.

What was helping me in this situation? I think it was years of personal development I had already undertaken around my emotional life, Men's Work and spirituality. Those experiences had taught me that I need not be afraid of the world or what it threw at me – and furthermore, if I chose to reach out for help from others it would certainly be there.

My exploration of writings within the American Men's Movement had begun in earnest around 1990, in the years following the end of my relationship with Muireann, my subsequent illness with Myalgic Encephalomyelitis (M.E.) and my attendance at the inaugural UK 'Men's Rites of Passage' event at Muriau Gwynion (as it was known, prior to adopting the name Cae Mabon) in North Wales in the summer of 1989.

With the air of a starving man, I had begun to seek the nourishment of emotional wisdom and an understanding of the world of relationships from the perspective of a quest to uncover my authentic Self as a man. I explored the works of John Lee, Robert Bly, Michael Meade, James Hillman and through them, Joseph Campbell, who had in his long life held a position as Chair of Contemporary Cultural Studies at an American University. Campbell was a scholar of the works of Carl Jung and deeply influenced Lee, Bly and James

Hillman a Jungian Analytical Psychotherapist and key figure in the development of Depth Psychology.

Campbell had suggested that from an existential perspective, "The purpose of a life is to find your bliss and follow it". It became apparent to me that my "Bliss" had changed over time. It was initially focused upon my career and ways of being in service in the world; through relationship challenges it had also grown to embrace the need for more balance and nourishment in my personal life; now it seemed it was expanding again to embrace physical health and continuation of life beyond the apparent inevitability of the final and inexorable dance with death. Over the next few years it would also deepen further to embrace a profound exploration of my spiritual journey and an astounding, ever expanding breadth of metaphysical experiences.

Even before my terminal diagnosis, I had been through what I thought was a profound 'Dark Night of the Soul', as my marriage to Lis ended and I chose to carry on, stumbling and wounded, with the task of being open to loving instead of hiding away from the pain of love. I realised there was no peace to be found in hiding away, even though staying open to the demands and ultimate healing of deep grief at losing my marriage to Lis, in the hope of having some kind of future beyond overwhelming emotional pain, was a very hard choice to make.

As Thomas Moore wisely stated (2004), in the context of the concept described by 16th century Spanish poet and mystic, St. John of the Cross; experiencing a dark night of the soul is like being taken on a sea journey, carried by the sea completely beyond any sense of control or direction. However in reality, despite the sense of helplessness, or if you have the wisdom to know what is required, even being open to the conscious choice of surrender,

*"You are **not** wandering all over the place. When you are on a night sea journey be taken, don't try to have it finished, don't try to figure it out, don't try to outsmart it"*.

So that first sea journey eventually brought me to an understanding that I needed to let go of resentment and to stay open to the possibility of future relationships, no matter how much pain I was experiencing.

For a while I enjoyed a short lived experience of closeness and intimacy with a new person in my life, Andrea. We got on really well, were very close for some considerable time and enjoyed (I think Andrea might not have used the word "enjoyed") an exhilarating motorcycle trip to the Picos de Europa mountains in Northern Spain. She eventually ended the relationship with me when it became obvious to her I had not really done the grieving I needed to do in order to heal sufficiently to be open to the challenge of a new exclusive intimacy. It hurt greatly at the time; Andrea was a beautiful person and very loving and I genuinely loved her, very much, but she was right – I had not sufficiently grieved the end of my marriage. The collapse of my relationship with Andrea pitched me into a very deep and dark place. I missed her greatly at the same time as I was still grieving Lis, I felt like I was being haunted (or was haunting myself) by the ghosts of two women.

In terms of profundity and impact, that first 'dark night of the soul' was therefore a searing and frightening experience. However, it was by comparison, just an echo of the deeper dark night of the soul I was yet to undertake.

As I was to find out, it feels like a stark choice is being offered, as Moore suggests that any "flight from darkness" will in reality,

"Infantilise your spirituality, because the dark nights of the soul are supposed to initiate you into spiritual adulthood. You have to use your intelligence every step of

221

the way. The spiritual life is both deep and transcendent; it should make you a person of character and discernment, emotionally tough and intellectually demanding, as well as loving and compassionate. It should give you insight into the deepest of your questions and problems, and give you a vision that extends beyond the everyday issues".

So it felt like a stark choice on the surface, yet I have come to understand in my own way, the presence of grace in the depths of grief, and the beauty and extent of God's love for me, in offering a hand of friendship and companionship to help me step up into that place of spiritual adulthood through the pain of choosing to fully live through the sea journey of grief.

As Robert Bly put it in "Iron John", (1990) using the Greek term "katabasis", you are required to "descend into the ashes" and the way back to life is to "exit through the deepest wounds".

I do feel that I have done that, and with God's grace, in so doing I feel that I have found a place of profound freedom and emotional liberation. I would like to offer an explanation of how I have come to that place in the pages and chapters that follow.

***

Is experiencing the "dark night of the soul" an inevitable aspect of choosing to be more fully present in the world?

I'm not so sure choice comes into it as, at least on the surface, on both occasions that I felt myself undergoing the "sea journey", I felt pitched into it by forces apparently beyond my control. If I take that view too far I can begin to sound like a disempowered victim of circumstance. In reality I think the challenge, in finding oneself in such

situations, is to surrender certainty and control, whilst remaining committed to a mindful and intelligent witnessing of one's own process and options for moving forwards. With this in mind, as the Book of Ecclesiastes suggests, there is a time for everything, or "every purpose under heaven", including both surrender and also action. We need to wait and be prepared to be in a place of not knowing long enough for deeper truths to emerge, before we act in manner as decisive as possible.

I think that may be much easier to do later in life. My experience of 'M.E.' happened in my thirties, when I was still hanging on to vestiges of the "puer aeternus" or eternal boy. Subsequently, although I learnt a lot about surrender I was not prepared enough to truly enter a "dark night of the soul". By the time my marriage to Lis ended I was in my early fifties and feeling much more broken as a person – broken enough to journey through a "dark night of the soul" and make contact with the "senex" or wise old man aspect of myself as a lifeline to deeper learning and spiritual growth. I received the cancer, heart failure and terminal diagnosis in my late fifties, when I came to know the "senex" aspect extremely well, as I moved through the deepest and darkest experiences I could ever imagine.

Only in recent months have I come to appreciate that this has been and still is a shamanic journey. I feel the dark night aspect is over, whatever happens to me from now on, because the split Self within me has been healed. In so doing, I feel I have been gifted with a new breadth of vision and understanding that is vast, compared to what existed, or what was apparently accessible to me, before. From this new place of insight and inner-sight, I can see that for me, one aspect of healing the split Self was to achieve a balance between both "puer" and "senex" aspects of the personality or perhaps of the soul.

The experience of exile, ordeal, trials, revelations and return to the community, brings a lighter and more humorous touch and also a kind of grounded sense of peace with the wise and discerning aspects of the Self, which is committed to facing and living life as it is, not as one might have hoped it would have turned out to be when one was younger. This is a good place to review and discern anew what one's bliss might be – and to honour it through self-expression at both the level of the "puer aeternus" and also the level of the "senex".

Here there is little to be afraid of except an unnecessary preoccupation with fear itself. Fear begets fear, courage begets courage, life begets a joy of life and death also begets life, if we choose to face death squarely and look it in the eye, long enough for a conversation to emerge between death's wisdom and our power of choice – I chose to live as fully in the moment as I could and let go of both the past and the future. It is a place where nourishment is endless and anything is possible including a return to health – I have changed and the world has changed around me.

***

John in Picos de Europa

Above: Undampened Spirits
Below: Rod Gibson

CHAPTER 11:

The road towards authenticity and integrity

I feel that I made a serious choice to set off down the road towards authenticity and integrity after my relationship ended with Muireann in 1986. The process was consolidated and deepened much further by my involvement in the embryonic UK based Men's Movement at the end of the 80s, throughout the 90s and beyond, up to and including the present day.

As I have written, I could not understand at the time of my break up with Muireann how I could care so much for someone (and in reality love someone), yet still feel so distant and afraid. At the time, I don't think I knew what love was, but I knew I was deeply troubled. Looking back, I think what was *"washed away"* (see poem "For Muireann", Chapter 6, p.132) in the rain that night was not *"magic, hopes and dreams"*, but simply an infantilised version of them in terms of my own lack of emotional and spiritual maturity.

It is clear looking back, that deep and profound emotional wounds brought me to the work of the Men's Movement. As I was recovering from the worst effects of M.E., I decided to go off on my own that summer exploring the West Coast of Scotland, prior to attending the inaugural 'Men's Rites of Passage' with Everyman in August 1989.

I travelled as far north as Scourie in Sutherland in the North West Highlands, the last part of the journey north being a wild sea ferry crossing at Kylesku as, in those days, the road abruptly ended then began again at the other side of the bay.

I felt deeply at home and in touch with my own rhythms as I explored the western seaboard and the Highlands. At Scourie, after the sea crossing, I turned south east and travelled the length of Loch Shin down towards Lairg and then Inverness. The further I travelled away from the Highlands, the more my mood darkened, reaching a low place in Inverness and a place of profound solemnity and what felt unmistakeably like grief as I explored the battlefield at Culloden Muir.

I heard no birds singing that day at Culloden and I was deeply moved by the place. Even though I had not been there before, at least in this lifetime, it seemed that I knew the place with a sense of horrible familiarity and dread. I knew I had to lift my spirits and I vaguely knew a place called Findhorn was situated to the north of Culloden. So I travelled there and the physical beauty of Findhorn Bay and the energy of the local Findhorn Community restored something deep inside me.

Attending the Men's Rites of Passage in North Wales immediately after that trip, was a gear shift from travelling alone to a journey into community, this time in the company of other men. Perhaps significantly, I left Inverness for the journey towards home intending to call in on my parents who had a caravan at that time on a permanent site in Scarborough. Some part of me wanted and sensed I needed to make some sort of meaningful contact with my father before I got to the Men's Event in North Wales. Ironically, even though I drove direct from Inverness to Scarborough to ensure I met my Dad, by the time I arrived I had missed my parents by 30 minutes; they had already left for home. I just accepted the pre-Event meeting was not to be. So I took half an hour's break and then drove back to Bradford. The next day I set off for North Wales.

I had been involved in Men's Groups in the 1980s at a time when it appeared men spent a lot of time apologising for themselves to women. During this time, as Robert Bly had suggested, women were very good at pointing out the shadow side of men, but not very good at seeing it in themselves. The work of John Lee, Robert Bly, Michael Meade, James Hillman, Joseph Campbell and others really called out to me at this time. They articulated and echoed a desire for men to find the positive and generative aspects within themselves and begin to live them in their lives, without apology, without feeling the need to justify being a man and with a sense of personal responsibility for their own actions, and a voice of personal authenticity as a mark of choosing to live out that responsibility in the world as emotional adults.

This view was around in 1989 when I attended the very first 'Men's Rites of Passage' run by Everyman at a place then known as "Muriau Gwynion", near Fachwen in North Wales. Muriau Gwynion was an embryonic encampment, situated next to the Padarn Country Park, on the shores of Llyn Padarn, opposite the town of Llanberis. The event was facilitated by Alex Wildwood and Eric Maddern. Eric owned the Muriau Gwynion site. I found it to be a very powerful experience of companionship, and an introduction to the power of community, and particularly as experienced in Men's Gatherings.

It was also a place where I made deep contact with the anger I felt towards my father, with whom I'd had a very tempestuous relationship since early teenage years. I felt I had been subjected to years of psychological abuse by a man who appeared to deal with his sense of shame by attempting to project it onto me, in a most psychologically violent manner for over 20 years. But as I was later to realise, shame had been in turn dumped onto him by previous generations, certainly as far back as my great grandfather, yes also bearing the name John Holt, who was a miner, an alcoholic and himself a man deeply traumatised by poverty and emotional violence.

I was sitting in a circle of men listening to a man called Pete who was attempting to articulate something. There was something about Pete's energy I did not like. He seemed arrogant, pushy, intense, self-preoccupied and very angry about something. How much of this was actually real, and how much was my projection of my own father's energy and presence, I'm not sure. As he talked he stopped and seemed to be thinking. Another man (whom I liked) attempted to give his views on what Pete had said so far. Pete cut him dead with a snarl and a furiously delivered, "I've not finished".

I felt something unlock deep in my guts as a visceral sideways movement, some kind of primeval power had been released – I cut right across Pete looking him intently in the eye and said, "Don't do that. You will not dominate this place. Other people have just as much right to speak as you. And I tell you this, you will NOT silence me! I will have my place here; you will NEVER silence me again!"

As I spoke, Pete (of course) turned into my father in my eyes and in my perception I was speaking out at last after years of fear and silence in the face of my father's violent energetic domination. Pete sat there looking ashen faced and very shaken. I heard the Belgian men sat around me growling encouragement and support as I spoke out. As I continued to speak my face distorted with power and a tremendous energy – my face began to distort and vibrate so much with energy that I could hardly speak by the end of what I had to say. I had to work very hard just to pull my facial muscles back into shape in order to form the words to prevent them sounding absolutely unintelligible. Having said what I felt empowered to say, I was still reverberating with energy and adrenalin but the fury had passed. I sat quietly and no one spoke for quite a while. Then Alex did his best to bring the proceedings to a close.

It must have been pretty tough on Pete, but significantly I made no attempt whatsoever afterwards to apologise or seek him out to reassure him. I figured with a powerfully assertive feeling, that he was perfectly capable of taking care of himself.

As I look back, I can see that for years, my pattern around my Dad had been to be silenced by a sense of overwhelmingly heavy fear and by the implied violence of his moods, to feel contemptuously angry towards him and at the same time, confusingly perhaps, feel deep compassion and sadness for the obvious emotional pain he was enduring within himself.

I had often, far too often, in the past forgiven my Dad, crucially without expressing the depth of my anger first, after his outrageously dominant outbursts – and the cycle had repeated itself yet again a few days, or if I was very lucky a few weeks, later. For my part, I know now that my contribution to the process of repeating patterns was not to fully express my fury, anger, grief and rage. Without that crucial part of the process, the eventual forgiveness is inevitably incomplete and shallow.

In my experience it is not possible to fully and genuinely forgive anyone if you have firstly not brought out and experienced the full depth of your anger and rage. This time there was no rescuing on my part. For the first time as an adult I felt liberated from his terrifying dominance and the tyranny of his violent moods and my authentic voice could be fully heard.

On return from Muriau Gwynion, I attempted a clumsy sort of reconciliation and forgiveness process, without explaining or talking about anything that had happened to me there, which my father found very difficult. However, the following year with the hope of real reconciliation within me, I visited my parents at Scarborough where they were on their regular caravanning holiday. I did experience a very powerful moment of grace when walking on the beach with Dad, talking about my embryonic plans to go freelance as a psychotherapist and organisational consultant.

I was amazed to hear him give me his blessing and say he wished he'd had the courage to do something like that when he was my age. My hopes rather soared after this until two days later when he spoke cuttingly and contemptuously to me in the car and I felt a violent emotional crash, and once again a rising anger and rage within me. I left Scarborough in a fury and also in deep sadness, and headed back to West Yorkshire.

I left the country shortly after that on a holiday to France with a Canadian friend, Sandra, and on my return felt unable to contact him. As it turned out I saw him alive for the very last time in Scarborough that August. We did have a slight but very awkward telephone conversation on my return (he phoned and asked me if I had been trying to phone him. "No", was all I said). By the end of September he had died.

My late adolescent-like fury and also the negligent medical profession had both overlooked the reality that my Dad had advanced heart disease; the GP diagnosed it as "severe indigestion". When Dad spoke at this time it was often with fear and anger although he himself was not aware of the true reality of his condition. That only emerged after his death and was written on his Death Certificate. His heart gave out one morning whilst gardening. He was 68.

I visited Dad's body at the Co-op Funeral Service premises in Chesterfield. I felt at the time it was a profoundly strange and visceral experience. I had been shown into what I thought was an annexe where models of coffins were displayed. There was a dummy in the coffin in front of me and I was waiting to be shown into the inner sanctum of the Chapel of Rest. I was therefore very surprised when the undertaker said, "I'll leave you now" and left me alone in the room. I realised this was not a 'demonstration coffin' and the figure in the coffin was not a dummy, it was my father's body. It took me quite a while to believe what I was seeing. I did not recognise the figure in the coffin. Dad had fair / sandy hair and used no hair gel, often sweeping his hair back off his forehead with his hand; a typically characteristic mannerism of his which I knew very well. This figure had slicked back hair. I only began to see my father's face when my eyes locked on to a bruise at the side of his temple. I remembered that I had been told over the phone by my brother, that he had keeled over in the garden from a massive heart attack and had hit his head on a paving stone as he went down.

As I looked at the bruise I began to recognise features all over his face. But it was not him. It was merely an empty husk. At that moment, I also absolutely knew that death as an ultimate state did not exist. My father's troubled, sad, verbally violent and angry spirit was still very much alive all around me, but it was not locked into the empty vessel I saw laying in front of me. I kissed my Dad on the forehead and placed three acorns from Muriau Gwynion in the coffin alongside his body. They were there in memory and honour of him, my brother Glyn and me. They were also an attempt to honour the male line of descendants in my family.

As I left the funeral parlour all I could taste was death on my lips from the undertaker's embalming fluid. I walked in a daze through Queen's Park and over the footbridge into town, faces loomed in front of me and to my eyes every single person I saw over the age of 12 was in some stage of physical death. I did not know whether in conventional terms I was any longer alive or dead. However, I was certainly emotionally spent.

A few days later I had a series of dreams: my telephone rang and there was no sound when I picked it up; the next night it rang again and when I picked it up I heard my father's voice, but I could not recall on waking what he had said. The next night I dreamt I was in a tall building looking down a corridor towards a pair of lift doors; the bell rang and the doors opened but there was no one there. On the final night I was back in that corridor again; the bell rang and the lift doors opened and my Dad was standing there. He came out of the lift and walked towards me but before he reached me, I woke up. I don't recall seeing him again in my dreams after that.

I struggled to deal with this unfinished business for years afterwards, with help from Brenda (my Spiritual Director now for over twenty years), and my Men's Work; in particular, in recent years through exploring many painful and dark places at Cae Mabon (formerly Muriau Gwynion), first as a participant on the Men's Rites of Passage and other Events, and then latterly as co-facilitator of "Mandorla Men's-Work Events".

It was not until early in 2010, at a writing workshop just down the coast from Scarborough at Flamborough that I could write in an expression of acceptance and forgiveness about my relationship with my father:

Small moment, big difference, passing person.

Scarborough, North Bay, August 1990.

How many times have I walked in step with you

On this beach, or anywhere?

I can't remember this happening before.

Mostly I walk without you or your back turns.

38 years have passed. Only now, sharing my thoughts

and hopes for the future do you really hear me.

Or is it that only now I really hear you?

"Yes, I wish I'd had the courage to follow

My dreams when I was your age. I think you should do it".

A father's blessing in an endless desert of conflict and estrangement.

It burned bright, I followed it, I did not realise then,

that in a moment you would be gone, back into the shadows.

But this time you did not drag me with you.

Thanks Dad for that moment, that flash of freedom.

I came to my current co-leadership role in Mandorla via further experiences as a participant in more Men's Rites of Passage Events, first with Alex Wildwood, then with "Everyman", then with Ron Pyatt as a co-facilitator with "Everyman - Wild Dance". Mandorla developed out of the old Everyman connection. My involvement with Mandorla came from an invitation from Simon Roe to be involved with a new team set up to deliver future post-Rites of Passage Events. We eventually pulled together a Team of six: Simon Roe, Sebastian Kelly, Phil Atkinson, Pete Dominey, Patrick Harrison and me.

We had been running our current reincarnation of Mandorla since Autumn 2007. Our first Event was entitled, "Feeding the flame: Authenticity, purpose and power". We had subsequently run two Events per year as follows: "The Snake Prince: Men and the Feminine" in May 2008; "Darkness and gold: Reclaiming life, meaning and authenticity from the ashes of broken dreams" in September 2008; "The Fire Within: Finding a path of understanding, integrity and freedom in the companionship of men" in April 2009; "Time, death and purposeful life" in October 2009.

The forthcoming Event in May 2010 was called, "Into the Wild". I was certainly experiencing a sense of wildness and danger in my life at this point. By then I had yet to endure the disappointment of my conversation with the Consultant Surgeon and my Oncologist, but I knew I was very ill.

Looking back, these Event titles have an unmistakeable ring of authenticity, in terms of describing the path I and others in the Mandorla leadership group were following. It had become apparent to me that what we were offering was different to previous experiences: the team of six lived out these themes during the planning stages and took them to Cae Mabon, where we were effectively inviting others to come and join us, hopefully as equals, in our process and turn it into a bigger collective process of dialogue and deep listening in a community of men.

The feedback we received from participants bears out both the success and also the power and enduring impact of Cae Mabon - Mandorla events time after time:

'P. B.'

The processes are very deep, and I know from the previous two events that it takes weeks and months afterwards to see just what has changed within me.

Being with other men in an authentic, caring, shared work: I have a greater confidence in saying who I am, and what I want – and what I don't want. It is as if I don't need to please other people, or look after them so much, because I have discovered that I am already loved, just for being me.

The walk up the hillside in the dark: why do I always think of myself as solitary, alone, isolated? There are other men in front of me and behind me. Their process matches mine in every way: we are not alone. The more I move out into authenticity (being me), the more I find I am not alone.

It was so affirming to hear other men talk about their Shadow side, and speak about how tormenting it is, to have the shameful, unspeakable, mean-minded, raging Other Self so close in everything I do, say or think. I gained more respect for myself, and more respect for other men. I saw the gold in them.

I loved the rituals! It's a kind of play, playing like a child, without shame or self-consciousness or rational put-downs, and going anywhere my intuition wants to take me. The result is always powerful: this time I let go of the dreadful weight of failed marriages that was hanging round my neck. It sounds so easy (naive) to say, "I let go" but in fact it was that easy, because my imagination was allowed to find me a way -- a way that I could never have found with my rational mind.

The effect of the events is cumulative: this time I could relate to the "Goddess" carved in the tree because I made a new, realistic relationship with Goddess last time, in the "Snake Prince -- Men and the Feminine" gathering. Only through that relationship within myself, could I (this time) release the women in my failed marriages, and release myself too.

The body work: I have gone a long way with "talk therapies" before, but the breathing and body work takes me deeper and faster than anything else I have known, into an unconscious, pre-verbal world of anger, betrayal, loss, terror, need, rage and love. I have no words for what I experience, find, and heal there. And I know that I am not alone when I am there: my partner-men in the work are in that mysterious world with me.

Dancing and chanting for three hours. What the hell! I loved it, I lose myself in it, my body dances for me, and time passes without counting. And I felt physically more alive the next day. The drumming, the fire, the threshold and the shrine, the other men – an experience that cannot be put into words.

I cannot really tell you how thankful I am, for the work of all the facilitators -- for your raw honesty, and willingness to be part of the process and to stand alongside us. I could not have found "my way" without the insight, strength and vulnerability of you all. Thank you!

'M.'

The wonderful timelessness of such a great exploratory weekend in the Company of Men; great stories; welcome opportunities to touch deeply important stuff inside me that is inaccessible in regular life away from the mountain retreat. Restorative for me and a much needed re-charge. No criticisms; brilliant to be able to trust a group of men I didn't know. I come away with new understandings about trust/mistrust inside me. Nobody was ever going to break my whittling stick, yet I thought you might...

Keep the work going.

Warm regards, 'M'

'J.W.'

I've just arrived home.

Time Death and Purposeful living.................. scary stuff.
This was for me indeed a journey in to uncharted waters.

I found this challenging to say the least, there was a moment during the birth thing where I felt I might take off and just keep running like Forest Gump, I'm glad I stayed.

I was deeply moved and humbled by what I heard, saw and felt.

I learnt a great deal and feel it will take some time for me to fully assimilate and integrate all that I learnt.

This experience has added a little more stillness in to my being and for this I am deeply grateful.

To me this work is far beyond the everyday, it feels real in a way that modern living often doesn't, no bullshit.

I would love to do this stuff more often.

Thank you

'J.W.'

The work and my five friends in Mandorla had become very important to me as a source of meaning and bliss in my life. This work and the depth of relationship it offered, was certainly a central aspect of experiencing my bliss as far as I was concerned, so the thought of possibly having to give up this work due to illness was very painful for me.

A number of the current team had been involved in running earlier incarnations of Mandorla or Everyman, where the emphasis had largely been on a 5 day Men's Rites of Passage. At these Events, leaders were offering a space for men through group work, dialogue and individual ritual, to move from a place of psychological adolescence towards a deeper place of male psychological adulthood. We were often given the projection of father figures by participants, as we helped individuals and the group with their process of engagement in psychological development.

Magical moments happened there too. I remember one occasion when I was co-leading an Everyman event with Ron Pyatt. We were working outside in a sand circle, near the replica of an Iron Age roundhouse. Ron was attempting to physically hold up a man who was deep into his own process of individual ritual and deeply collapsed into Ron's arms, pulling him towards the ground. Ron spoke out in a moment of truth and frustration, "I just can't get a handle on this". In the same moment, without me really knowing what was going on, my hand reached down into the sand and I pulled out a drawer handle from two or so inches underneath the surface of the sand. "Here's your handle" I said to Ron, handing the object over to him. Ron, the man, others helping and I all collapsed into laughter and the man then moved on powerfully with his own internal process. As a character once said in the Bob Hope / Bing Crosby movie, 'Road to Rio', we were, "in the groove Jackson!"; the current and the sense of healing were strong.

With Mandorla we were attempting a different approach, where (at least in my mind) we already assumed participants had moved into psychological adulthood. We sought to offer a space as stewards and elders for other to join us, to find their own steward and elder energy within, in the task and process of co-creation around themes of authentic experience of male adulthood.

Otto Scharmer (2007) describes something very similar. We always sought to deepen experience as the Event went on, from the *"Level One"* space of repeating old paradigms and old mental models, through *"Level Two"* (Seeing) and "Level Three" *(Sensing)*, to *"Level Four"* which Otto Scharmer calls "Presencing", an environment of co-creation.

Otto describes this Level Four place as an environment of five distinct movements:" *"Co-initiating"* by "listening to what life wants you to do"; *"Co-sensing"* where in the place of greatest potential you listen *"with your mind and heart wide open"*; *"Co-presencing"* in a place of *"individual and collective stillness"* in order to *"connect to the future that wants to emerge through you"*; *"Co-creating"* through a process of prototyping in order *"to explore the future by doing"*; and finally *"Co-evolving"* an intuitive ecosystem that interconnects people *"through seeing and acting from the whole"* (Page 18).

I feel we had on occasions reached the threshold of Level Three and sometimes Level Four by the middle of the third day, before the forthcoming night's communal ritual space. Our work up to that point always sought to deepen attention, dialogue, listening and experience.

The morning of day three had through a gradual development of these events, come to be the time when I took a lead role as a facilitator and group therapist, where I led a form of group witnessed individual therapeutic dialogue, working with one man at a time in a group of nineteen. These sessions usually lasted around three hours. I would typically work with one man who requested the floor space, exploring his issues through dialogue, reflection and sometimes movement, until he felt he had completed what he wanted to complete – then silence would return until another man requested floor space and we repeated a similar sequence. Very often an issue brought up by one man would reflect very similar issues or challenges current in the lives of other participants. I find this is often the case in therapeutic group work.

It is in this space where I have so far found my deepest bliss around Men's Work. In this communal space, I listen deeply to what each man is saying and I follow my intuition around the only question that seems relevant to me, which is:

"What is needed here right now?"

Sometimes what is needed appears to be empathy and compassion; sometimes gentle or vigorous encouragement; sometimes assertive challenge through naming what appears to be a powerfully toxic internal narrative driving the speaker; sometimes irreverence and humour.

One man at a recent Mandorla Event was talking of his wife's disapproval around his behaviour and apparent thoughtlessness. She had given him instructions to 'Stop, look and listen' every day. If he didn't, she intimated, it would have dire consequences for the future of their relationship.

My response was to say it reminded me of signs children are encouraged to read at level crossings that warn them of the danger of advancing trains. Could he possibly choose three or four other words that were not so infantilising or apocalyptic, and instead would both help him and also validate him in his desire to be more constructive in his relationship?

Through dialogue, we came up with, "Enjoy adult resonance", and a notion that it would be helpful if he should choose to act as if he was already the most thoughtful and receptively mature marriage partner that had ever lived. We had a lot of fun in the group working that one out!

From subsequent feedback, it seems that the approach we came up with had proved useful to him in his relationship.

***

What does it take to "descend into the ashes" as Robert Bly describes it, in order to contribute towards healing the Self by "exiting through the wound"?

Bly contends that somewhere in mid-life, we will descend anyway, whether we choose to or not. But choosing is an act of power which is likely to give that descent meaning and a sense of personal purpose; whilst not choosing invites the intervention of one's shadow self in turbulent and provocative mood or the apparent intervention of the forces of external whims of fate.

I think I was fortunate enough to have an early hint of what was required through experiencing dealing with M.E. in my mid-thirties. I gradually learnt the wisdom of surrender, waiting and the requirement of eventual mindful action to respond, when the time arose where I was called upon to act in a decisive manner.

Without that and my experiences of both personal development work and also men's work, I think I would have been ill equipped to face what I was eventually called upon to face in respect of the challenges of my apparent terminal illness.

I surrendered to the force of the descent into the "dark night of the soul" and was open to undertaking a stormy "sea journey" when I accepted that I was seriously ill and in some form would remain in some state of permanent disability thereafter. I did something very similar when I opened up my heart and allowed myself to believe that I was truly loved and supported by others.

In allowing others to bless me this way, I came to know what it was like to genuinely bless oneself. From that new place of understanding and self-acceptance, it became much easier to turn and face the possibility of my own death and begin a constructive dialogue with that own particular aspect of myself and eventual wise companion in my everyday life.

Somewhere in the above process, perhaps through receiving a consistent blessing from others, I learnt to let go of destructive and toxic self-criticism and the compulsion to shame the Self. As the cacophony of those internal voices diminished, I was able to expand my appreciation of who I was and who I am at the level of the authentic Self. In so doing, I came to love and trust myself with much more consistency and appreciation of the person I am. From a place of relative calmness, even with the constant presence of physical pain, I began to ask myself what was needed from me in terms of conscious and mindful choice: when to ask for specific help from the medical profession; when to open up to offers of

*hands-on and other forms of healing from others;
when to respond to others requests that I continue
with the work I was doing, for example, my
involvement in men's work; when to say yes to
more robust and challenging forms of alternative
healing; when to act in response to the challenges
and demands of personal relationships and the
potential for embarking upon a life partnership in
a relationship of the heart with a life companion
and lover.*

*Through all of the above, I came to know my own
particular wounds, to accept them, to grieve them
and to move on into a greater sense of emotional
freedom.*

***

Above@ Llyn Padarn – photo taken during Mandorla Event
Below: Dad aged 67

Above: Stone Age Roundhouse at Cae Mabon
Below: Cob Cottage at Cae Mabon

CHAPTER 12:

The path of service – intention is everything

Intention is everything in terms of making active choices in the world. But intention without mindfulness is for me, too close to abdicracy, and sometimes too close to things that are much worse. This would be especially so, if I were to hold the view, for example, that "God will guide me in what to do" but at the same time I was not very discerning in differentiating between God's apparent guidance and my own impulsive ego-centred perceptions, beliefs and actions.

On one level, I may want God or The Universe to show me how to be of service. But I also feel, as an implication of the requirement to act with spiritual responsibility that I need to be very alert and receptive in order to hear the response clearly. I then need to make very conscious as well as intuitive choices about how I seek to manifest that in my life and in my contact with those I feel God wants me to serve.

I want and choose to be of service in the world in my work. The word "choice" suggests I am exercising adult personal power and discernment in relation to what to do, how to be, or go about what I do. It seems to me however, to be a very delicate balance between: asking for guidance; surrender (of ego) and willing receptivity to God's influence; responding to my intuition with faith that what I am visioning is the right path; openness to being surprised and to the unfolding of mystery. These are active and mindful choices to be a spiritual adult and being prepared, as poet David Whyte suggests, to "step out of the boat" and have faith, or be open to receiving the deep conviction that I will not drown as I seek to walk towards the vision co-creating itself in front of and within me.

I would connect all these things to a deeper and deeper understanding of the Self, in terms of coming to understand what my bliss is and choosing to connect to the best of my ability with what to me feels like the voice of my authentic Self. In my experience, this happens gradually over time, maybe over the course of a lifetime as it unfolds.

Furthermore, my authentic Self will also include an awareness and crucially, acceptance, of my own shadow aspects.

Jung developed the concept of the human "shadow" as, "One of the archetypal components which play specific roles in the psychic development and social adjustment of everyone" (1994). The Shadow is a frequently disowned aspect of the Self, containing what we have been told or what we tell ourselves is bad or unacceptable about us; and as Robert Bly has pointed out, often also containing what he calls precious "psychic gold" which the world needs access to in order to become a healthier place.

The Persona or so called acceptable public face we present to the world, is often as far removed from what we perceive to be in our Shadow as it possibly could be. So the Persona is certainly not likely to be a reflection of the authentic Self as I would understand it.

I think by now I know most of my own shadow aspects and it has become part of my conscious choice, and mindful intention, to be aware of when it is active. If I am wise, and honest with myself, I am most likely to notice it when someone really annoys me. The chances are they are exhibiting an aspect of my own (at root fearful) shadow self, which I am acting out unconsciously in the world. But instead of recognising how and where I may be doing that, which can be a painful thing to admit to myself, I may be more easily inclined to project my rage or disapproval or contempt on to some external person who may be exhibiting some behaviour which could be an aspect of my own shadow behaviour.

This is known in my professional world as 'projective identification', and is very destructive if instead of recognising what is happening and dealing with it in myself, I choose to pretend in the terminology of Transactional Analysis, that I am 'OK' and they are 'Not OK'. In my way of looking at it, projective identification is the tendency to distance oneself as far as possible from some unresolved or unintegrated aspect of the ego – we cannot own or resolve it because it is too threatening to our sense of ego-self, and it would throw us into cycles of misplaced guilt or shame if we were to acknowledge it as unresolved or unintegrated in our wider authentic Self. It is far too threatening to acknowledge given such concerns, so instead we are likely to project it outwards on to others and see it as a totally unacceptable aspect of the Other. We will be hypercritical if not downright violent towards those we see as carrying such unforgivable flaws. The more disturbed we are by a particular aspect of our own ego or conscious self, the more powerfully we are likely to project it onto others and the more vociferously we are likely to condemn them. The more we do that, the more other people's gaze and focus is directed away from ourselves and psychologically and emotionally speaking the more comfortable we are likely to feel.

Recently I was watching the TV Series "Divine Women" where the historian Bettany Hughes was exploring the presence of the sacred feminine in early religious history (2012). It was a fascinating and powerful programme. Not only did it show how influential and central women were in the early development of the Christian Church, it also showed how women were eventually excluded from the priesthood through both the First Council of Nicaea in AD325 and also the influence of St. Augustine.

The story of St. Augustine (354-430; Bishop of Hippo in North Africa) in particular fascinated me. It appears that prior to returning to the fold of the Christian Church, through the efforts of his mother St. Monica, he was leading an extremely promiscuous life. St. Augustine once back in the Christian community eventually developed the doctrine of "Original Sin", and identified the ultimate responsibility for the 'Fall from the Garden of Eden' resting with 'Eve the temptress'.

As I watched this I could not help but conclude this was a powerful form of projective identification of Augustine's disowned sexual shadow aspects onto women. The result has been devastating for women in Christianity: over 1700 years of discrimination and exclusion including the severe distortion of the true nature of Mary Magdalene and her role and significance in the early Christian story.

It has also been devastating in terms of the effects the concept of "Original Sin" has had on both religious and secular human experience and self-awareness. As I have previously written, I believe it powerfully and toxically distorts the true significance of the Crucifixion and the opportunity that devastating event created to enable human beings to let go of apocalyptic thinking and instead embrace an adult, spiritually responsible developmental transition in to a world of joyful inclusivity, adult spiritual and ethical responsibility and openness to the abundant presence of Grace. This occurs through transformation, when old fear based punitive paradigms are dropped. As Matthew Fox implies, a kind of death is always required to move from what James Alison would refer to as the 'apocalyptic', to the 'transformational'.

Augustine's theology, influence and personal process, seem in direct contrast to those of another influential Christian figure, St. Ignatius Loyola (1491–1556). Loyola was

252

also a man who lived on the edge before he embraced his religion. But in contrast seems to have owned and reintegrated his shadow aspects much more successfully. The results of this process seem very clear when Loyola is often cited by Matthew Fox and others as a direct inspiration behind Creation Centred Spirituality which appears to be inclusive, inter-denominational, open to indigenous native American and other similar spiritual traditions, a prime motivator behind South American liberation theology movements and also open to the return and rise of the sacred feminine, post-patriarchy.

Karen Armstrong (1993) regards Augustine's theology in relation to "original sin" as a reflection of deep sadness and clearly influenced by the fall of Rome to barbarian Northern European tribes. She describes how his doctrine became central to the way Western people came to view the world. Augustine claimed that God had judged and condemned the whole of humanity to eternal damnation because of Adam's one sin: allowing himself to be corrupted by 'Eve the temptress'. Her view is that a religion which sees the humanity of men and women as *"chronically flawed"* can only lead to alienation of people from themselves. This is seen in its most acute form where that religion denigrates sexuality and in particular denigrates women.

Matthew Fox takes this theme further in his book, "A New Reformation" (2006). He regards this Augustinian theology as perfectly expressing the "Punitive Father ideology". He says, *"To teach people, especially young ones, that they are anything but images of God and heirs of divine creativity and responsibility is very dangerous. It leads to low esteem, low expectations, diminished compassion, increased fear, feelings of inferiority and inadequacy – the perfect set up for addictions not only to alcohol and drugs and shopping and sex, but to a religion of the Punitive Father and to its representatives"*(Page 26).

Peter Russell (2009), suggests the, *"essence of enlightenment is a shift in perception"* (Page 96). He contends that the admonition, 'Sinners repent, for the Kingdom of Heaven is at hand" is not simply confirmation of the concept of original sin. If earlier Greek texts are studied it is clear that the word translated as "sin" ("amarto"), is a term derived from archery, meaning having missed the mark, or the target. Russell suggests the target we are seeking is *"inner fulfilment"* but we aim in the wrong direction to achieve it.

I heard something similar from my spiritual director Brenda who has studied early Greek and Aramaic texts. She, like Peter Russell, contends that the commonly understood word "repent" is a mistranslation (particularly by the 17th Century King James Bible) of the word "metanoia", which simply means a change (or transformation) of mind. So, "sinners repent" could be more accurately translated as, *"You who have missed your target, and not found happiness in the"* (external) *"world around you, change your thinking"*, because you will find the happiness you seek in the world within yourself".

Jacquelyn Small covers similar territory in her book "Awakening in Time" (1991). Taking a Buddhist perspective she contends that a shift from unconscious to conscious living will necessitate a realisation that *"all is"* in the *"mind"* (Page 116) in terms of the power of its chosen assumptions to create a living environment around ourselves and with it an apparent "reality". When the mind abandons its assumptions it renders visible the truth of primary experience. The New Testament refers to this process of a change of mind as "metanoia".

Despite the inaccurate use of the word "repentance" to describe this process, there is still some usefulness in exploring the Latin root of the word, as it reveals that the original Latin word "repoenitet" means, *"A mental revolt that affects one's whole way of being"*. For Small, metanoia is, *"An ancient and universal concept underpinning all true spiritual paths"* – it is a *"felt experience"* (or in my words a "lived experience") *"that accompanies any kind of mental conversion"* (P116).

Of course, such a change of mind also invariably includes a change of heart. Small quotes words attributed to Christ:

"As a man thinketh in his heart, so is he". We become *"A new creature and old things are passed away: Behold all things are become new!"* (Page 116).

Small contends that metanoia is, *"The shift from being intellectual only to becoming filled with the soul-quality of creativity or active intelligence. Instead of being a passive recipient of others' ideas (a form of co-dependence), we begin to formulate wisdom gained from our own direct experiences with life, our truth"* (Page 116).

I believe the linguistic and conceptual distortion of "original sin" has spiritually paralysed many people who live within religious paradigms and has also severely amplified feelings of low self-esteem and lack of self-worth amongst many mental health clients in post-Christian culture.

Yes, it is true that Britain is a varied and multi-cultural society, and perhaps very few people anyway would regard themselves as particularly Christian in outlook or beliefs, however much of what ends up in the British therapeutic and mental health culture is nevertheless deeply influenced by the American Psychiatric Association, particularly through the intermittent release of their DSM (diagnostic manual). American populist culture is predominantly right wing and neo-conservative Christian. It is another form of what Ian

255

Taylor describes as *"authoritarian populism"*. This is a culture which Matthew Fox claims is enmeshed in the theology of the "punitive Christian God" and all that flows from it in terms of its interpretation of the concept of "original sin".

Writing in 2006, Fox says, *"Deep ecumenism and interfaith movements allow Christians and others to renew their spiritual roots. But the primary obstacle to reaching an interfaith identity, as the Dalai Lama has observed, is "a bad relationship with one's own faith tradition". Those espousing the theology of the Punitive Father who seeks obedience at all costs harbour a bad relationship with their own faith tradition. They know Original Sin but not Original Blessing. They cannot participate in the interfaith movement"* (Pages 17 - 18).

I find what Matthew Fox says about the "two Christianities" he experiences in the USA, to be very powerful and I also feel we have permeated our own culture similarly: *"There are two Christianities in our midst. One worships a Punitive Father and teaches the doctrine of original sin. It is patriarchal in nature, links readily to fascist powers of control, and demonizes women, the earth, other species, science, and gays and lesbians. It builds on fear and supports empire building.*

The other Christianity recognises the Original Blessing from which all being derives. It recognises awe, rather than sin and guilt, as the starting point of true religion. It thus marvels at today's scientific findings about the wonders of the universe that has brought our being into existence and the wonders of our special home, the earth. It prefers trust over fear and an understanding of a divinity who is source of all things, as much mother as father, as much female as male. It is an emerging "woman church" that does not exclude men, and tries to consider the whole earth as a holy temple" (Pages 19 - 20).

In my view, the doctrine of "original sin" has bred negative self-pathologising, self-imprisonment and passive subjugation to oppressive external control, loss of connection to the authentic Self and those of others, exclusivity, toxic piety and spiritual arrogance and perpetration of acts of human evil.

I'm sure I could add many more things to that list including 'intention' where it is neither mindful nor connected to the truth of the authentic Self, nor adult in its manifestation and active commission in the world.

It seems that we need to be very careful when we choose to describe ourselves as "acting with intention" in our lives and in our work.

***

In a much broader sense perhaps than themes already explored in the preceding chapter, what has been my primary 'intention' in my life? Clearly it has changed over the years as my focus on life and my preoccupations have also changed.

The earliest memory I have was the intention, in childhood to grow up as quickly as I could because I wanted the adult freedom to be who I was, and I experienced childhood or some aspects of it as absolutely stifling and frustrating.

My next recalled intention was to be the best Cub Scout it was possible to be. Apparently I was so taken with the idea, the first weekend of my Cub career, I slept that Saturday night wearing my Cub uniform under my pajamas, in preparation for attending the Armistice Day Memorial Sunday ceremony at our local cenotaph, with our Cub troop. My Mum came in late at night to see if I was sleeping and was alarmed to see my face had turned beetroot red. I was persuaded to ditch the uniform for the rest of the night, but I wore it with some sort of pride for two hours the next day, stood to attention in the pouring rain. On returning home I received a lecture from my Mum on the obscenity of glorifying war through quasi-religious services. I didn't fully take that on board until I was 16 when I recognized the Cubs were in my words, "just another shit paramilitary organisation". This view was easy to adopt as at the age of 10 I had resigned in disgust from the Cubs because they had not made me a senior sixer and I felt they should have done!

When I was 12 and the Deputy Headmaster at our Grammar School told me I was stupid, my intention was to trust only myself in future, because I knew he was wrong as I told myself that I "thought too much to be labelled stupid".

When I was 18 my intention was to love Jane forever and never get a mortgage or get my hair cut ever again. I eventually failed on all fronts with that range of intentions.

When I discovered the work of Joseph Campbell, my intention was to respond to his suggestion to "follow my Bliss" as best I could for the rest of my life. I'm still doing this, and it proved to be a lot more challenging than I thought, until I gave up relying on, or being persuaded by, others to define my bliss and started to define it for myself whatever the cost. Over time it has become much simpler and much easier to do as I recognized it was mostly about just allowing myself to be... my authentic Self.

When I was told in so many words by the Oncologist, that I was going to die, my intention was unequivocal and my language was profane. I intended to live and I've not been doing a bad job of that so far. As a result it is just possible that I am going to live a whole lot longer than I would otherwise have done. The power of intention wedded to the power of receiving faith in the Self from one's Self, from unseen sources and from others, can apparently change the course of a life and move it away from death, back to life again. Central to this intention has been valuing my love for and the love I have received from my partner and those friends and family who truly love me. I'm not naïve enough to think this can happen for everyone. Sometimes the world's brutality takes over and demands the ultimate price from those who should never have to pay such a price. But I'm sure many others with greater material life chances could choose to go on living if they held such a clear intention and were blessed with as much grace as I seem to have been.

**

CHAPTER 13:

And the road goes on forever - living with fear of death

As I reflect on my descent into serious illness with pure right ventricle heart failure and carcinoid syndrome, I recognise that I reached an absolute low point around December 2010 to February 2011. It was a very dark time for me.

During that period, particularly as I moved into the latter stages around February 2011, I almost chose to die; I felt I could not really go on much longer with the physical, emotional and psychic pain of it all. I think I had begun to lose any real sense of meaning in my life, which rendered any thought of a viable future impossible to hold on to. I knew I was, in Hakomi terms, "self-reliant" and a past master at the art of "burdened and enduring" living, but without a core sense of meaning, all those particular strengths came to nothing. I had thought a lot, and talked a lot to colleagues in Mandorla, about the need for resolute stoicism, but my stoicism was wearing dangerously thin whenever I thought about what the future might hold for me.

Somewhere in the middle of, and leading up to this, I had to work through a fear of death, but in the context of the above, also a growing fear of carrying on living.

'Fear of living' is an interesting idea; generally I am a bit of a risk taker in life, so I do not think under normal circumstances that it is a natural way of being in the world for me. I suppose it began to show itself when my symptoms were at their worst: firstly prior to the prescription of any painkillers by my Cardiologist, and later during the December to February period, when I was relatively free of the excruciating pain of earlier, but I was still facing a very uncertain future, feeling very ill indeed and then getting considerably worse by February 2011 when I appeared to have contracted an extremely virulent form of adult chicken pox.

I think as human beings we try to seek solace in even the smallest of things when our backs are truly against the wall. For example, during the pre-pain killer period, being in considerable and relentless pain during waking hours and occasionally allowing myself to think, "well at least I won't feel the pain when I am asleep", I could draw some modicum of solace. Superficially it offered some level of emotional comfort and anticipated respite until I realised with a gradual certainty that I was actually sleeping less and less. So at my worst even this sliver of comfort felt taken away from me.

Attempts to sleep were pretty much an ordeal night after night. I came to absolutely dread going to bed. I could not lie on my back without severe heart pain, but I could not sleep lying on my side either, as it seemed to amplify the abdominal pain emanating from the tumours in my liver. I felt like I was being repeatedly kicked in the stomach by an angry horse. All this time I felt exhausted and desperately in need of sleep and the peace of unconsciousness. But continuing to lie in bed, hoping for something that refused to arrive, became a very futile and dispiriting experience.

In the end, in an attempt to preserve some kind of psychological sanity, all I could do was to go downstairs instead and sit upright in a reclining chair, waiting for exhaustion to overtake me and hopefully lead me into oblivion. As a result I got very little sleep - maybe on average three hours or so of very broken and interrupted sleep each night. The cumulative sleep deprivation sent me almost into a twilight world in waking hours.

Under those circumstances, I found sleep in any kind of normal sense, absolutely impossible. I dealt with it as best as I could, by sitting upright in the chair downstairs all night and propping myself up with cushions. From time to time I would fall unconscious then wake up, half awake and half dreaming, in agony sometime later, half fallen out of the chair or twisted around and laying half horizontal near the floor.

On the many occasions I sat there, either upright or on the floor, absolutely exhausted but also wide awake, I became much more intensely aware of the incessant pain from oedema which made my legs feel like they were on fire or immersed and entangled in vicious stinging nettles. I was also very short of breath and from time to time felt I would suffocate. I just could not get any air into my lungs.

I think I ended up in some kind of semi-permanent altered state: where I believed I would never fully understand what was happening to me, because I could no longer use my brain and intuition to figure this out as my whole range of senses were drowned out with extreme discomfort where no reflective space or opportunity to even approach such a place of reflection existed; where I would never receive any kind of tangible relief ever again, but because of the relentless nature of the pain I also found myself apocalyptically coming to believe that I would not be allowed to die either. I felt stuck in a never ending wasteland, not living but simply half existing in a space between life and death.

Death at that point would have been for me an end to mental and physical torture and a place of divine and blessed peace. But all I could see and experience from that point was endless pain stretching away from me and back into me, forever. That, and the time of onset of adult chicken pox in February 2011, were the times of my most profound fear of life, or as I saw it at the time continued and intense conscious suffering.

I looked so horrible, with suppurating sores all over my face and body, that it was hard to let myself be seen by anyone, not least my clients or supervisees as I grew to feel irrationally ashamed of my appearance. It was a harsh world of adult emotional and physical pain and a sense of being rejected and abandoned by the world, where the child-self within me knew full well it would never receive any comfort or reassurance from anywhere, ever again. Furthermore, financially I felt I had no choice but to keep on working as best I could. It seemed on one hand that I could not afford to live, but on the other hand I was not receiving any opportunity or help to die either.

Neither did the fear of death restrict itself simply to physical death; over time it also encompassed fear of death of relationships and - or loss of love forever in my life. All in all, it became somewhat of a white knuckle roller coaster ride, where at times I felt I had to fight hard simply to hang on to any tangible sense of Self including my sanity.

Thomas Moore (2004) would probably describe all this as a "Dark night of the soul", and for me it was certainly a sustained period of one of the darkest experiences I have known. I had no choice but, in Moore's words, "when you are on a night sea journey, be taken. Don't try to have it finished. Don't try to figure it out. Don't try to outsmart it" (Page 13).

It was most definitely a process of surrender on one level, but as I very gradually adjusted to the pain and its harsh rhythms, I was also slowly able to become more mindful again, about my circumstances and I became increasingly aware, that at some point I would be called to act, and in so doing I would also have to act decisively with courage and clear intention if I was ever going to heal on any kind of level.

As my illness silently and unknown to me, progressed in the period prior to the onset of these dramatic somatic changes, I was doing my best to stay grounded and optimistic. I had begun a friendship connection with "K" whom I met through my work at a time when I was not really aware of being seriously ill. I was more aware of slowly emerging from my grief around both the end of my marriage to Lis and also the painful but sweet short lived relationship with Andrea.

K was clear from the beginning when she realised I was not in a relationship, and assumed therefore that I was available, that she wanted a relationship with me and changed aspects of her working life to make this more possible. Nevertheless, I had already said I felt it was too soon for me. I did want a friendship, but I could not promise anything beyond that. Inevitably I suppose given K's feelings, it soon became a very intense friendship, although the intensity came more from K than from me. On one level she seemed to accept what I said but clearly and frequently stated she wanted more.

I genuinely liked K and enjoyed her company, lively energy and sense of fun. I don't think I ever gave her false promises nor pretended to feel anything I did not feel. Nevertheless over time I felt drawn inexorably into an intense dynamic that carried a lot of my familiar shadow aspects that were still very active at that time. The most obvious of these being a tendency to unhelpfully blur what I termed "compassion" and "emotional rescuing". As a result, I stayed silent through not wanting to hurt someone, especially a woman. I became involved in a physical dimension to the relationship whilst at the same time feeling guilty for having sexual feelings at all given my emotional ambivalence. I also blew hot and cold about the desire for and involvement in sexual contact and lack of assertiveness around the reality of my true feelings.

To be fair to myself, on more than one occasion I did make considerable attempts to assert myself to say I felt we could not continue with a physical connection and that we really only could continue to meet as friends, but I found it hard to sustain these assertive pronouncements. On one or two of those occasions K reacted with intense, semi-hysterical, emotion which I found very hard to deal with in any kind of constructive way for either of us. Had I not been so progressively and rapidly falling into serious illness at the time, I might have acted differently.

As it was, I chose to stay with the "connection" (K got very annoyed I called it by that name), and in reality we did eventually develop a relationship that lasted a considerable time, during which despite everything, through my active choice to stay with being open to loving K as much as I was able, I grew to genuinely love her.

The choices I made then, made it all the more painful to let go when I eventually did so, in October 2011. What made it even more difficult was growing also to love K's three daughters whom I gradually got to know well over that time. I was especially close to her eldest daughter, who spent hours talking to me about her hopes and dreams for the future. I was genuinely moved and inspired by her infectious enthusiasm for life. When K and I parted in October 2011, I felt I had profoundly lost a genuinely loving connection to four people.

However, I also received a lot of help and support during this period up to February 2011. K herself offered a great deal of support in her own way, particularly through introducing me to the power of prayer through recitation of the Sikh "Shabads". For a long period of time K phoned me each morning to offer an opportunity for the two of us to jointly recite these Sikh Prayers in Punjabi. I found this gave me a sense of continuity and groundedness, especially as the physical symptoms of my illness became more complex and difficult to deal with mentally. But it also became a process where I felt I had some sort of misplaced sense of duty to continue with it.

I was also contacted out of the blue, via a mutual friend, by an ex-colleague Cathy, with whom I had worked, and whom I had helped, many years previously. She had heard of my illness and now working as a Reiki healer and Homeopath, in partnership with another healer Julie, she offered to give me regular healing sessions to help me deal with the cancer and the heart failure. I felt considerably moved by their generosity in offering sessions free of charge - even though I chose to pay Cathy and Julie, their gesture was typical of my experiences at that time of people giving me help with spontaneous open heartedness. Such gestures amplified and if it was needed, restored a great deal of faith within me about the inherent goodness of human beings.

This turned out to be a very deep and important connection and in terms of the level of generosity offered, it was typical of the way genuine friends rallied round at the time of the onset of my illness, when it was clear to anyone who knew me that I was facing something very challenging indeed to deal with, whilst still attempting to earn a living and be of service in the world in my work.

The consistent care, support, and love of my relatives, friends and colleagues in Mandorla and other professional and personal support groups, has been both vital and invaluable.

✳✳✳

Why is 'fear of life' such a powerful presence in the world?

I think this is something to do with our human habit of living and thinking apocalyptically. Our

whole social media focus and discourse seems to be deliberately rooted in drama and the adversarial notion of someone or some people being to blame for our current state of affairs, including immoral or criminal social behaviours, whilst the rest of us are innocent victims.

I seem to recall from my social work student days that Geoff Pearson (author of "The Deviant Imagination" [1975]) had also written a book called "Hooligans: A history of respectable fears" [1983] in which he pointed out that the familiar argument, "things are much worse now than they were twenty years ago", was repeated regularly in the media of the day and that this has been going on pretty consistently since the 1800s or even earlier: that what was being said about 'criminal behaviour' then, was very close to what is described now, and that the implied 'golden age' of twenty years previously has never really existed.

Sometimes this attempt to define so called 'reality' is blatant and very political, for example, David Cameron's assertion that the Government that preceded his own was so bad that we are now living in a place he describes as "broken Britain". Hence the need for severe measures of control, especially of the underclass, by way of stringent cuts in welfare benefits. After all, "we support the strivers, and the opposition supports the skivers". Dog-whistle politics indeed! What is the reality? Perhaps, comparatively, the moral values of the corporate and banking sector have created much more damage to our social fabric than our media has even to date acknowledged.

Apart from the dubious ideological and political aspects of the above, that kind of discourse pitches our society headlong into the psychology of the "Drama Triangle", where someone else is to blame, and it's certainly not us. So we project on to them all the dubious moral and behavioural traits we employ but simultaneously deny in ourselves, and doesn't that feel good?

Well no, ultimately it does not, because it creates a climate of deep fear of personal change, and unwillingness to exercise adult personal responsibility for our own actions, and we remain stuck in disempowered self-created misery or vindictiveness, which in the long term poisons us and disables us just as much if not more than it disables and poisons others.

Ultimately I regard this as a fear of living and thus a fear of one's own power to choose to think, be and live differently, in a world of mutual support, encouragement and faith in ourselves and others. I feel we block so much help from unseen sources through this kind of apocalyptic thinking that we make life on this planet so much harder than it need be.

And then we have an annoying tendency to blame God for such injustices in the world! Yes, natural disasters happen, but human beings also make their own political and economic decisions about where vulnerable people end up living – on flood plains, or in places of physical danger. We create more apocalyptic phenomena than we give ourselves credit for!

***

Dave P., Pete, John, Roy, Dave M., and Simon

CHAPTER 14:

Facing fear and feeling death's friendship

In October 2009, I was a co-facilitator with my Mandorla colleagues on the Event, "Time, death and purposeful life". Through dialogue, research and preparation for the Event, I revisited the writings of Carlos Castaneda, particularly Castaneda's book published in 1972, "Journey to Ixtlan: The Lessons of Don Juan".

These writings and our discussions helped me to recognise and understand the wisdom of developing a benevolent, loving and accepting relationship with the archetypal figure I could regard as a manifestation of my own death. Castaneda suggests "death" is our truest friend and wisest source of wisdom about how to be and how to live: to that end we do well to seek a daily dialogue with our own death.

In my experience, my "death" has so far shown itself in many forms.

For example:

- Sometimes I feel death in its broadest sense as an anticipation of the end of my time in this life on this earth;

- Sometimes I feel death in an aspect of my own shadow self where fear is present and influences me to pull back, avoid risk, think apocalyptically or project my own insecurities on to others as their problem rather than my own;

- Sometimes I feel death as I sense something passing away from me never to return, whether this is a connection with someone, a loss of physical ability, or an opportunity to experience something I once loved to undertake but am no longer capable of doing;

- Sometimes I feel death as an accumulation of wisdom and a sense of growing peace with who or what I am becoming or in terms of my authentic Self, perhaps what I am returning to after years of anxious wandering and sense of loss.

Sometimes I feel death in its broadest sense as the end of my time in this life on this earth:

Although I was not, and as yet am still not ready to leave this life – when I seriously took on board the possibility in 2010 that I may only live another 3 years or so at most, I became very focused on what was important to me. It took me a while to realise it, but it was the beginning of receiving an absolutely priceless gift of emotional freedom, of which I will say more in the next chapter.

In terms of settling my affairs, did I have a lot of reconciliation work to do for past actions that I had come to regret? When I thought about it, the answer was mostly "no", since I recognised what motivated a lot of my anxious thoughts around past actions was probably some unhealthy form of attempting to sanitise my reputation, so when I died people wouldn't see me in such a bad light as they may have otherwise done. Letting go of that particular worry helped me considerably to move into a place I now regard as very healthy, where I do not hold very much at all in the way of anxieties or fear about what people might think of me or how they might judge me. In fact I have come to regard this as one powerful element that I allowed to die within me: fear about my personal and professional reputation. It has become one of the central aspects that have helped me immeasurably move away from the 'Via Negativa' into the 'Via Positiva'. As Matthew Fox suggested, a kind of death is always required and that was one death into which I was happy to surrender.

I also gradually came to realise that if God wanted me to put things right, people would reappear again in my life for me to do so. This has happened with one or two people, and not others. Where people have re-appeared I have mostly found myself pleased to have the opportunity to be with them again and we have both taken an opportunity to sit together in some sense of mutual acceptance and forgiveness without much need for words. Where people have not reappeared I take it that my task is to accept the responsibility for the things I have done to hurt them, accepting how and why I lived out my own shadow behaviour and then asking for forgiveness and forgiving them for whatever wrongs I may have once felt they did to me.

I recall when Lis and I were still married, I was absolutely furious about something she had said to me and was experiencing it as proof of her lack of love for me. I was sat alone in our bedroom, immersed in fury and self-pity. I heard a voice plain as day say, "John, you have to let go of that resentment". I'm not really sure where the voice came from, but to this day I still feel I was in the presence of a voice speaking that was both full of love and compassion for me, and also very assertive.

Being a little addicted to the erroneous idea that I was the wronged party, it took me a while to live out that advice, but I am so grateful I did. Because now I can see Lis and I were both acting from a mutual place of fear, and at the same time our relationship was a precious gift to both of us. Now in the light of my possible death, I can see just how trivial that fear is compared to the genuine love I feel for Lis, and the absolute delight I experience in spending time in company with her and her excellent partner Dan.

In terms of the future, how much does it really matter? If I want to be part of the change I want to see in the world, why not do and be it now? Why wait? I may not be around when the future turns up and I won't have done anything much either.

So this has become a commitment to live as fully in the present as I can, coupled with continued mindful awareness of continuing to the best of my ability to follow my bliss. The present moment is absolutely full of possibility, promise and creativity – do it, be it, live it, change the world for the better in whatever way feels authentic to you. In my experience when you fully embrace that, the help, energy and encouragement you feel coming back to you is enormous, powerful, frequently joyous and celebratory. I am allowing myself to be as present as possible in the here and now moment, whilst staying active around holding a vision for myself and the way I choose to be, both now and in the future.

I am particularly moved by the work of Dewitt Jones (*see www.dewittjones.com),* a noted American photographer who has worked for National Geographic Magazine. In his DVD, *"Celebrate what's right with the world",* published by Star Thrower in the USA (2001), he suggests that what we believe is what we see, and that what we see becomes our reality. In other words, our perceptions and beliefs colour everything… like begets like as I have already suggested.

Furthermore, as I have so often found in my reading and explorations, different people, from very different perspectives in terms of occupation and life experience, tend to say very similar things about how we can know life at the level of the authentic Self.

For example, a lot of the points made by Dewitt Jones appear to echo Matthew Fox's description of the 'Via Negativa', where I am likely to be locked into a way of seeing that simply reflects some form of paranoia. It is a way of seeing that will highlight apocalypse, chaos and the need to attack others and-or defend myself from them as best I can, in a diminishing world of increasing scarcity. However, if I choose to seek out, in a more expansive and inclusive fashion which chooses as a starting point, what might already be right with the world, then I am already much closer to Fox's notion of the 'Via Positiva', where I have the opportunity to begin to experience a world of abundance and from a place of metanoia, I can begin to contribute to universal nourishment of myself and others through acts of authentic alignment with my deeper human qualities. In so doing I both invite and support transformation within myself and amongst others.

I can vision a better world for myself and also as an act of giving and blessing for others; in so doing I may contribute to a collective and powerful form of healthy co-creation within the human community. I can do that because I am choosing to place greater emphasis on what is already right with the world, rather than what is wrong with the world.

Sometimes I feel death in an aspect of my own shadow self when fear is present:

Fear can creep up on you, like an oncoming tide where one minute you feel you are standing on safe sand in warm sunlight then all of a sudden you are surrounded by water and the light is fading fast. What is rushing in with the tide is the accumulation of all your past so called "failures" and a growing conviction you do not, or no longer have the ability to face what life is now throwing at you. Soon you will go under. Yes, you will if you believe it.

This can happen through a chance word of criticism or sudden experience of insecurity, where all your deepest fears flow back in to haunt you and convince you that you are still a helpless child after all. Yes, your traumatised child self may suddenly be running the show but she or he need not be allowed to do so. Take a deep breath instead, and remember you can choose to reassert your adult ability to be active and competent in the world. Your frightened child self will eventually be reassured.

The above line of thought occurred to me when Carol and I were in County Mayo, Ireland, enjoying a peaceful time exploring the shoreline where a river estuary met the Atlantic Ocean. Everything seemed fine and the oncoming tide seemed a long way away. Suddenly we realised we were becoming surrounded by water as we were unknowingly actually standing on a sandbank. I first felt fear, then a sense of incompetence and then we struck out for the shore in an act of survival. It was a sobering lesson to remain vigilant of one's surroundings and not take anything for granted.

My brief feeling of incompetence was a symbolic reflection of a powerful example of suddenly meeting one's shadow, which had involved Carol and I on the outward journey to Ireland. We had passed through check-in and security at Liverpool John Lennon Airport. It had been a difficult process. I had made a mistake a few days previously when attempting to book our flights on line in the cheapest way possible, only to find at the check-in desk that we had to pay an extra £110 each way for baggage. I'll leave the reader to guess which airline was responsible for that particular policy!

Not only had this been a big shock, it had severely delayed us and left little time to clear security and board the flight. As we entered the duty free area Carol and I both went off to find the toilets prior to the flight, arranging to meet back next to the bureau de change desk. As I looked for the signs for the gent's toilet I didn't notice in my somewhat agitated state that there was one situated next to the bureau de change, instead following signs across the duty free area and down the stairs.

On completion I was on my way back when my mobile phone rang and Carol was speaking to me in a panicky voice asking (it felt like demanding) to know where I was. I eventually located her at the foot of the stairs and she told me she was really angry with me because she had been "waiting for ages" at the bureau de change desk. I tried to explain myself and instead thought I heard her say I was "useless".

I was already feeling bad about my previous apparent incompetence with the booking, and to hear I was "useless" flooded me with feeling and memory of the times my father (gifted at mathematics and skilled with figures) had contemptuously dismissed me and my abilities as "useless". I felt angry and hurt. Carol felt angry and hurt that I had apparently abandoned her. We seethed in each other's company for a good half an hour until we slowly came round into adult space again. Reflecting afterwards Carol recognised her deepest fear of 'abandonment' had been triggered, and I recognised my deepest fear of 'financial insecurity' and an accompanying sense of overwhelming incompetence had also been triggered.

What came as rather a revelation to us both was how quickly we both engaged in shadow projection of our deepest fears on to the other from the poisoned well of our own distorted personal narratives, which without dialogue symbolically spoke to each other in such a way that they toxically matched, and in so doing, co-created a

277

simultaneous parallel reality of non-communicated self-fulfilling prophecies: both apocalyptic, both rooted in scarcity consciousness. And the both of us really do love each other!!

Co-creation can be mindful and collaborative, or silent and toxic – we choose what realities we live by.

Sometimes I feel death as I sense something passing away from me never to return:

I have always loved mountains and also the majesty of nature's remote places. At times I have felt very close to my authentic Self and to what I perceive as God, as I have sat awestruck on the top of a high peak, looking out at and on the world, feeling what UK climber and mountaineer Joe Simpson once called the "beckoning silence". I have tended to feel this most in very remote places – on the Aiguille du Midi in the Mont Banc Massif; on the Aonach Eagach Ridge in Glencoe in winter; in the caves of the Mesa Verde in the State of Colorado, USA; sitting on the summit of Sgurr Alasdair in the Cuillin Hills of the Isle of Skye. I can see myself possibly visiting accessible tourist places like the Mesa Verde again, but due to my health situation and need for regular access to prescribed medication, I find it hard to envision me, after a strenuous journey under my own steam, sitting again on a mountain top, looking out at the magnificence of nature.

In a daft kind of way it was always my ambition to climb the Matterhorn in the year of my 70th birthday. I think I have gently let go of many such ambitions. Something may happen in future, but I am not over invested in it anymore. Literal mountain tops may pass away from me, but I may still sit and experience the world from many more symbolic mountain tops before my time on this earth is over.

When it comes, I fully expect to be on the final mountain, with my own death, as Carlos Castaneda has already written in "Journey to Ixtlan" (1972):

"And thus you will dance your death here, on this hilltop, at the end of the day. And in your last dance you will tell of your struggle, of the battles you have won and lost; you will tell of your joys and bewilderments upon encountering personal power. Your dance will tell about the secrets and about the marvels you have stored. And your death will sit here and watch you."

"The dying sun will glow on you without burning, as it has done today. The wind will be soft and mellow and your hilltop will tremble. As you reach the end of your dance you will look at the sun, for you will never see it again in waking or in dreaming, and then your death will point to the south. To the vastness". (P189)

Sometimes I feel death as an accumulation of wisdom and a sense of peace with who or what I am becoming or in terms of my authentic Self, perhaps what I am returning to after years of anxious wandering and sense of loss:

I trust myself now. Mostly, I do not bullshit and I do not deceive. If I find myself doing so, I am generally quick to recognise why and what aspect of my shadow self still requires integration and to be owned responsibly by me, in a mindful and loving way. By and large I now have the wisdom to love myself and I know this simultaneously gives me the ability and the gift to love and bless others.

Despite years of believing otherwise, on some occasions more forcibly than others, I know I am fine and well in my soul and blessed, as I always have been. I just didn't realise it, thought I deserved it nor chose to accept it before.

My authentic Self is intact and knows me well. It accepts me and loves me and celebrates who I am and what I choose to do and be in the world, when I am following its wisdom and guidance accumulated over years of living.

The difference now is that I am actively and mindfully choosing to live as much as I can in the most alive place accessible to me in this life, the present moment. Here, life is rich, generous, and potentially endlessly creative. Why choose to be anywhere else?

***

What is "death" really?

In the world of apocalyptical thinking it is the end of all things: hope, ambition, optimism, human aspiration, the future, life itself. All that remain are ashes, pain, grief, bleakness and broken dreams.

However, viewed from an "eschatological" (or developmental and transformative) perspective, it is simply the end of one thing and the potential beginning of another or other things. It is a time of anticipated transition, a shift in energy and in human terms, perhaps also a shift in perception – "metanoia" in its truest sense. But in my experience the potential can probably only be fully realised if one really is willing to let go.

Not too long ago, I had a conversation with my spiritual director, Brenda, who had done some recent research on the origins of the word "Apostle". Apparently in the Greek, and possibly Aramaic, context it meant to "let go... of everything". I'm not much of a theologian, but I seem to recall Christ had said to the Apostles something along the lines of, "Let go of everything and follow me".

If we take that metaphorically and symbolically, it seems the wise aspect (or "Christ" aspect for some) of the Self – the "authentic Self" in my terms, knows that in order to embrace metanoia, one must let go of all previous certainties. Matthew Fox says pretty much the same when he suggests that a kind of death is always required, to move from apocalyptic ('Via Negativa') to eschatological – transformational ('Via Positiva') being and living.

My experience of this process has been at times apparently paradoxical: I knew I had to let go of control and surrender to "the Dark Night of the Soul" in order to even create the possibility of healing from serious illness, whilst at the same time, I needed to be fully mindful of the need to act decisively and unequivocally when called upon. I acted with true intention around decisions in my professional life, personal relationships and around my choice of the harder path of healing using Homeopathic remedies.

I also let go of 'knowing' in the midst of my adult chicken pox crisis and of the certainty that I could return to earning my living in the way that had so fulfilled me up to that point. I let go of the certainty that I could forever use my cognitive abilities to continue to practice my craft in the helping professions. As I had discovered with M.E. years previously, the point of genuine surrender and openness to help from unseen sources, was actually the precise turning point in my healing.

For me, "death" has meant opening up to life on a scale I had hitherto not known. I now experience *the world with more insight, more emotional resonance, and more breadth of vision, more openness to faith, than I had ever done so before.*

When I 'let go', I did so in a way that reminds me, on reflection, of the Robert Frost poem that inspired the title of M. Scott Peck's book, "The Road Less Travelled" (1978).

The poem (Frost, R. 1920) read,

"Two roads diverged in a wood, and I – I took the one less travelled by,

And that has made all the difference".

***

CHAPTER 15:

Grace and Illness Part 2 – breakthrough

By January 2011, despite the pain, I had got used to the daily experience of living with my own possible demise or recovery. I was taking regular allopathic medication: Lanreotide injections to block production of and damage to the heart from the hormone 5HIAA (Serotonin); Bumetanide and Spironolactone for abdominal and lower limb oedema; Tramadol for tumour pain. I was also regularly receiving Reiki Healing from Julie, Acupuncture from my acupuncturist Danielle and Homeopathic Remedies from Cathy in the form of Crataegus for the heart functioning and Taraxacum for tumours in the liver. I was also doing daily Sikh 'Shabads Prayers' five days a week with K.

I decided against following a strict Gerson Diet for the tumours when I discovered this would involve frequent juicing of raw organic vegetables and organic fruit. Even though I quite liked the idea of organic vegetables and fruit, the discipline required, not to mention the time necessary, to use a suitable organic juicer every few hours of every day, every week, for years, seemed just too much and too overwhelming for me to deal with. But if I am honest, I would have to say that the real clincher was realising I would unfortunately also need to undertake organic coffee enemas up to four times day. I recognised in no uncertain terms, that was not my cup of tea, so to speak! I had asked my acupuncturist Danielle why it needed to be organic; I asked, "Given where you put it, does it really matter if it's organic or not?" She assured me organic was essential – she pointed me in the direction of very interesting website photographs of results people had achieved from this procedure. They were horribly fascinating and strangely compelling; nevertheless, I declined this course of action anyway!

So instead, and with an internal sigh of relief at what I had narrowly escaped, I asked Cathy to take me further in to homeopathic healing processes around the tumours. Cathy is a very gifted homeopath and works at physical, spiritual and metaphysical levels. She had been prescribing a number of helpful remedies previously that, one by one, addressed my illness on a deeper level, bringing an increased sense of well-being and symptom relief. However, it felt like we had reached some sort of plateau, where limited progress was available unless I elected to follow a much more radical course of action.

It had then got to the stage where Cathy felt we needed to go much deeper to effect a fundamental shift towards the possibility of a permanent recovery from the cancer and secondary tumours. She shared with me that in her opinion, the cancer was probably curable but it would either take a very long time with gradual application of homeopathic remedies, or we could take a much more direct and intense route with the possibility of a greater chance of success. She warned me that there were likely to be very powerful effects from the process if I were to choose the more direct route. I heard Cathy's advice and warning with concern but also with a sense of stoic fatalism: if I was going to get better, I simply had to take up this challenge. Although I had become used to the more regular medical and complementary medicine processes, I knew I was still very ill and it felt to me that I was simply holding the power to reduce my life expectancy in check for a while. I could follow Cathy's gradual route, but there was no guarantee that I would not be overtaken and overwhelmed by the spreading of cancer whilst I was in the middle of that process. I decided that I absolutely needed to take the risk, so I did. Cathy prescribed a particular remedy that was based on Wild Nettle – she was working very intuitively at this time and her choice was uncannily accurate in terms of the process I needed to undertake. The somatic response to this remedy was almost instantaneous, but I hadn't nearly enough anticipated what an absolute ordeal it would turn out to be for me.

Barely a week into the new homeopathic regime, I was dismayed and somewhat alarmed to find that I had developed full blown adult chicken pox. I had experienced most childhood illnesses: mumps, serious influenza, measles; tonsillitis; something akin to glandular fever – but I had never had chicken pox. It is apparently very unpleasant in childhood, but if you have the misfortune to develop it in adulthood it can be a very onerous experience indeed. I could not believe how rapidly it spread all over my body from the first few hours of discomfort and understated changes to my skin pigmentation, to entire body coverage of blisters and suppurating sores.

Cathy's view was that the virus had been locked in my vital organs since childhood, contributing considerably to the severe compromising of my immune system and therefore probably a forerunner of the development of carcinoid syndrome. It was a necessary and good thing that the body was now releasing it via illness. I recognised the likely truth of this view, but nevertheless its effects were simply devastating.

I was covered in less than twelve hours in suppurating sores and blisters from head to toe; I felt extremely ill and worst of all I became feverish and delirious to the extent that it quickly became obvious that I was also experiencing serious neurological imbalances.

I had become used to relying on the power and flexibility of my cognitive abilities to help me make sense of most things, and more often than not to come up with a creative response to whatever challenges I was facing, but this development was something I had not experienced before to this devastating degree. Admittedly, when I had Myalgic Encephalomyelitis in the 1980s, I lost some level of cognitive functioning for a while: mostly I remember a period when I was forming words and sentences quite normally and intelligibly in my mind, but when I came to speak what came out was gobbledegook and gibberish. It felt embarrassing at the time, especially when I was attempting to chair meetings, but I went off sick very shortly after that and that particular symptom quickly disappeared. This however, was altogether different and much more frightening to experience.

The most fear-filled aspect of this new development was that I felt I was literally losing my mind and could no longer use my brain. It simply would not function anymore. I was until this point, still carrying on working as best I could given the considerable physical pain I was constantly experiencing. I could not afford to stop, and although I looked and felt terrible, until the awful realisation I eventually had of also experiencing neurological imbalance, I could still work quite effectively with both clients and supervisees.

However, by the second week of my considerable discomfort and then subsequent apparent onset of severe neurological changes, I quickly recognised that with the addition of this neurological dysfunction, not only could I not continue anymore with day to day work, I began to think that maybe I would never again have the brain capacity to do the work I had spent years training to do and years refining through accumulated experience and development of my craft.

I recognised I had to stop, albeit as it turned out in retrospect, only for a further week or so. I basically took emergency leave whilst I attempted to stem the rising panic I felt within me and also tried to work out what to do for the best for the future, given the apparent loss of my cognitive abilities and all that went with it in terms of employment and livelihood.

As I think back on this time I know it was and still remains the most disturbing and frightening aspect of my journey so far – even worse than a near death experience that was to follow in early July 2011. Why? Because I felt I was witnessing with full and terrifying consciousness, but with absolutely no power whatsoever to do anything about it, a rapid descent into what felt to me like pre-senile dementia or perhaps Alzheimer's disease. I remember sitting down repeatedly with a pen and paper trying to write in order to understand what was happening to me. I spent hours doing this, with more and more effort and increasing layers of absolute cognitive confusion.

All I could produce on the reams of paper were sentence after sentence that read, "I don't understand". Each time I saw Cathy that was also all I could say. She looked extremely concerned but took very deep breaths and encouraged me to stay with the process. I tried to talk to her, and to K, to describe what I was experiencing, but unlike now, I just could not find the words to articulate the experience. All I could do was repeatedly look at Cathy or K with panicky and uncomprehending eyes and say, "I don't understand. I just don't understand no matter how hard I try".

Thankfully three or four weeks after the onset of the initial symptoms, the worst was over as my faculties gradually recovered, even though the suppurating sores persisted for a very long time afterwards. I had been doing quite well using lotions and massage to help the open sores on my legs heal, that had been created by the earlier oedema – but once I developed chicken pox sores, the wounds on both legs opened up again. To this day, three years later, I still have the wounds although they are now very gradually healing.

In the midst of those awful days I simply wanted to die. Even someone with a lifetime's experience of stoicism and being "burdened and enduring" was finding it next to impossible to endure this ordeal. I really could not face going on anymore. I would never seriously consider taking my own life – it just doesn't seem to be in me to do so, perhaps my authentic Self was by then still just too strong to go down that road, despite the fact that I felt completely adrift from my authentic Self at that time, but it is true to say that on a number of occasions I absolutely longed for death to overtake me.

I think once or twice I even prayed to die, but thankfully God did not grant that particular prayer. Even as I began to recover, my faith was severely shaken but ultimately not broken. Talking to Cathy months afterwards she confided that the severity of my symptoms had really shaken her, and almost caused her to lose her own faith and belief in herself and her accumulated wisdom. Fortunately for me, she did not lose her faith and she kept encouraging me not to give up, although, like mine, her faith was tested to the limit in a most powerful and demanding way.

Since then, I have been on a powerful road to recovery that had a further severe test awaiting me in the forthcoming July. It helps me to realise that when we choose to be adult in the world, step up to the plate to stand alongside God if we can, we may well be severely tested and our faith, or perhaps more accurately our willingness to receive faith from unseen sources, may be tested to the greatest degree of all. It seems to me, that if a severe test of faith is confronting me, then this may well be one way that the world of the spiritual adult is differentiated from the state of infantilised spirituality that many of us are growing out of as we seek a more authentic understanding of the world and our place within it.

There may be many other paths to faith, which help the shift from infantilised to adult spirituality, but that was not the one I chose. I think for me, it turned out to be as it should have been, because for me at least, faith and its accompanying twin trust are everything at the end of the day. It seems whichever road is taken, one way or another, we are being called powerfully into spiritual adulthood and away from spiritual infantilism. That being the case, if we cannot hold faith or be receptive to faith, in the midst of the darkest hour, it seems to me that we will not be able to step into that spiritual place of co-creation alongside God. It may be true for many, as I feel it was for me, that I had to be ready to go through what writers like T.S. Elliot have previously described as a fiery crucible, a holy fire.

My experience of this particular faith path has been that with the right attitude it becomes an almost alchemical process of metaphorically turning base metal into gold. If I was completely unprepared for what I eventually went through, I feel what could have happened was that I would have simply burned up and expired. It was in my experience, uncompromisingly tough, but degrees of faith and various aspects of trust are what pulled me through time after time. I feel that nothing else would have saved me. Furthermore, I feel faith and trust have also given me every joy and freedom I now experience: especially emotional freedom.

There were moments of tough love during this trying time. We held a pre-Mandorla Planning Weekend at my house. Phil was the first to arrive, giving me a hug and offering his usual enormous sense of warmth and also this time, a new energy of deep sympathy, commiserating with me on how awful the experience must be for me. Ten minutes later, the others from the Mandorla team arrived. Phil met them at the door with an upbeat greeting of, "Hey lads, come inside and have a look at Spotty Muldoon!"....... Bastard!!!

Some considerable time after the chicken pox infection, I was driving from home to my regular (some of them would say I am anything but "regular"!) attendance at the Leeds Men's Group which meets fortnightly on Sunday evenings throughout the year. It has become a lifeline and source of fantastic support for me. The Group has three of us from the Mandorla leadership team as members and also a high number of other members have attended Mandorla Events, some having attended many times. Even outwith Mandorla, we are a solid Group in our own right with, in my opinion, a collection of excellent, honest, supportive, challenging and emotionally loving men.

It was a beautiful early summer's evening as I was driving through rural West Yorkshire from Ilkley into Otley, on my way to Leeds. I looked over to the right and saw dappled light spread across deep green fields and just drank in the view with deep nourishment. Almost immediately I also heard a voice inside my head say, "Enjoy it whilst you can, you could be dead soon". I startled myself as I spoke out loud in reply. It sounded like the unmistakeable voice of my authentic Self, "Yes, thanks for your advice and now keep your counsel. I'll go when God and I are ready and not a moment before". Immediately in that moment, I felt all the weight of life and death lifted from my shoulders and I was flooded on an emotional level with a sense of complete freedom and a profoundly deep feeling of peace within my whole being.

I stayed intensely in that space for hours afterwards, talking of the experience when I got to the Men's Group later that evening. A sense of lightness and ease stayed with me for a good fortnight or so after that, until the power of it very gradually faded into the background of my daily rhythm of life.

When the title of this book revealed itself to me, I knew immediately that "Fields of Freedom" was what I had seen that early summer evening as I drove through rural West Yorkshire towards Leeds. I saw those fields again in a different form in Ireland, at the excavated Neolithic settlement of Ceide Fields which I will describe in Chapter 16.

This West Yorkshire experience coupled with my experiences at Ceide Fields in County Mayo, underlined the appropriateness of the title my authentic Self had chosen for this book. The memory and lived experience of that moment of communion with "Fields of Freedom" has become a new threshold from which I now experience the world.

***

What is the reality of choosing to take the shamanic path, the one that Joseph Campbell refers to in effect as, the ultimate deal in life?

"Follow your bliss. The heroic life is living the individual adventure. There is no security in following the call to adventure. Nothing is exciting if you know what the outcome is going to be. To refuse the call means stagnation", and in my case I think it would have simply meant physical death.

It seems to me that the significance of taking such a step rests on one's intention to be as authentic as possible, whilst being mindful to neither be over inflated in an egocentric sense, nor unnecessarily deferential about one's abilities and personal strengths.

When I started writing this book, my initial motivation was simply to be a witness to my own experience: it was an act of self-comfort on one level. I was trying to understand what was happening to me and find some solace in the answers I hoped to uncover through observation of and reflection on my own process. At some point, I realised what I was discovering might be of help to others and then, perhaps because of the extreme nature of those (particularly initial) experiences, I felt on some level I may have been in some way 'called upon' to witness and report on the whole process as a way of helping others facing similar frightening circumstances to empower themselves and honour their own authentic experiences, hopefully with reassuring encouragement from me.

Perhaps it was possible that what was happening to me was no accident of nature, and perhaps because of my self-awareness and some ability to express myself in writing, I was potentially in a position to help many other people. It was then that Joseph Campbell's idea of a "shamanic journey" began to make some real sense to me. Perhaps in some way, my 'job' was to go to extreme places within my own interior world in order to bring something back of value and benefit to the community of which I am a part.

If so, what is it, what 'diamond' have I brought back with me from this journey? I think I have brought back:

An awareness that fear is not to be trusted as a guide of what to risk and what not to risk in life: that the apparent death sentence I received was not by any means the full story; that it is in some circumstances, possible through choice and mindful intention, with the help of 'grace' to change one's future for the better. I also suggest that it is vital to never give up; that we are loved much more than we ever think can be possible; that we are in spiritual reality 'blessed' and we are not nor ever have been 'miserable sinners'. If we choose to believe and see the best in ourselves and others then our reality changes for the better and we can simultaneously help others to do the same. It seems to me now, that fun is possible even in the midst of pain and not knowing because we live in a 'both-and' world, not an 'either-or' world.

Finally I believe that we are powerful creators and co-creators of our own realities because our authentic Selves know our own truth and challenges much better than any expert, politician, doctor or theologian could ever know them. The most profound and sustainable change always comes from within.

***

CHAPTER 16:

Power, authenticity and surrender - dancing the final dance with death

What has been my biggest learning on this journey? It has been to recognise the power of love, faith, trust and the ultimate freedom and constant presence of choice to recognise and honour the voice of the authentic Self. Through this, and the decision to face my fears as directly as humanly possible, I came to know that I was able to return to life from the deepest depths of despair and apparent hopelessness: to be renewed again, but as a changed person with significantly expanded abilities, sense of awareness and a much deeper perception of the realities of the world.

What has made this possible? My experience has included unmistakeable milestones all the way on this journey to the deepest part of myself and back again into what may for others still be the everyday world, but for me is a very changed world yet still with familiar features. Perhaps all the choices of direction I made were critical ones. Perhaps they were all examples of 'the road less travelled' and had I made different choices, I would not have been led by my authentic Self and the wisdom and help of others, to the place of being I have eventually come to know. As T.S. Eliot implied in the final poem of "Four Quartets": "Little Gidding" (1943), after all our wanderings we return to the familiar place, the place we left behind, but only now, do we finally know it and see it as it actually is: *"and the end of all our exploring will be to arrive where we started and know the place for the first time"*.

I can still see many milestones, many forks in the road that were taken on this journey:

- facing fear and thinking about my possible death
- developing an uncompromisingly raw relationship with my experiences of both physical and psychological pain
- going to the deepest part of my sense of abandonment and alienation from a healthy life only to find I was not alone after all
- understanding different forms of love (love that possesses and controls which pushes me further into a behavioural response of self-reliance and love that liberates and empowers which encourages me into commitment and continued intimate connection)
- choosing what may sometimes be the hardest path as an ultimate reflection of the deepest love of the Self and others, which necessitates allowing an aspect of one's familiar life patterns to die
- having, holding and receiving faith and trust in the Self, in others and in the future...

All of these milestones and distinctive division of paths helped me to recognise what is really required to move from the '*Via Negativa*' to the '*Via Positiva*', which is no less than replacing habitual paranoid and defensive thoughts and reactions with metanoia and a knowledge that what was required of me, was a willingness to enter fully into living in the now, absolutely without need for any guarantees about the future.

I was deeply impacted by the final stages of my inward and almost shamanic journey, which clearly for me meant passing through the clashing of apparent opposite aspects of the Self (in my case this was in the form of the "puer auternus"- eternal boy and "senex" - wise old man) until I

296

reached a place where those parts were reconciled and balanced and the split that existed formally was healed. I am left with the conviction that this enabled me to come back to life from a place of apparent absolute bleakness.

This meant I needed to understand that two apparently contradictory aspects of the Self needed to first be held in dynamic tension alongside and hopefully in relation to each other, long enough to recognise they were not irreconcilable either-or elements. Instead, the deeper reality was that they absolutely needed to coexist and finally integrate as both-and aspects of the way I express myself and live in the world, if I was ever to deal successfully with a life threatening and possibly terminal illness. Too much puer auternus would lead me into unrealistic and infantilised ways of being without the wisdom to let go of the things I needed to shed in order to begin to heal; whilst too much senex would leave me stuck in an old man's way of being without any real zest or enthusiasm for life needed in order to remain determined to really, really live.

To do all this, I was required to know what fears and unrealistic hopes must be dropped and what choices must be made, in order to be able to breathe new life instead of half living a life of suffocation or ungrounded and futile optimism. I also recognised that the ultimate core of love, faith, power, choice and freedom, centres on one's trusting relationship with oneself. At the end of the day, profound change comes absolutely from within. As Eliot's work implies, this is an internal experience of going through and coming out of a crucible of fire; renewed again, rather than consumed by the flames.

In terms of the depths of this fire experience, I would say that the pre-pain killer time in 2010 and the period around February 2011 were aspects of my darkest hour, perhaps the darkest hour of my relationship with myself. However, it is also true to say that for me, these episodes were followed by the inexorable dawn of a new and slowly unfolding world beyond fear. It was a relationship with and beyond fear which at the time existed both inside me and also around me in the world as I experienced life's rhythms and changes. I feel that it was also a reflection of relational dynamics which existed inside other people as I perceived them, that impacted upon me, and in different ways my responses also impacted back upon them and how they perceived the world. I think what I am saying here, is that the changes which began occurring in me also began to impact on other people's own perceptions of issues around illness, life and death. It may be that my experience of this crucible of fire and my fortune in being able to return from it, and articulate something of its visceral nature and the ability to survive it, began to offer some semblance of hope to others I spoke to who were in similar or equally challenging life and death situations.

Perhaps that was the moment I began to fully realise that if I wrote honestly and truthfully about all my experiences on this long and arduous journey, my words and reflections could offer the potential of a healing guide for others facing similar life challenges. I knew if I was to do so, I would need to write about things that I would have preferred not to have made public. There are clearly risks involved in revealing personal information to the depth that I felt I might need to reveal, in order to remain fully truthful. Fortunately, one of the aspects of my ego-centric self that I had already recognised I needed to let go, was any deep concern about how I might be judged by others. By this time, I no longer had the same level of, frankly dubious, over-investment in my personal and professional reputation.

In that context I am able to share the following: In late February 2011, whilst in the midst of my acute pain period, I was deeply touched by a communication I received from a supervisee, who shared with me her awareness of my severe illness and what she saw me choosing to do – which was to carry on despite the pain, fear and illness I was feeling and continue to choose to serve others in my work. She saw me very clearly in ways that no other person had, possibly with the exception of my spiritual director Brenda. She thanked me for my courage and commitment. I could not say then that I was feeling particularly courageous – I was carrying on because, in truth, I saw no other way forward and I had already decided I was not going to take my own life.

As I look back I can now also see that despite the ordeals I was going through, at least at that time, I was demonstrating faith and trust in some sort of positive vision of the future, and I was also visited by faith, in that the world, including my supervisee, was offering me the gift of her faith in me and her willingness to value me.

I had been working with my supervisee for about six months at the time. I had warmed to her from the beginning as a person with obvious wisdom and I also felt in the presence of someone with a big, loving heart. She recognised my accumulated experience and skill in the role, and yet I also felt we talked from the start as spiritual equals, albeit coming from very different spiritual traditions.

Over the following three months I became more deeply aware of a resonant soul level connection to Carol, my supervisee. Her advice and help in our brief discussions about natural healing were immensely encouraging for me in my struggle with serious life threatening illness. I was as mindful as I could be of the need to maintain professional boundaries, and I did not seek to increase the frequency nor nature of our contact.

However, I could not deny that something was seriously deepening in me around my feelings towards Carol. I thought about it a great deal and in my own mind I felt I had then made a clear choice, in perhaps the short time I had left on this earth, to see through to its development or conclusion, my connection - relationship with K. It was clear my connection to Carol had some profound significance for me at a soul level, but it seemed to me, other than maintaining our professional relationship, that I would not be acting on those feelings of significance, certainly not in this lifetime anyway.

I am sorry, or in retrospect, if I'm honest, pleased to say that my authentic Self had other ideas. Towards the end of June after completing a supervision session, I surprised myself by hearing me say spontaneously to Carol, "There is something I feel I have to share with you".

I had been very aware towards the end of the session, where my symptoms had been acutely painful, that I was feeling very preoccupied that, after all, my death might not be far away. I suddenly felt a profoundly overwhelming sadness, and a deep conviction I would not live to have many more meetings with Carol, nor anyone else. I then felt an aching sense of poignancy that I needed to share something with Carol of what her presence in my life had meant to me. I knew I could not die in peace if I did not speak out, despite whatever rules I might be breaking in doing so.

I knew at one level, strictly speaking this was beyond what was acceptable in a professional relationship, but the desire to speak out in some way and say something, was too powerful for me to hold back. Maybe this would signal the end of my professional career, I was prepared to accept that, but from where I was in that moment, all I felt sure of was that very soon I was going to die.

I think it was the nature of what I said that surprised me; it came out in a way that I had not pre-empted nor anticipated. I said to Carol, "There is something I feel I have to share with you. I feel I would not die in peace if I didn't share this with you. I know I can do nothing about it in this lifetime, but if there is such a thing as reincarnation I can tell you I am going to marry you in the next lifetime. What would you say if I asked you to marry me then?" Carol said, "I would say yes".

Perhaps a word of explanation is required here. Although my words were absolutely spontaneous, they reflected a very long held belief in reincarnation. I have regarded it as natural phenomena as far back as I can remember. It wasn't particularly part of my mum's spiritual perspective and as a traditional Methodist, it was certainly not part of my Dad's spiritual perspective either. I seem to recall that even as a child, when I thought of life beyond death, I assumed it was life beyond death for a while until we chose to come back again in another physical body and in another lifetime. These assumptions were significantly deepened when I was at Art College. One of my closest friends there, Kath came from a traditional Catholic family background (strangely as did most of my friends at the time). She was very down to earth and grounded and also very psychic. She had an intuitive knowledge of people and what made them tick; she also appeared, in the modern vocabulary, to "channel" complex and profound spiritual knowledge which took reincarnation as an obvious fact.

So as I found myself contemplating my own death, I could see myself after the death experience, in another dimension. I could not bear the thought of going there without at least sharing with Carol how I felt about her – I felt if I did not do so, I may never see her again. On some level it felt like an echo of previous lifetimes, when I had known Carol and we had been forcibly removed from each other by others, never to meet again in a physical form in each particular lifetime. This time, it felt like a moment when I had to speak out.

On the surface, this dialogue was, hand on conscience, somewhat irresponsible but I hope understandable. Professionally, it certainly appeared to fly in the face of my BACP code of ethics, so in that regard I seem to have "sinned". In another way, it changed nothing beyond my perhaps dubious professional ethics in that moment, given that Carol was committed to staying in her relationship of many years, and I had already chosen to spend the rest of whatever time I had left honouring my connection to K to the best of my ability. After all, I did love K and Carol loved her partner. Who was I fooling, really?!! In reality, of course, everything changed after that.

However, honouring our professional and ethical responsibilities as best we could, we did recognise that we had to quickly bring our professional relationship to an end. I had discussions with my own clinical supervisor and my group supervisor about the need to end my professional relationship, especially if it seemed likely that Carol and I would develop a friendship. That did seem very likely, and so we formally ended our working relationship almost immediately. We resolved to keep in contact as friends.

Earlier in the year, in late April 2011, I had gone to Ireland with my Peer Supervision Group. We stayed at a cottage in County Mayo, close to the sea. It was a fairly busy itinerary, which also offered an opportunity to me to work on and develop my writing, focused on my illness, a personal narrative about my life to that point and my professional – spiritual learning and development, both over time and also in the light of receiving a terminal diagnosis.

I initially felt, and through discussion with colleagues, intended to hold as a potential audience for the book, fellow professionals. However, it has become very clear to me, over time, that the book is also as much for clients and indeed for anyone facing a terminal diagnosis, either their own or that of a loved one, as it is for fellow professionals.

Not all my peers in the Supervision Group agreed with me on this, but by now I know the voice of my authentic Self and in dialogue with it I get the unmistakeable response, that my developing intuition is right. This is a much more universally relevant book than I had originally thought.

By early July 2011, despite my illness, I had the opportunity to visit County Mayo again, to do further writing on the book. I originally invited a long standing friend from my Art College days, Andy and his wife Lynn, to accompany me. I already knew from my visit the previous April that I needed to be in community with others, as well as in County Mayo, in order to write creatively. I found it next to impossible to do this work at home, and even less likely to do it well if I was attempting to work in solitude. Hence I decided to offer the invitation to Andy and Lynn.

At that time, my contact and connection with K was very distant. Although I was doing my best to remain open to the possibility of a relationship, it seemed that a friendship was the kindest and most compassionate connection I could offer myself and offer her, given my struggles to feel at peace with the idea of a committed exclusive relationship. I felt genuine love for K but in all honesty, which I shared with K at the time, I felt uneasy about offering anything more concrete for the future. It seemed we were open to continuing a connection with a basis in friendship, but nothing more solid was directly demanded of me nor offered by me.

Plans were made to set up a trip, but at the last minute, Lynn was unable to come along. Andy was still open to the opportunity and I mentioned in passing to Carol that I would be away in Ireland for a week in July, working on the book. Carol spontaneously said, "Oh, I wish I could come along", I just as spontaneously answered, "Why don't you then?"

Carol had a brief discussion with her partner and decided she would. I did not realise it at the time, but her decision marked the start of an incredible spiritual and metaphysical journey, certainly for me, that I feel I am still on to this day. I know that Carol would say something very similar, if asked.

My abiding memory of that trip to Ireland, despite the powerful drama that subsequently unfolded, was that the three of us never stopped laughing. Andy got on like a house on fire with Carol, and I felt very much at home in the presence of both of them, having known Andy since I was 18 years old.

Even on our way to the cottage I got completely lost driving the car and impulsively suggested we head off on a road over the moorland. The road soon turned to a track and then to a muddy quagmire. I insisted we would be fine, that we were on the right road and the cottage would be "just around the corner". I also encouraged everyone not to panic. We were all in hysterics – possibly panic induced, but for some reason we all found it incredibly funny. In the end I gave up my stubborn resistance to the possibility we were on the wrong road, and did a ninety six point turn on the muddy track, which took a considerable time. Returning to the main road it took a mere five minutes to recognise the road we should have taken and we arrived safely a few minutes later. I felt very much at home in Ireland. It was almost as if I held body and cognitive - emotional memories of being there in County Mayo before, in that landscape, with those two people. I had been struck the previous April by a prior expectation that Mayo would feel very foreign, and an absolute amazement that it seemed I knew the place on some level like the back of my hand (but obviously not quite like the back of my hand given my navigational adventures on the way there!).

Carol and I talked a lot about the energy that was obvious between us. A few days into the holiday she asked me if we could share a bed together, without any expectation of sexual contact. I thought about where this would leave me in relation to K and was very aware of the current distance between us.

Subsequently I thought long and hard about the rights and wrongs of what Carol was asking me. It took me quite a while, but eventually I concluded that this was not only natural and right, it was somehow required as part of a powerfully unfolding mystery that seemed to surround us.

Carol confided in me much later, that her motivation for asking was simply to spend as many moments close together as possible in this brief period of time we were sharing. Her thoughts were repeatedly turning to this question, "When would we ever get chance to do this again? This is priceless and treasured".

Despite there being no expectation nor seeking out of sexual contact between us, it was clearly a path of choice that was not likely to lead me back into a desire for a more concrete future commitment in my connection with K. Given where K and I were at in relation to each other, this felt very sad but seemed to emphasise that my connection to K was not strong enough to create the outcome that she continued to desire, which I wished I could naturally offer her, despite K keeping her distance from me during the period before I went to Ireland.

Subsequently Carol and I did share a bed over those few nights in Ireland and simply talked and held each other as we lay awake and as we fell asleep each evening. I felt a deep sense of communion with Carol that I could not easily explain. That sense of communion had been present from soon after we landed in Ireland.

When we had landed at Knock Airport at the start of our time in Ireland and picked up the hire car, I had experienced a strong motivation to drive to the Shrine at Knock prior to setting off for the North Mayo coast. At Knock I sat in the chapel at the Shrine and Carol was alongside me, with Andy close by. I began to feel an almost indescribable sensation of lumps of grief and physical pain being pulled out from within my being as I sat contemplating the religious tableaux in front of me. It felt like both my grief and my tumour pain were being gently but powerfully removed. This had only lasted for a few minutes, but in that time I felt a profound presence of deep relevance and purpose in me being there, in Knock, at that moment, with both Carol and with Andy.

Later Carol told me that although she had never seen the actual Shrine at Knock before nor any photographs of it, what she saw behind the altar we were facing, was the same tableaux she had seen surrounding me a couple of weeks earlier when she had given me a Reiki healing session in my home in West Yorkshire.

We slowly and leisurely explored the surrounding area over the next few days. I felt tired and weary to my soul on one level, whilst simultaneously very much alive and interested in the world. I remember catching sight of myself in the bathroom mirror on the Saturday morning, four days after our arrival in Ireland, and was very shocked to see how gaunt and lined my face looked. I almost did not recognise myself. I looked like a very ill old man.

That same Saturday afternoon, we visited the local beach at Bunatrahir Bay, Ballycastle. We wandered down along the strand and where a small river flowed down to meet the sea, we stood and watched scores of Swifts flying and swooping through the air. I was transfixed by the beauty of their flight and felt myself almost flying with them; certainly I was aware at the time that I didn't feel very rooted to the earth at all.

I remember saying, "I shall never forget this moment" and as soon as the words left my lips I felt a powerful pain spreading across my abdomen from left to right and up into my chest area. Suddenly everything seemed to turn black, with a kind of dull explosion, strangely similar to the sensation I remember feeling when the house brick hit me between the eyes, when I was four and a half years old.

I began to feel waves of extreme pain and nausea and started to stagger, almost losing my footing in the sand. I can't remember seeing much, but I was acutely aware of Carol and Andy's deep concern, even panic, as they tried to walk me back towards the car. I don't know to this day how I was able to stagger back to the car, without collapsing, but I did so with a great deal of help from Carol and Andy.

Somehow, they manoeuvred me into the passenger seat at the front of the car. Carol jumped into the driver's seat and Andy got in the back. I felt myself starting to go out of consciousness and my head moved to the left as I lay slumped in the car seat. The car was parked in an area cut out of the hillside, and as I looked out of the car window I could see tall grasses at eye level, moving with the wind.

As I watched the grass, I felt myself transported to a battlefield somewhere, laying on the ground seriously wounded, looking up at grass and smoke. It was a very powerful and present sense of being in another place. People were dying and calling out all around me. I knew I was fatally wounded. I felt I had been here at this point on many battlefields in the past, in many previous lifetimes, and I knew I was going to hear a voice, as I had always done before at this point of deep silence.

Then I heard the voice speak to me, it said very calmly and very clearly, "Do you want to stay or go?" I knew I had heard those same words so many times before, and I knew that each time I had heard it before I had said "I want to go" and I had died there. This time, I felt such a powerful pull of love and grief and energy from both Carol and Andy, it shook me out of my past inevitable pattern. I said, "I have to stay". The voice replied, "Alright, but there's a lot of work for you to do".

Recently, Carol was reading a book by Neil Donald Walsh (2006), in which he describes what apparently happens when a soul is at the point of death: he describes this as "stage three" of death when the soul is asked a profoundly important question, *"This will be the most important question you will ever be asked, and your reply will be the most important statement you have ever made and the biggest moment of free choice you could ever imagine"*. He claims the question is *"Do you want to stay?"* (P256) I felt a powerful sense of recognition when Carol read out that section of the book to me.

I don't know how Neil Donald Walsh received this information; his claim is that these are "channelled conversations". What I do know is that I was definitely asked that question – and my awareness of the profundity of the moment was also an echo of what I had experienced and written many years before, about the choice facing me at the age of eleven, when I found my maternal Grandfather dead in bed and knew I would be the one who had to break the news to my Mum. I have slightly amended the words. This time it was not the "child in me" that was dying, I was dying: "In this deep silence, the whole world waits. In this deep silence, I know that I am dying".

After my response to this question, I returned slowly to full consciousness, with Carol physically hanging on to me, sobbing, but absolutely determined to not let go and it seemed to not let me go either. I felt very similar energy from

Andy sitting in the back of the car, and I have a memory of him holding on to my shoulders.

The pain subsided and the darkness left me. I felt exhausted but safe. I was back in the world again and I was not going anywhere without these two loving souls who were with me in that profoundly silent moment of near death.

I suddenly felt I needed to go to the local bar and get some Guinness down me. Probably not the best thing to do after a near death experience, but I insisted I did not need a hospital! We made our way in the car back to Ballycastle and entered Polke's Bar on the High Street. I had my Guinness, Carol and Andy had their own fortifiers, after which we wandered out again on to the High Street.

Looking down the road I could see a Catholic Church on the left hand side. Andy did not want to go in, but I asked Carol if she would accompany me and we entered St. Bridget's Church, Ballycastle. Carol slowly showed me around all the statues of Saints, explaining who each one was.

We stood at the front of the Church, in front of the altar. Carol was holding my hand. I looked down and saw a carpet of stars spread out in front of me. I looked up and saw the Sacred Heart Christ figure looking down on us both. At that moment, I felt the whole world and my consciousness expanding as if forever. Carol and I seemed to be travelling through space and time together. It seemed to me, together, as we always had done for many life times before. It took quite a while for that sensation and possible memory to fade, and then we slowly made our way out of the Church, back to the car and drove back to the cottage.

I was in a state of quiet and slightly shocked convalescence I think, after what had happened at Bunatrahir Bay. I sat around a lot, my energy somewhat spent. At some point I fell asleep in a chair by the fire. Later

Carol told me I had slept for around 4 hours. In all this time, I felt Carol close by, on occasions holding me, on other occasions just being there along with Andy as a collective very loving presence.

At one point I awoke and went in to the bathroom. As I washed my hands, I glanced up at my reflection in the mirror. I had to look again, and again, before I confirmed to myself that all the lines that had been in my face only hours previously had completely vanished. It seemed to me I looked a good ten or twenty years younger than I had a mere few hours previously.

Later that evening, Carol and I went to bed. I sensed she was falling asleep as we talked and soon I realised she had fallen out of consciousness. I lay there all night propped up on my elbows, just looking into her face feeling a profound sense of love for her. I was so very aware that soon we would be travelling back to England, and this precious time together felt to me like it could be lost forever, as we returned to our respective lives. I just could not sleep. I had to be conscious and just see her face as long as I possibly could.

Every moment was timeless and also transient, never ending and soon to be gone. I felt such love and sadness it was almost unbearable, but I just could not turn my eyes away. In fact I did not for one moment remotely feel like turning my eyes away. Instead, I was transfixed. I saw in front of me the face of a beautiful nineteen year old young woman. A face I felt I had known forever and seen in so many places, so many different lifetimes previously.

This time round it felt I would only be with her for such a short while before the cloak of infinity enveloped us again and we were once more lost to each other.

At that moment Carol stirred from a state of deep sleep, "What is that bright light?" I told her there were no lights on, but she sensed an intense light in the room and was shielding her eyes. Carol spoke again from a semi-sleep state, "Oh he's absolutely beautiful; he's so tall and strong. I can see his leather breastplate across his chest. He looks like a Roman Soldier but he's much bigger than that".

She fell into deeper sleep again. A few minutes later she stirred and said, "There are pyramids here, gable ends, and stones everywhere. So many stones, there's just too many for me to lift. There are just too many stones, but we have to find it. We have to find the place". She then fell back into deep sleep once more, and didn't stir until morning.

The next day, I told Carol what I had witnessed. She recalled the figure instantly. She described a very large being dressed like a Roman Soldier, but rather than a military demeanour all she felt was a deep well of compassion and love emanating from this powerful presence in the room.

In later months, Carol reflected that after this experience she had begun to have very frequent metaphysical insights that had not been made available to her previously. It seemed that some latent abilities had been powerfully unlocked. Carol had told me that on many past occasions she had previously heard "murmurs" of this nature but it had felt like "indistinct voices underwater". The nature of it felt profound but it was not really audible. After this experience at the cottage, voices and images were always very clear and distinct.

Later in the day, Carol became most insistent that we needed to visit the Neolithic site at Ceide Fields, situated a little further down the Mayo coast from Ballycastle. None of us had been there before, as we drove south from Ballycastle on an unfamiliar road. Rounding a sharp bend we saw on our left in a field a gable end of a ruined building, then another. As the road rose up an incline towards the Atlantic coast, we could see on top of the hill a pyramid structure.

"Oh my God", Carol said as we drove on. "Is that Ceide Fields?" It was, and we pulled off the road into the car park.

We walked up the path to the visitor's centre and exhibition entrance. Looking inside I could see what looked like a massive ancient oak tree, upright in the centre of the entrance area. Somehow I felt that I knew the tree. As I walked towards it I knew I would find the shape of a hand print slightly above head height, around the back, on the left side of the tree. I walked round the back of the tree and my hand rose up to meet the wood, resting in the indentation of a hand print that seemed to perfectly fit my own hand. The tree was over 5,000 years old and had been excavated from a turf bog during archaeological exploration and restoration of the site.

We explored the visual and modelled display showing aspects of Neolithic life, complete with life size human models. I had the most peculiar sensation looking at the human figures that they were not models, they were alive, and somehow communicating a human connection towards me and with me. It was an unsettling experience.

It was getting late and Carol was very anxious to visit the Neolithic site behind and beyond the Visitor's Centre. She went on ahead of me as I could only walk very slowly. I saw her ahead of me up on the hillside and eventually joined her. She was standing next to a boulder field... "Too many stones for me to lift" echoed in my head from the previous night.

I looked across the field and could see the Atlantic Ocean and Downpatrick Head in the near distance. Somewhere close by between where I was standing and the promontory of Downpatrick Head, hidden by the curve of the coastline, was Bunatrahir Bay where I had gone through a near death experience not much more than twenty four hours previously.

Carol looked down at the stones in front of us and said, "This is where we were buried all those thousands of years ago". She went on, "I know you and I agreed to come back for another lifetime this time around, and it was always meant to be that we would come back here and I would be here alongside you again, to offer healing to you. It is not time for you to die now".

As I heard these words I felt my whole visual and energetic field, swirl through what seemed like 180 degrees, and I experienced a surge of energy entering my body. We left Ceide Fields shortly after, and as I moved back towards the Visitor's Centre Car Park prior to departure, I felt much more energetic and alert.

Back at the cottage, I was sitting indoors talking to Andy. Carol called us outside to look at the sunset. We took photographs of each other and of the sunset. When viewed later, many of the photos had strange swirls of light in them, some five or so appeared to spell out letters.

At one point, standing outside the cottage, we all looked down simultaneously at a camera. As we looked up no more than a second later we all saw a large bull in the field in front of us that had not been there previously. It seemed to appear instantly from nowhere. Over the next twenty minutes the bull roamed around the cottage garden and whilst not too wild, did have a robust engagement with a bush! We called the local farmer who came to retrieve it.

The next morning at 7am, I was standing in the large room at the back of the cottage, looking through french windows towards the sea. Although the doors were closed I distinctly heard laboured breathing coming from outside. I opened the doors and could see cattle in the field beyond, some eight hundred yards or more in the distance, at the side of a hedge. The laboured breathing grew deeper and louder and then I heard a bull amongst the cattle begin to bellow and moan as if in intense passion or pain.

The bull stood up and began to thrash about in the field, then made repeated attempts to break down the hedge. After a couple of minutes it succeeded and came crashing through the hedge into the cottage garden. It looked wild, angry and out of control. It moved down to the corner of the garden and started digging out great sods of earth with its hooves. Eventually it saw another bull in the next field, across a dirt track and faced it in a kind of stand-off, bellowing and shouting as its rival reciprocated with its own wild verbal barrage.

By this time, Carol had also entered the room, and we watched as the stand-off went on for a good twenty minutes or more – we phoned the farmer again! Ten minutes later the farmer arrived and with a bit of persuasion using a large stick, steered the bull away back into the original field, prior to attempting to mend the hole in the hedge. The Irish Gaelic name for the place we were staying is translatable as, "place of the cattle on the hill". Somehow, it seemed the energy of the place had been stirred and activated after our return from Ceide Fields!

Later that afternoon, we flew back to England. It was very hard parting company with Andy and absolutely excruciatingly difficult to say goodbye to Carol. At this point, we were moving into a friendship beyond our previous professional relationship, but there was no prospect at that time of a viable relationship together. And that hurt a great deal.

Shortly after my return from Ireland, K confided in me that she had been seriously reflecting about our connection and felt I had been right about the growing distance between us. But rather than suggesting an ending as I had been expecting, she told me she wanted to take a powerful step towards choosing to commit to a life together. I know my immediate response was a very quiet and understated one. I think I was in a state of shock. It took me two days to find the courage to share with her the essence of the powerful connection I felt I had made with Carol in Ireland.

K was unsurprisingly very angry, accusing me of deep betrayal; I was being accused of an act which I have to say does not ring true to me to this day. She was telling me I was in effect distorted in my thinking and needed to be prepared to offer commitment to our relationship. As part of this she said she wanted me to end all contact with Carol, at least for the whole of the remaining summer and into early autumn, "To give our relationship a fair chance to deepen". I asked for time to think this through, knowing precisely what I felt, and the next day I told her I could not accept such conditions. I was open to K and deepening our relationship, if it was meant to be as a natural development, but I would not do so by cutting off all contact with Carol.

I also talked this through with Carol when I got a chance to see her. At that time we were both still saying we wanted to stay with our respective partners, and it was only right that over the coming months each of us should fully explore the depth of our commitment to our partners, whilst she and I maintained a friendship as best we could. Looking back, I can see the desperate naiveté of two people doing their best to be responsible to other people in their lives; but I would not for one moment doubt the sincerity of what we said to each other.

K and I agreed to give it our best shot over the following few months. K however, also insisted she wanted me to make a final decision about a "life partnership" with her by the end of October. I was very sceptical about the helpfulness of imposed deadlines; I don't think real love responds well to the imposition of deadlines, and I said so – but for better or ill, I agreed to do my best to reach a decision by the end of October.

All I can say, is that in the time that followed I did my very best to be as open and loving towards K as I possibly could. I was always open to potential transformation of the situation, but as I told her, the connection to Carol felt very strong and not a temporary distraction. I genuinely didn't know whether my connection with Carol was meant to be a friendship or something more. So given what I had already agreed to, I opened my heart to K as deeply as I possibly could over the next few months. I felt myself slowly being torn apart. My heart continued to feel a deep and resonant certainty about its connection to Carol's heart, but I was not at all sure what I should be doing about it in terms of the way we might choose to be in relationship with each other. Should it be as friendship; should it be much more; should we walk away from each other for the good of all concerned?

In parallel with this, my love for K really did grow much stronger, but the sense of being deeply troubled when I contemplated a life together with K never once left me. It felt inevitable that I would have to say "no" come the end of October, I often said as much to K, but in honour of all the things we had shared together on our respective journeys I kept my heart wide open to her just the same.

By mid-October I felt I was losing my mind and my connection to my own authentic voice. I had touched a depth of love for K that I had previously never known, and yet I was still troubled. I was still open to transformation, but I felt come the 31st October, I would lose my connection with K, and as she had already made clear, if I chose not to be with her, she would have to cut off all contact with me, "in order to deal with this emotionally".

I knew this would therefore also mean I would lose my connection to K's three daughters; all of whom I liked, or more accurately by this time loved, particularly the eldest to whom I had grown very close, and where I felt very deeply connected. I felt the prospective grief of losing four people I loved, very acutely, in the final week before the end of October.

The last weekend of October proved to be an unbearably poignant, sad and in its own way a beautifully human experience. The love I felt for K that weekend was enormous and unfathomably deep – but I knew within my heart I had not felt a transformation that would enable me to be at peace with saying "yes" to a lifelong relationship with her, whether or not Carol and I remained friends or even remained in touch in to the future. I felt I was about to lose not only four but quite possibly five loving connections in my life, forever.

I had to accept I could lose absolutely everything if I stayed true to the authentic voice I felt in my heart. That weekend K and I slept together – she was hoping against all odds that I would say "yes" the following morning; I knew with a desperate certainty that all I would be able to say was "no". I held K tight and close to me all night, barely sleeping, awash in a surging and moving sea of grief and sadness.

The next day I told her my truth – her tears flowed immediately and she seemed heartbroken, but absolutely clear she could not see me anymore. Nevertheless we spent the whole painful and heartbreaking day together until around 7pm.

Finally I held her in my arms in the street outside, for what felt like eternity, as she steeled herself in preparation to drive away. I'm sure in those moments that neither of us wanted to let go, but eventually we did what seemed unavoidable. K walked to her car, in tears, got in and drove away apparently out of my life forever.

***

What exists beyond our preoccupation with "fear"?

I posed this question to Carol and she replied, "Freedom!!" She is absolutely right. When I think of how I have experienced that freedom it is undoubtedly in the, unmistakable once experienced, form of emotional freedom.

Suddenly the weight and pressure of life is lifted and I can really breathe deeply again, and taste again the beauty and promise of life and truly living when: I realise that I am free to think what I want, to act how I want to act, to experience life as I choose to experience it, not in the way others tell me I should or must experience it; To "let go" of any previous anxious preoccupation with what the world might think of me, or how it might judge me or attempt to define me; To follow my own truth and the consistent wisdom of the voice of my own authentic Self.

That kind of freedom is anathema to some because they regard it as dangerous. It IS dangerous for them because it tells them that they cannot any longer control the person who now lives in a place of emotional freedom.

So instead of owning their own particular fear of life they put a great deal of energy into convincing the person they formally controlled through emotional manipulation, that they are selfish, self-centered and uncaring. Their aim is to undermine that sense of emotional freedom in the other to such an extent, that their own distorted and fear-based view of life becomes viewed yet again as so called "common sense" by their intended victims. They would much rather pull the emotionally free back into apocalyptic misery, than face the challenge of living their own life with a measured sense of adult responsibility for the world they create around themselves.

I think it is precisely because on some deep level we know that we will face that kind of opposition from many others, that it is so very hard for us to take that step beyond fear into emotional freedom.

However, once we truly make that step, we become aware that we are given enormous energy, who knows where from – from our own authentic Selves, or from unseen sources or both – to sustain us in this new world and this place of new possibilities, which would otherwise never have revealed itself to us. This is simply unknown to the fearful in my experience, because from a place of fear, it cannot be either seen or experienced, except perhaps through the intervention of grace, in the form of a fleeting glimpse of what could be if we thought, felt and acted differently.

Such freedom comes at a price – often the price of opposition and venom from those more fearful than ourselves, and also at the cost of leaving behind our own restricting but in some psychological way, comforting familiarities which imprison us in other people's worlds, alienated from our own authentic truth. The price demanded may be high, but the rewards are to truly live and be fully human. That is always a price worth paying in my book.

Fortunately, in my search for freedom I support Chesterfield Football Club, known as The Spireites, and have done so since I was 14 years old. Believe it or not, this has helped me in life. We may not be *very successful in the footballing world of fame and fortune, but we have something absolutely priceless nevertheless, it is this saying:*

"We are Spireites and we do what we like!" Amen!!

***

Carol

Above: John and Andy, aged 21
Below: John & Carol after near death experience

CHAPTER 17:

Fields of Freedom - living one's craft, loving the world ......and being loved

I was brought up in a mixed faith family: my Father's history was around non-conformist Methodism and Trade Unionism; my Mother's history was around Spiritualism and a working class radicalism of compassion and relating from the heart towards others, especially those less fortunate than we were. The common values shared by both their families were an absolute commitment to a kind of community based socialism and a belief in a better world for all, not just those who were born to privilege and an expectation of plenty.

Despite those obvious links however, those histories often didn't see eye to eye with each other out there in the real world beyond the safety of my immediate and extended family. In addition I remember vividly from childhood, how my Mum almost lost her (Catholic) best friend, Lily, because the Priest had told her Spiritualism was "the Devil's work" and she must end the friendship with Mum immediately. Mum's friend whom I knew as "Aunty Lily" defied the Priest and refused to end the friendship. She and my Mum remained great friends for the rest of their lives. I regard this as the power of love over dogma and fear.

My Mum and in their own way, some others in my family were great spiritual teachers although I think that they did not really know it. I remember Mum's friends and acquaintances being frequently drawn energetically into confiding in her and asking for information about what they feared: death and beyond, or simply attempting to work through their lost and frozen grief about a family member separated from them by death. We had frequent visits when I was at home with Mum and I got used to hearing her talking in the kitchen to her worried friends about the world beyond death.

As for me, I have never feared death in the way that many seem to fear it, perhaps because of those frequent experiences and listening to what my Mum often said to people. I came to regard what she said as fact and a natural way of being for the human species. So I was already more than half prepared for the spiritual truth that we need to both embrace death as our wise counsel and equally also to live joyfully if one can in what others have called the "precious present" of now.

Like my paternal grandfather, Heber Holt, I have also always felt drawn towards trade union radicalism for the greater good and its often attendant spiritual-philosophical framework of Methodism-Socialism. Granddad Holt was very active in the local community, and had been so ever since my childhood. For years, through a local private bus company, he arranged community day trips to various tourist destinations across England and Wales. I went on many of those trips and it felt like an extended family outing on many occasions, complete with a wooden crate of pop bottles at the back of the bus and bags of crisps with salt contained in little blue paper packages inside each bag. After my Grandmother died all that came to an end, and he moved into a one bedroom flat in the centre of the mining town he had lived in all his life. I remember one day being with Granddad Holt on a street in Staveley, near where he lived. I knew he came from a big family but I never met all his siblings. That day we turned a corner and came face to face with his brother Walter, who it turned out was an identical twin, with virtually the same timbre and sound to his voice. I remember being very confused watching two versions of my

Granddad talking to each other, as if facing a reflection in a mirror. It was a pretty surreal experience!

I was always struck by the enormous number of Christmas cards he received every year; to read the contents was to recognise how deeply loved he was by so many people. He was certainly not a saint, he had a tendency to be involved in lots of personal and public social situations where he strongly felt he should be active, but others might have preferred to be left alone to deal with their life issues! Some might have said he was a bit of a busybody and I can't say I agreed with his views on everything either. I understood his insistence that when we went to the cinema together, I should not stand dutifully at the end for the National Anthem, as was customary when I was around 10 or 12 years old. "Sit down! Living off the workers' backs", he said vociferously as he tugged at the back of my coat, pulling me back down into the cinema seat from which I had just dutifully arisen. However, I could not agree that The Beatles were responsible for the downfall of Western Civilization and everything that was wrong with British society in the late 1960s and early 1970s.

When I was 21 he gave me a book, "50 Years March: The Rise of the Labour Party" (Williams, F., 1949). I knew what this meant to him and I was deeply touched. I still have that book. When he died, I was very moved and amused to hear that at the age of 84 he was still President of the local Young Methodists Society. In fact, that was what started me off crying at his memorial service in the local Methodist church the day of his funeral. I started to laugh, standing towards the back of the congregation and a couple of seconds later I was in floods of tears, which I could not stop no matter how hard I tried. I was delighted many years later, to find when I bought my house after Lis and I split up, that the next street was named "Heber Close". He was a good man and I still feel a great deal of love for him.

I grew up hearing from my Mum and from her sister my Aunty May (or "fagash Lill" as my Dad called her, deliberately puncturing Aunty May's attempts to appear glamorous and sophisticated!) about extraordinary metaphysical phenomena, almost from the age I could talk, so much so that I regarded it as natural and normal. She and her sister also regarded death as a mere phase and threshold from one reality to another, the latter being full of joy and honesty and human communion. My own path felt deep energetic resonance with both these traditions and I was also drawn towards Taoism and Buddhism, especially the emphasis on the natural way, the need for balance and for not over-efforting.

Since my near death experience on the strand near Ballycastle, in Ireland, in the summer of 2011, I have in addition been drawn powerfully and increasingly towards recognition of and desire to connect with the sacred feminine. There appears to be little reference to the sacred feminine in Western tradition, except in a very diluted form in some aspects of the Catholic faith, especially its mystical aspects and its recognition of the importance of both Mother Mary ("Our Lady") and in more subdued fashion, Mary Magdalene, along with numerous female Saints. This awareness even in diluted form draws my attention and interest.

Over the years, I have always felt strongly drawn to certain male writers almost always from the Catholic tradition: Matthew Fox and the development of Creation Centred Spirituality – following the much earlier influence of St. Ignatius Loyola; the contemporary Thomas Moore (author of, amongst other works: "Care of the Soul / Care of the Soul in Medicine / Dark Night of the Soul"); and latterly

James Alison (especially his reworking of the doctrine of "original sin" and his perspective on the philosophy of Rene Girard, who developed "mimetic theory" which mapped out the human tendency towards "resentful desire", "coveting" and eventually "envy, scapegoating, exclusion & violence".)

I am not naive about the considerably repressive aspects of some of the more dogmatic interpretations of Catholicism, I could hardly be so, given my awareness of Matthew Fox's assertions that there is a pressing requirement within the Catholic faith to reassert the need for a "New Reformation" (2006). As described previously, Fox suggests, *"There are two Christianities in our midst. One worships a Punitive Father and teaches the doctrine of Original Sin. It is patriarchal in nature (and) links readily to fascist powers of control.... The other Christianity recognises the Original Blessing from which all being derives. It recognises awe, rather than sin and guilt, as the starting point of true religion"* (P19). The God this Original Blessing represents is an inclusive God, not a God of punishment, exclusion and fear.

Nor am I unaware of the tendency of some Catholics, and for that matter many other self-identified Christians, to take the Bible's teachings literally rather than symbolically. However I have never been a literalist and I don't rest easily with notions of dogmatism nor fundamentalism in any of their manifestations, in any religion, whether they are so-called Christian, Jewish, Hindu, Buddhist or Islamic in their particular forms of fundamentalism.

But I am repeatedly drawn back to Catholic writers and sacred feminine icons, because I feel much of what is written from, or sympathetic with a mystical early Christian tradition echoes my own truth, and that the worst aspects of Catholicism stem from patriarchal colonisation of a spiritual movement around 300 years after Christ's death. It was this

327

colonisation which appeared to go to great pains to remove any references to the sacred feminine from scripture and religious tradition.

Certainly as far as I could ascertain, my experiences in Ireland were inevitably within the framework of mystical, sacred feminine, pre-Christian, Celtic and Catholic theology. They led me to read more about very early Christian and pre-Christian movements including the Essenes, who appeared to have strong connections to the British Isles including Ireland.

Shortly after we returned from Ireland, I asked Carol who she thought the figure was who appeared to her in a half dream state. She did not know; I suggested she asked whilst in a meditative state. She did and immediately heard the name, "Clarion", which meant nothing to her.

We used an Internet search engine to check the word "Clarion" and came up with innumerable references to Archangel Michael. Two months later, whilst in a bookshop in Gloucester, Carol found an illustrated card with a representation of Archangel Michael. The illustrated card portrayed an image, very similar to the one she saw in her personal vision in the summer in County Mayo.

On the 11th November, 2011, eleven days after my break with K, Carol and I visited the crypt at Lastingham Church in North Yorkshire. At precisely 11.11am, I had a strong altered state experience there of energetic fields converging and grounding themselves in the space in front of the altar. We both sensed that we had been there many centuries before, together, prior to an involuntary and violent parting imposed by others.

All I could sense in that moment on the 11th November was a powerful process of completion and return to balance between our two personalities. It seemed to mirror the expansive and flowing energetic state I had felt in the RC

Church in Ballycastle, County Mayo after my near death experience in the summer. This time, I had the feeling of my soul being finally at peace.

Later the same day we visited Whitby on the North Yorkshire coast. A sense of peace, coupled with a tangible awareness of living in extraordinary times surrounded us both. On the way home in the late evening we drove off the A64 into Malton, for a break in the journey and a meal. As we approached a set of traffic lights on green in the centre of the town, a car suddenly hurtled across our path from our right; I slammed the brakes on immediately and we missed collision by a hair's breadth. Shaken, I pulled into a side road and asked Carol for a cigarette!

As I sat there it became very clear to me that I had to put my cards on the table, there and then, about our future together. It seemed to me that the near collision was a bit of an omen. I needed to speak out very clearly about my feelings for Carol: somehow it suddenly seemed to me that time was getting short again and even though on one hand the escape from a massive collision was an example to me of the ever present power of grace, nevertheless I also felt that I may not be given many more opportunities to share the true depths of my feelings before the sands of time in this lifetime finally ran out for me. I recalled how I had previously vowed never to ask Carol to leave her partner – I said out loud, "Carol, I'm going to fight for you. I will use all the strength in me to be with you permanently in this lifetime".

During early November, Carol persuaded me to hold a big party for my forthcoming 60th birthday which was the 27th November. I had not been keen on the idea, I wasn't so sure I felt great about becoming 60, but as Carol said, "You were not supposed to be here so let's celebrate the fact that you still are here". On reflection I realised that she was absolutely right and anyway what's so bad about being 60?

Subsequently, first of all, I held a relatively small gathering on my birthday at my house, attended by around sixteen of my friends.

In January 2012, Carol and I hosted a much bigger event at the Irish Club in Bradford, attended by around sixty people: those I had not had the space to invite in November, and those who had not been able to attend the original event. In truth I enjoyed myself so much at the initial gathering that I wanted to repeat the experience, So I didn't take much time to decide that a further event would be perfectly in order! Around ten people from the original event were also able to attend in January. Unsurprisingly the two events were both astoundingly moving and powerful for me. I was able to say all the things I wanted to say, to very many of the people who had meant so much to me in my life to date.

I made a speech which I would like to reproduce, as follows:

"This is my second 60th Birthday Party. The official one or unofficial one – I can't decide. The first one was the day before my actual birthday on the 27th November last year. Yes, complicated isn't it?!

I could only invite a few people in November as my house was not big enough, so I decided to organize a second party for January, so I could invite all those people who mean a lot to me. Some couldn't be here tonight but I can still see their faces in my mind's eye and I'm saying this to them too.

There's no difference between those who came in November and those of you here now, because you are all very important to me and all extraordinarily human. I have been very blessed in my life to have such dear friends. All of you understand what it means to live from the heart. I think it's the only way to be in a world such as this one.

I've had a lot of time exploring stuff around my heart in these past 18 months since I received a challenging medical diagnosis. I am dealing with both heart failure and cancer, and according to some people my time left is rather limited. But I can tell you that I would change nothing if I had the chance to live my life over again.

Why? Because the last 18 months have taught me what love really is, and why my friends mean so much to me.

Love to me is total commitment and total freedom. I have known many of you a long time and that is my way of living commitment. I want all of you to be the very best 'you' that you can ever be. That's all I would ever ask of you. That is how I live out freedom. I believe in the end, it is all about living as our true selves, being and doing from the heart.

My Granddad taught me about Socialism, my Mum taught me about Spiritualism; my Dad taught me about being a Warrior of the Heart and my Brother taught me about Loyalty. All my family and friends have taught me about the preciousness and beauty of human life. My dog is teaching me by the way to make friends with pooh.

I don't live in a value free world and I have values which are who I am. I care about other people and people will always come first for me before power, profit or personal ambition and personal gain. If this life is not about the heart connections between people it has no meaning. People matter. Friends matter. Choosing life over self-aggrandisement matters. Speaking out and being the change we want to see in the world matters.

People who really know me well from way back will say I am shy and the thought of having to speak in public like this would bring me out in a cold sweat. They are right, it is true, yet it is important to me given my health situation to go beyond my fear tonight and speak out. I don't know if I will ever get a chance again to say what I am saying to people I care about, so tonight is the night it has to be done.

I would hate to think I would leave this world without you knowing my true feelings and without the opportunity to say thank you to all of you. So thank you.

Last but by no means least; I want to say a special thank you to Lissie my ex-wife who is here tonight, and the love of my life Carol. It didn't work out for Lis and I together but I don't think we will ever stop loving each other. It simply wasn't meant to be for us to stay together.

Years later, when I met Carol, and when Lissie met Dan, I understood why it wasn't meant to be for Lis and I to remain together. I have been truly blessed to love you both. God has been very generous to me.

Carol and I feel like we have known each other for thousands of years and I think we have. It seems like we have been sent to heal each other.

I know Carol and I will be working together, from the heart, in the time we are being given. And despite the medical diagnosis I'm planning to be around for a long time, but in the end I will go where I am asked to go at the right time. I feel that time is a long way off... and if it isn't I shall simply demand a second opinion.

Carol and I are writing books at the moment: we are off to Ireland on Tuesday for a week to do more writing. My book is called, "Fields of Freedom: Breaking through Fear in Personal and Professional Life", and Carol's book is called, "Having Hope when No Hope Remains". We both know from experience what we are writing about and we hope the books will help others. It seems to be part of what we are being asked to do. And we do it with joy and thankfulness.

Tonight is all about joy and thankfulness for me too. I hope you all have a great time tonight and please remember to live the lives you were meant to live. The world needs you".

On Sunday, 22nd January, 2012, I attended Mass at St. Bridget's R.C. Church, Ballycastle, County Mayo, with Carol. The same church Carol and I had visited in July 2011, after the dramatic events on the strand at Bunatrahir Bay.

This time, I had pre-planned my visit. It was my first Catholic Mass after I had decided some weeks previously that I wanted to become a Catholic or at least make closer links with the Catholic faith. It was also the first time I had received Holy Communion since that decision. It seemed that Carol and I were welcomed with ease into the congregation of locals. From my previous memory of attending a Mass in England during my Art College days with my Catholic friend Mick, by comparison an Irish Mass appears to be at least ten times quicker than a Mass in the U.K. The priest and the local congregation rattled through the procedure, ceremony and prayers like there was no tomorrow. Maybe there is no tomorrow, all there is, is now; as Van Morrison says in his best Belfast accent, "It's always noy. It's always being noy!!"

Carol is a Catholic Catechist, which means she is qualified to teach and instruct in the way of the Roman Catholic faith, and to prepare converts to become full members of the Church through sacramental preparation. She had been doing this for a long time as a member of her church in her home town. So she had spent time previously giving me instruction, since I declared my interest in Catholicism and perhaps becoming a Roman Catholic. Subsequently, we have discussed different aspects of the Catholic faith at length together. With this in mind, I felt a strong pull to attend Mass whilst we were in Ireland in January 2012.

As the service neared completion with Holy Communion, I prepared myself and then stood up from the church pew, moving into the aisle, I genuflected and moved down the line with the rest of the people from the congregation to receive

The Host from the priest. Carol went immediately before me, I followed. The priest placed The Host, Body of Christ, in the palm of my hand and I took it into my mouth and swallowed as I walked back to my seat. As I did so, I immediately felt an enormous energetic explosion and powerful surge of energy which moved down my body from my head directly into the tumours in my abdomen. My whole body shook as I sat down and I felt overcome with powerful emotion. Energy surged up and down in my body and Carol reached out from beside me and took my hand. Not only did she know what was happening, as she told me later, she knew it was going to happen, "Or at least I had a very good idea!"

I sat a while alone in the Church after the Mass ended, somewhat stunned by what had happened, but knowing it was absolutely meant to happen there, then, in that moment. It felt like a very powerful and perhaps final healing.

Carol couldn't find a loo after Mass and asked if there was one at the Church. She was advised by a lady outside the Church who was enjoying a cigarette to, "Go to the pub instead". We headed for Polke's Shop and Bar in Ballycastle High Street, re-introducing ourselves to Shopkeeper-Landlord Brian, whom we had met the previous July. As I savoured a pint of Guinness, and read a report in the paper of Chesterfield F.C.'s first win (away at Colchester United) since September 2011, Carol was relieved in more ways than one to find the toilet.

As we sat in the pub Carol told me she had been advised by Spirit to encourage me to return to the beach at Bunatrahir Bay. Carol had asked me on the previous Thursday, a day when we appeared to be grounding some form of metaphysical energy at the feet of St. Patrick's statue on Downpatrick Head, if I would return with her to the strand where I almost died. I felt I could not, the place still haunted me.

She gently explained that Spirit had prompted her several times during the morning and also in Mass, to ask me how I felt about going back to the beach today. She said she had been shown after Mass, that this was a time of liberation and freedom from fear, she heard the words, *"Help him to see there is nothing to be afraid of, to conquer fear, to behold great beauty and be set free"*.

When she heard this, Carol thought simply of looking at the waves in the Bay from the seashore. She also felt that it was as much a test for her as it was for me to share this information with me, in that she had to face her own fear of mentioning the idea twice. She would have not previously pushed the idea, preferring to honour my previously spoken wishes. However, Spirit was very insistent and she took the risk to raise it again. She may well also have been nervous because of what had happened the previous evening.

The previous evening, Carol had been on the phone to her friend Debbie as we sat together in the healing - therapy room in the cottage. Debbie had spent the whole day in bed with what had sounded like some sort of transformational spiritual exhaustion, feeling something like a baby moving about inside her. She told Carol she had felt very strange, thinking an awful lot that past lives and present lives ran together simultaneously in the here and now.

Earlier the same day, visiting the cliffs near Ceide Fields, we had told each other something very similar – we kissed on the cliff top and both Carol and I felt we were, back where we had been, then as now. At the same time Carol's phone was receiving a text message from Debbie which read, "Have you ever thought that the past and future exists in the present, and we can be in all time zones in the same moment?" A portal in the fabric of time where then was now and now is then; simultaneously on the coast of County

Mayo and back in West Yorkshire. It had been - was - is a powerful and profound moment.

As I had sat, attempting some writing for this book and listening to Carol talk with Debbie, I had felt the stirrings of abdominal pain, I could not settle to my writing and I got up pacing the room. Carol had ended her conversation shortly after and asked me if I was OK. As I had begun to talk about my restless feelings, the pain in my abdomen grew more and more intense until it reached a pitch I could hardly bear to endure. I sat down and the pain continued to intensify as it began to take my breath away.

Carol had put her hands on my abdomen and asked me to do breath-work which was very difficult for me. I was being wracked with regular bodily convulsions. Carol had asked me what it was about, "It's old stuff, very, very old stuff" I said...

In my mind's eye I was repeatedly seeing images, visions of the scene at Calvary at the time of the Crucifixion. Auto-suggestion probably, but it felt like every time I was convulsed in pain that it was sequentially linked to Christ's body being pierced with a spear, and I was somehow reliving standing there at Golgotha on the bleak hillside, witnessing the very Crucifixion itself as a grief stricken follower of Christ. As I allowed these images to stay in my mind's eye and chose not to dismiss them from my mind as the ramblings of a madman, the pain subsided and left me.

What pain still remained with me however, was possibly emanating from echoes of a previous life, but I'm sure that it was also still very much more in my body from this lifetime, in the form of somatic resonance with my broken relationship with Jane, and also from the end of my marriage to Lis. These were also still linked to much hidden fears I still had around things not working out for Carol and I despite everything that was-is-will be. Somehow acknowledging this was a way of releasing its power over me.

Subsequently, when Carol spoke again in Polke's Bar, and mentioned visiting Bunatrahir Bay, I now felt very open to doing so. We left the Bar and drove down towards the car park next to the beach, where I had distinctly heard the voice asking me if I wanted to "stay or go" and had silently chosen to stay and live on in this lifetime.

The place was packed with cars when we arrived. As we walked on to the beach we saw makeshift horse-jumping fences every sixty yards or so, all the way down the beach. In the distance we saw people on horseback riding down the beach towards us. As they rode past us along the strand, I must have counted fifty or more horses and riders of all sizes, ages and abilities. It was an incredible sight as horses and riders ran past, wheeled about, ran into the sea, and ran through the waves.

At one point a horse refused a jump, and the rider I was watching then attempted to take it into the sea. It ran around in circles in the surf, trying to unseat the rider and wheeled about and stopped facing towards us as the waves lapped against its legs. It seemed to stare intently at me and at Carol. Then it began to move, coming straight for us as we stood on the beach. I stood feet planted in the sand, thinking, "I'm not meant to move, I'm supposed to stand my ground here", as the horse galloped straight towards us.

I stood in the sand and did not move until the last second, as I did, the horse veered slightly off to my right. It felt almost other worldly, a feeling of freedom, power, movement, grace, energy and choice. I was also engaged in some deep process of trust in relation to my own judgment and intuition. At that point the rider (or perhaps even the horse!) said "sorry" and rode on. In fact as I recollect it, I did hear the horse speak, not the rider and it definitely said "sorry" as it galloped past my right shoulder.

I was transfixed by the sight – a place full of movement and life where the previous summer I had only felt the presence of death, as my life seemed to ebb away.

The place was full of people, horses and movement but in a space of no more than five minutes the horses and riders left as suddenly as they had arrived, sweeping round a corner at the end of the strand.

Carol and I stood on a virtually deserted beach. As we made our way back to the car park, only three cars remained, our own plus two others. By the time we reached our car, only one other vehicle remained and we drove off down a deserted road on a circuitous route back to Ballycastle.

I was deep in reflection as we drove away from the strand. My mind was flooded with images of movement and power. So was this the end of my pain and illness? Could I believe that? I don't know, but perhaps at long last, Deo Gracias, the agony was – is – will be over.

Above: John & Carol November 2011
Below: Seascape near Ceide Fields

Grandad Heber Holt

LATE THOUGHTS:

The bloody-minded approach to continued living,

(With help from unseen sources)

A good friend told me that traditionally the last thing one writes in a book as an author is the Preface or Introduction. Being the somewhat unconventional and bloody minded sort however, in the form of "Early thoughts", it was the first thing that I wrote.

My bloody mindedness has had a long history. I remember at the age of around 17, after an infuriating argument with my Dad, going into the kitchen and reaching up in to the cupboard to get myself some breakfast cereal. It was a new package and as I took it down from the shelf I read the message on it which said, "Open other end". My response was precisely the same one that I muttered spontaneously under my breath, when my Oncologist inferred that I only had a few more years left to live. "Fuck that!" I said as I tore open the cereal package at the wrong end.

I made a mess all over the kitchen floor, but it made me laugh out loud at my rebelliousness and changed my mood from impotent adolescent rage to a pre-emptive glimpse and experience of adult self-knowing. In that moment and for a while afterwards I was emotionally free of fear and resentment.

It was a lesson I had to learn again many years later – that sense of freedom is still with me, and for some people, I suppose I am just as irritating as I was at the age of 17. I like the 17 year old within me – I think in some mysterious way he has saved my life.

I started the book in May 2011, at a time when the future looked to me to be very uncertain and very bleak. As I finally near completion of at least the writing part of the book prior to the process of eventual publication, it is now late January 2013.

Much has changed in the intervening period. As I write, my apparent terminal illness has been in remission now for well over eighteen months. From what I was told by my Oncologist in 2010, I would not have expected to still be here. Yes, it could all collapse tomorrow, but it is not going to collapse now unless I choose that or unless God's plans for me turn out to be very different from the way they appear to have been unfolding since 2010.

Fortunately, my bloody-mindedness has been a key factor in what has unfolded, along with the almost constant presence of what I have come to regard as Grace – I call it this because I feel frequently blessed by the world, both seen and unseen, and the more grace I experience, the more able I appear to be to bless myself and to bless others. The more I bless myself and others, the more I am blessed. This is especially so when I see many of my psychotherapy clients moving through profound and positive change towards self-empowerment and growth of the power and wisdom of the voice of their authentic Selves. I recognise that, in some part, my willingness to hold a bigger vision of their potential than they can hold for themselves in the moment is a significant contributory factor to this process.

I have also felt that 'blessing' at the deepest moments of despair, often through immediate synchronistic experiences: for example, turning on my TV in the most extreme depths of my physical pain and the first image I saw was my biking friend and ex-colleague Rod Gibson, who had died many months earlier, talking to me in the guise of 'special consultant' to a team of wrestlers on the TV Programme

"Scrapheap Challenge". Yes, by then, in my own way of lived experience, I knew a lot about wrestling, scrap heaps and challenges. Rod's Team won: I think I, and the voice of hope from the depths of my despair, are still winning.

As I consider my role particularly as a psychotherapist, (although this can also apply to my work as a clinical supervisor, coach, coach supervisor or facilitator) I consider that what I do is this: I believe in people and I encourage them to believe in themselves. When they do, I see profound changes in them as they appear to recognise a growing sense of personal power. They do so by tapping into confidence in their ability to find healthy ways to look after themselves in this world, from a perspective of an adult minded sense of the authentic Self. I feel proud of them and of their choice to act with courage in an uncertain and often very frightening world.

I especially celebrate the emergence of the voice and wisdom of their authentic Selves – often different from my own, with different beliefs and different frames of reference. The Independent Practitioners' Network once described the vast range of available approaches to therapy as a rich and diverse "ecology of skills". I feel there is an equivalent richness and diversity evident in ways of being human, which emerge when different clients are able to access and begin to articulate a sense of awareness at the level of the unique character of their authentic Self. I think God loves variety – I feel this when I hear my clients beginning to articulate their own unique voice at the level of the authentic Self.

None of us are the same; no one has the complete handle on ultimate truth. "We only have one world" but often we seem to "live in different ones", as Mark Knopfler once described in the song, "Brothers in Arms". If I am not really in touch with my own authentic voice then I may be easily drawn into seeing the world from an apocalyptic perspective, where the notion of needing "brothers in arms" is a matter of apparent wisdom in an adversarial world. From here it is not difficult for me to experience division and a tendency to brutalise both myself and also others. But if I choose instead to live in a world of potential cooperation, partnership and co-creation, such differences can only enrich and free me from the imprisonment of previous fears: especially if I can acknowledge and celebrate difference. If I see the world more from this new perspective then I can help in my own way to contribute towards unlocking the staggeringly diverse range of human potential available to me and others.

I feel we can change the course of our own and others supposed destinies by changing the way we see the world and our place within it. We can change the future for the better. We are more powerful than we think we are. As I say in the book, in my opinion, the most profound and sustainable change always comes from within.

What unlocks that potential transformation - that "metanoia" – is conscious choice. For me "metanoia" means a complete change of mind: choosing to move away from what are likely to be old and habitually adversarial habits, or ways of seeing life, towards a more cooperative and inclusive view of human action and interaction.

An example of this would be my continued work with healers Cathy and Julie, in partnership with Carol. The four of us are aware of how much can be unlocked through following processes of metanoia in ourselves and offering help to others to make increasingly conscious and self-responsible choices in their life path and life's work. To this end, we are continuing to consider how best to offer a place of rest and renewal, along with encouragement, to other practitioners working from the heart in the helping and healing professions.

In the context of the journey I have already been making with the help of Cathy, Julie, Carol and others, I feel I have been helped greatly, not just in terms of a physical turnaround in my health (which at the time of writing, amazingly, looks very much like a period of sustained remission from illness), but also in the development of my spiritual awareness and metaphysical abilities.

The latter expanded considerably from July 2011 onwards, mostly through the development of my deeply powerful relationship with Carol, hopefully now my eventual life partner Carol.

I think whether the conscious choice to move away from old habits is taken alone, or in close cooperation with others, it represents a willingness to move beyond fear.

We can choose to face our fears and move beyond them into a more cooperative world. We can choose to face our own nightmares and often as we do so, we are likely to notice that their impact and size diminishes. We can choose to let go of that which no longer serves the interests of our authentic Selves. We can allow what needs to die, to die, in order to enable new life to be reborn. We can believe in ourselves, bless ourselves and in so doing we are likely to simultaneously bless others. Through all these things we can let the power of grace and human love flow within and amongst us.

I realise "grace" has a theological meaning for many people and as a result of my many life experiences on my journey through and beyond and back from terminal illness, I would now tend to give it a theological emphasis.

But even from a more existential perspective, I think it is possible to understand grace as the occurrence of unexpected good fortune or a sudden emergence of a deepening perception of the Self and others. However we experience it, I feel it can help us to more easily befriend ourselves and our fellow travellers in life; it can also help us to befriend our own death, to seek its wisdom and good counsel, and in so doing I feel we can come to power, which may also be spiritual power, by living life in the most profound and rich way possible.

We can do this however long we are given to sojourn on this earth. When we act and allow ourselves to be with this level of mindfulness, courage and humility, I feel we are welcomed home, because living beyond fear is where we naturally belong. This is, and always has been, our birth-right!

John Holt

Past the white gates

Turn left at the bent tree

Lacken

County Mayo

Eire

January 16th, 2013.

Above: Carol and Marlon November 2012
Below: John Holt February 2013

ACKNOWLEDGMENTS:

There are a number of people I wish to thank for helping me create and complete this book.

I have received unstinting and unwavering encouragement from the start from Brenda Wall and Steve Page, both personally and professionally. There were times at the depths of my journey and physical difficulties when even my speech didn't make any sense anymore, but there is one thing I will say for Brenda and Steve in their own uniquely individual ways, neither of them even once faltered in their support and they never gave up on me. It helped me greatly never to give up on myself, even in the darkest moments.

As the process and story unfolded and people got to know what I was engaged in doing, many others offered words of support along with direct practical help. They include: Patrick Bond who gave invaluable feedback on earlier drafts of the book as well as offering use of excellent photographs of the scenery around Cae Mabon in North Wales, where many Mandorla events have taken place; Steve Lee who offered early ideas on book cover design; Steve Page for his excellent and patient editing; Sylvia Merrett for her sterling work on book manuscript preparation for publication and for her design skills; John Campbell and Benita Treanor for friendship, encouragement, creative collaboration and early discussions on the possibility of joint writing adventures around the theme of "craft development" in the coaching profession; a number of ex-partners for their extraordinary generosity of spirit in reading earlier drafts and agreeing to have references to them included (whilst I honoured their confidentiality by ensuring that names have been changed);

a number of friends for helpful and constructive feedback and in particular Sue and Pete Dominey for their honesty, love and friendship and Sarah Douglas for her enthusiastic and empathic support for a number of years.

In the earlier stages of the book's development I received considerable support from my peer supervision group and direct offers of practical help from my peer Karunavacha. I am grateful for their early help and guidance.

A number of people maintained continued interest in the book's progress, not least my colleagues in The Phoenix Partnership, my friends in the Leeds Men's Group and my co-facilitators in Mandorla. The practical help and encouragement I received from Mandorla colleagues Patrick, Pete, Phil, Sebastian and Simon, in the depths of my illness was pure gold, invaluable and very timely. I would also wish to include my old colleague Rod Gibson, who I am sure, was consistently helping and encouraging me from a place somewhere beyond this physical world – his presence and influence are a continuing thread throughout the book.

In terms of my road towards healing myself: from the devastation of the diagnosis of carcinoid syndrome, secondary cancers in the liver and pure right ventricle heart failure, to what appears today to be a period of sustained remission, I have many people to thank.

I would like to include: again, Brenda who has offered spiritual guidance and prayers throughout; K who helped me with her dedication to Sikhism, introducing me to and encouraging me to learn the Shabad prayers; Danielle Colclough who offered excellent help and support with acupuncture, diet and her advice on dealing with cancer (my brother reciprocated by reproducing a computer generated advert for what he called an "Acupuncture Repair Kit" based on the old Dunlop Puncture Repair outfits familiar to any cyclist in the 1960s and 1970s, which I was delighted to present to Danielle); the hospital Consultants who have offered me real help including Dr Clements (who very intuitively made the initial accurate diagnosis) and Dr Crawford (my Oncologist) both based at Airedale Hospital, Dr Sapsford (my Cardiologist) based at Leeds General Infirmary who has always been a delight to deal with; also I must reserve a special word for the wonderful staff at HODU (Haematology & Oncology Day Unit) at Airedale Hospital who knew me by my first name very early on in my regular treatment and who have always warmly welcomed me on every visit, exuding love, empathy and sheer human affection, not just to me but to all patients at HODU – even without my regular injections I think I would have benefitted greatly in terms of a healing process simply because of the way they are in their natural "being" and the obvious depth of care they live day by day – I never once failed to notice that I always came out of HODU feeling so much better than when I went in, whatever level of pain I was enduring or living through at the time.

I owe a great debt of gratitude to Cathy Presto (homeopath) and Julie Redman (Reiki healer and spiritual healer) who have been with me every step of the way, and along with frequent help from unseen sources, in my opinion have offered key elements which have decisively turned around my illness. In their own way I am sure they were central figures in bringing me back from the absolute threshold of death. I am delighted that Carol and I are now engaged in co-working with Cathy and Julie.

I am honoured to both acknowledge and also appreciate decades of loyal friendship from my oldest friends: Jim Antcliffe and his wife Suman, Andy Wilson, Mick Chambers, John Lawler, Julia Studley, Chris Willetts, Jim Caswell and his partner Ann, Peter and Renee Partridge, who have one way or another, all been a consistent loving presence in my life, every step of the way. Whatever difficulties I have faced, they have always been there, especially when the going became very tough indeed. They were never very far away and always helped, certainly when asked and often without me having to ask for anything.

I would also wish to thank my family of origin and my living relatives, in particular Glyn, Chris, Kerry & Tim, Liam, Chloe and Jamie for being such a rich source of belonging and meaning in my life. I also wish to remember my ancestors, no longer with me in a physical body, but so deeply influential in helping to co-create the person I have been able to become (or return to) after all my journeying.

Last but absolutely by no means least; I wish to thank my partner Carol who became a profound source of strength and inspiration, not only in the writing of this book but also in co-creating the deep meaning I am now finding in my life – Carol has offered me a joy greater than I have ever before known. We have had endless discussions about the book and the themes that have unfolded. I often found myself including aspects of such dialogue in the writing, soon after we had spoken, to the extent that I feel the book in very many places is a living record of the wonderful journey of exploration, deepening knowledge, love and co-creation we have shared and constructed together.

You have helped me more than you will ever know.

Thank you all.

ABOUT THE AUTHOR

John Holt is a Counsellor, Psychotherapist, Clinical Supervisor, Coach and Coach Supervisor, Organisational Consultant and Trainer, practicing in West Yorkshire. He is a BACP Accredited Counsellor & Psychotherapist, BACP Accredited Supervisor, BACP Registered Senior Practitioner and A.C Accredited Master Coach.

Information about John's *Therapy, Supervision and Coaching Practice* can be found at: '**John Holt – Authentic-Self-Purpose** '*www.johnholt-authentic-self-purpose.org.uk*.

For his **Creative Change Management Consultancy Organisation** please visit '**The Phoenix Partnership** *ww.phoenixpartnership.co.uk*

If you have enjoyed this book and would like to read more of John's writings please visit his Blog: *www.johnholtauthenticselfpurpose.wordpress.com*

APPENDICES

APPENDIX ONE:

HAKOMI "CHARACTER STRATEGIES"

What follows are summarised from teachings of the Hakomi Institute and can be explored further, within the public domain in an adapted form, in the Ken Keyes Jr. publication (Keyes, K. [1995]).

The full range of identified "Character Strategies" which were developed by staff at the Hakomi Institute, are set out below, with original "DSM" classifications in parentheses:

- **Sensitive / Analytic (Schizoid):** **'Defence'** = Minimise self-expression and emotional contact with others; **'Strengths'** = Eye for detail (as an aspect of "hyper-vigilance") and ability to view the world in analytical and strategic ways / sensitive, intuitive and psychic / original thinkers; **'Underdeveloped-complements'** = Ability to read and experience the world from an emotionally relaxed base with an emotionally self-expressive style of communication.

- **Dependent / Endearing (Oral):** **'Defence'** = Seeking support by acting childlike and in need; **'Strengths'** = Interest in others and tuned in to others' needs / non-threatening / easy to talk to / often affectionate; Underdeveloped-complements' = Self-motivation / exercising self-responsibility, personal power, action and decision making / identifying and voicing own needs.

- **Self-Reliant (Compensated or Denied Oral):** **'Defence'** = Mobilise self-support and prove self-

357

reliance plus tendency to act as an "emotional caretaker for others"; **'Strengths'** = Self-motivation and self-determination when not under undue pressure / emotionally empathic and pragmatically helpful to others; **'Underdeveloped-complements'** = Ability to identify own needs and act on them / allowing others space to find their own power and sense of discernment.

- **Tough / Generous (Psychopath 1): 'Defence'** = Domination and control whilst hiding vulnerability / organising perceptions, feelings and actions around using others or being used by them; **'Strengths'** = Willingness to take on leadership roles / be in public view / perceptive and adventurous; 'Underdeveloped-complements' = being real and honest or transparent with others / able to show vulnerabilities / ability to form equal relationships.

- **Charming / Manipulative (Psychopath 2): 'Defence'** = Charm others and seduce them to get what you need / playing psychological games with people's emotions / emphasis on being attractive and wanted; **'Strengths'** = Skilful with words / charismatic and creative / generosity and charm / perceptive and good actors; **'Underdeveloped-complements'** = Ability to communicate in a transparent and honest fashion / identifying and asking for needs to be met in a straightforward way.

- **Burdened / Enduring (Masochistic): 'Defence'** = Bear up and outlast pressure / masking feelings of guilt, inferiority, inadequacy and seeking to avoid both transparent mistakes and hurting others /

passive aggression; **'Strengths'** = Reliable and dependable / loyalty and thoroughness / ability to withstand pressure and focus doggedly on a task or tasks without being side-tracked or distracted / stoicism especially under duress; **'Underdeveloped-complements'** = Emotional and mental spontaneity and self-expression / ability to express anger in effective and healthy ways / willingness to take action and exercise self-responsibility.

- **Expressive / Clinging (Hysteric): 'Defence'** = Get attention and avoid separation / making a show of being easily upset and dramatic / seductive in an attention seeking way / caring and "motherly"; **'Strengths'** = Sensitive and flexible / expressive and empathic / stimulating, enthusiastic and spontaneous; **'Underdeveloped-complements'** = Feeling relaxed around other's need for distance and emotional space / relational insight / ability to negotiate separation and endings in a healthy manner.

- **Industrious / Over-focussed (Phallic): 'Defence'** = Work hard, keep going and don't let anything distract you / perfectionism, effort and striving; 'Strengths' = High achievers, successful fast workers / gets things done, responsible and down to earth / dependable; **'Underdeveloped-complements'** = Confident at being loved for oneself / ability to sit back and relax and be loved / ability and enthusiasm to complete tasks and let go.

APPENDIX TWO:

BIBLIOGRAPHY

AND FURTHER READING

FOREWARD: Steve Page

- Page, S., [1999] "The Shadow & the Counsellor", Routledge

- Page, S & Wosket, V,. [2001]"Supervising the Counsellor: A cyclical model", Routledge

- Bloom, W. [2011] "The Power of Modern Spirituality", London: Piatkus.

EARLY THOUGHTS, MAY 2011: My Last Will and Testament - A letter to fellow professionals both old & new

- Castaneda, C. [1972], "Journey to Ixtlan: The Lessons of Don Juan", Washington Square Press, Simon and Schuster

- Parkin, J.C., [2012], "F**k It Therapy: The profane way to profound happiness", Hay House

- Rodegast, P. & Stanton, S. [1985], "Emmanuel's Book: A manual for living comfortably in the cosmos", Bantam Books

CHAPTER 1: Envy and "En vie" - confrontations with a house brick

- Glasgow University Media Group [1976], "Bad News"; [1980] "More Bad News"; [1982] "Really Bad News", R.K.P.

- Macy, J. [1991], "World as Lover, World as Self: Courage for Global Justice and Ecological Renewal'", Parallax Press

- Taylor, I. [1981], "Law and Order: Arguments for Socialism", Macmillan

CHAPTER 2: Hyper vigilance, self-reliance and endurance

- Buhner, S. H. [2004], "The Secret Teachings of Plants: The intelligence of the heart in the direct perception of nature", Bear and Company

- Skynner, R. & Cleese, J [1993], "LIFE and how to survive it", Methuen

CHAPTER 3: Betrayal and retreat into the Self

- Bly, R. [1990], "Iron John: A book about men", Addison Wesley

- Peck, M.S. [1978], "The Road Less Travelled: A new psychology of love, traditional values and spiritual growth", Simon and Schuster, USA

- Tams, J. [2005], "Man of constant sorrow" on the recording "The Reckoning", Topic Records.

CHAPTER 4: Early conversations with power

- Cooper, M. & Mearns, D. [2005], "Working at Relational Depth in Counselling and Psychotherapy", Sage Publications

- de Haan, E. [2008], "Relational Coaching: Journeys towards mastering one-to-one learning", John Wiley & Sons

- Johnson, R. [2009] "He: Understanding Masculine Psychology", Harper Collins, Adobe Digital Edition

- Peck, M.S. [1978], "The Road Less Travelled: A new psychology of love, traditional values and spiritual growth", Simon and Schuster, USA

- Peck, M.S. [1987], "The Different Drum: The Creation of True Community – The First Step to World Peace", Arrow Books

- Scharmer, C.O.[2008], Blog entry on 24th August, 2008: www.blog.ottoscharmer.com

- Scharmer, C.O. [2007], "Theory U: Leading From the Future as it Emerges – The Social Technology of Presencing", The Society for Organisational Learning

- Senge, P., Scharmer, C.O., Jaworski, J., Flowers, B.S. [2005], "Presence: Exploring Profound Change in People, Organisations and Society", Nicholas Brealey Publishing

- Stark, M. [2002], "Working with Resistance", Aronson

- Williamson, M. [1992], "A Return to Love: Reflections on the principles of A Course in Miracles", Harper Collins

CHAPTER 5: Glimpses of freedom

- Beckhard, R., [1969], "Organisation Development: Strategies and Models", Addison-Wesley

- Boyle, J., [1977], "A Sense of Freedom", Pan Books, and [1984], "The Pain of Confinement: Prison Diaries", Canongate

- Eastwood, S., Davill, M., Holt, J. [1987], "Worth The Risk: Creative Group Work with Young Offenders", Save the Children & West Yorkshire Probation Service

- Fromm, E., [1942], "The Fear of Freedom", Routledge, Keegan & Paul

- Holt, J. [1985], "No Holiday Camps: Custody, Juvenile Justice and The Politics of Law and Order", Association for Juvenile Justice

- Karpman, S. [1968], "Fairy tales and script drama analysis", Transactional Analysis Bulletin 7/26

- Macy, J., [2005], "World as Lover, World as Self", Parallax Press

- Schutz, W. [1979], "Profound Simplicity", Bantam Books

CHAPTER 6: Grace & Illness Part 1 - where the road of starvation meets the water of life

- Campbell, J. edited by Kudler, D., [2004], "Pathways to Bliss: mythology and personal transformation", New World Library

CHAPTER 7: Showing the Self in the World

- Julian of Norwich. "Showings". [Published 1978]: Paulist Press, New York

CHAPTER 8: Bridging and integration of the split Self

- Alison, J., [1996], "Raising Abel: The recovery of the eschatological imagination", Crossroad Publishing Company

- Alison, J., [1998], "The Joy of Being Wrong: Original Sin Through Easter Eyes", Crossroad Publishing Company

- Buckingham, M. and Clifton, D.O., [2001], "Now, Discover Your Strengths: How to develop your talents and those of the people you manage", The Gallup Organisation

- Campbell, J., [1990] & Centennial Edition [2003], Edited Cousineau, P., "The Hero's Journey", New World Library, U.S.A.

- Fox, M., [1987], "Original Blessing: A primer in Creation Spirituality", Bear and Company

- Fox, M., [2006], "A New Reformation: Creation Spirituality and the Transformation of Christianity", Inner Traditions

- Gould, P. & Rebuck, G., [2012], "When I Die: Lessons from the Death Zone", Little & Brown

- Holmes, P., Paul, S., Pelham, G.; "A Relational Model of Counselling" in "Counselling" Journal, August 1996

- Julian of Norwich. "Showings". [Published 1978]: Paulist Press, New York

- Moore, T. [2004], "Dark Nights of the Soul: A guide to finding your way through life's ordeals'", Piatkus Books

- Scharmer ,C.O., [2008], (*www.blog.ottoscharmer.com,* August 24th, 2008)

- Whyte, D. [1996], "The Truelove", in the book, "The House of Belonging": Poems by David Whyte, Many Rivers Press

- Wosket, V., [1999], "The Therapeutic Use of Self: Counselling practice, research and supervision", Routledge

CHAPTER 9: Healing spirals - risk taking, competency and confidence

- Davill, M., Eastwood, S., Holt, J., [1987], "Worth the Risk: Creative Group Work with Young Offenders", Save the Children and West Yorkshire Probation Service

- Gramsci, A., [1971], "Selections from Prison Notebooks", Lawrence and Wishart

- Holt, J., [1985], "No Holiday Camps: Custody, Juvenile Justice and the Politics of Law and Order", Association for Juvenile Justice

- Jones, D., [2010], "Celebrate what's right with the world", (DVD) Star Thrower Distribution Corporation

- Senge, P. M., [1990], "The Fifth Discipline: The Art and Practice of the Learning Organisation", Currency-Doubleday

CHAPTER 10: "Following your bliss", or not

- Bly, R., [1990], "Iron John: A book about Men", Addison Wesley

- Czikszentmihalyi, M., [1990], "Flow: The psychology of optimal experience – Steps toward enhancing the quality of life", Harper & Row

- Moore, T., [2004], "Dark Nights of the Soul: A guide to finding your way through life's ordeals'", Piatkus Books

- Pirsig, R., [1974 & 1999], "Zen and the Art of Motorcycle Maintenance: An enquiry into values", 25th Anniversary Edition, Vintage

CHAPTER 11: The road towards authenticity and integrity

- Scharmer, C.O. [2007], "Theory U: Leading From the Future as it Emerges – The Social Technology of Presencing", The Society for Organisational Learning

CHAPTER 12: The path of service - intention is everything

- Armstrong, K. [1993], "A History of God", William Heinemann

- Hughes, B. [2012], www.bettanyhughes.co.uk/divine-women

- Russell, P. [2009], "Waking up in time: Our future evolution and the meaning of now", Cygnus Books

- Small, J. [1991], "Awakening in Time: The journey from co-dependence to co-creation", Bantam Books

- Stevens, A. [1994], "Jung: A very short introduction", Oxford University Press

CHAPTER 13: And the road goes on forever – living with fear of death

- Moore, T. [2004], "Dark Nights of the Soul: A guide to finding your way through life's ordeals", Piatkus Books

- Pearson, G. [1975], "The Deviant Imagination: Psychiatry, Social Work and Social Change", Macmillan

- Pearson, G. [1983], "Hooligan: A History of Respectable Fears", Macmillan

CHAPTER 14: Facing fear and feeling death's friendship

- Frost, R., [1920], "The Road Not Taken", Mountain Interval

- Jones, D. [2001], "Celebrate What's Right with the World", DVD, Star Thrower Distribution, U.S.A.

CHAPTER 16: Power, authenticity and surrender - dancing the final dance with death

- Eliot, T. S., [1943], "Four Quartets", Harcourt, USA

- Walsh, N. D., [2006], "Home with God: In a life that never ends", Hodder and Stoughton

CHAPTER 17: Fields of Freedom – living one's craft, loving the world ....and being loved

- Frankl, V. E., [1946], "Man's Search for Meaning", Beacon Press

- Williams, F., [1949], "Fifty Years March: The rise of the Labour Party", Odhams

APPENDICES: Appendix One

- Keyes, K. [1995], "Your roadmap to lifelong happiness: A guide to the life you want", Love Line Books

FORTHCOMING BOOKS

"Re-Lighting the Fire!: A journey of the heart"

"Constant Equilibrium: Finding natural balance through authentic living"

Printed in Great Britain
by Amazon.co.uk, Ltd.,
Marston Gate.